**HOLT**

**Elements of Language**

SIXTH COURSE

# Developmental Language Skills

- Grammar
- Usage
- Mechanics

**HOLT, RINEHART AND WINSTON**

A Harcourt Education Company

Orlando • **Austin** • New York • San Diego • London

# Contents


Using This Workbook .............................................................. vi
Symbols for Revising and Proofreading .................. vii

## Chapter 1
### PARTS OF SPEECH OVERVIEW: IDENTIFICATION AND FUNCTION

The Noun............................................................................... 1
The Pronoun A: Personal Pronouns; Reflexive and Intensive Pronouns...................... 3
The Pronoun B: Demonstrative and Interrogative Pronouns ............................ 5
The Pronoun C: Relative and Indefinite Pronouns ........................... 7
The Adjective ....................................................................... 9
The Verb A: Main Verbs and Helping Verbs ............ 11
The Verb B: Action Verbs and Linking Verbs............ 13
The Verb C: Transitive Verbs and Intransitive Verbs ........................................... 15
The Adverb ......................................................................... 17
The Preposition ................................................................. 19
The Conjunction and the Interjection ...................... 21

## Chapter 2
### THE PARTS OF A SENTENCE: SUBJECT, PREDICATE, COMPLEMENT

Subjects ................................................................................ 23
Predicates............................................................................ 25
Direct Objects ................................................................... 27
Indirect Objects................................................................. 29
Predicate Nominatives ................................................... 31
Predicate Adjectives ....................................................... 33

## Chapter 3
### THE PHRASE: KINDS OF PHRASES AND THEIR FUNCTIONS

The Prepositional Phrase ............................................. 35
The Participle and the Participial Phrase .................. 37
The Gerund and the Gerund Phrase ......................... 39
The Infinitive and the Infinitive Phrase ................... 41
The Appositive and the Appositive Phrase .............. 43

## Chapter 4
### THE CLAUSE: INDEPENDENT AND SUBORDINATE CLAUSES, SENTENCE STRUCTURE

The Adjective Clause....................................................... 45
The Noun Clause............................................................... 47
The Adverb Clause .......................................................... 49
Sentence Structure A: Simple Sentences and Compound Sentences ..................................... 51
Sentence Structure B: Complex Sentences and Compound-Complex Sentences ......................... 53

## Chapter 5
### AGREEMENT: SUBJECT AND VERB, PRONOUN AND ANTECEDENT

Subject-Verb Agreement A: Singular, Plural, and Compound Subjects ....................................... 55
Subject-Verb Agreement B: Intervening Phrases and Clauses; Indefinite Pronouns .......... 57
Subject-Verb Agreement C: *Don't/Doesn't;* Collective Nouns; Amounts ................................ 59
Subject-Verb Agreement D: Nouns Plural in Form; Titles and Names; Relative Pronouns................... 61
Pronoun-Antecedent Agreement A: Number, Gender, and Person; Compound Antecedents ..................................... 63
Pronoun-Antecedent Agreement B: Indefinite Pronouns; Relative Pronouns............................. 65

## Chapter 6
### USING PRONOUNS CORRECTLY: CASE FORMS OF PRONOUNS; SPECIAL PRONOUN PROBLEMS

Personal Pronouns A: The Nominative Case, the Possessive Case ............................................... 67
Personal Pronouns B: The Objective Case ............... 69
Special Problems in Pronoun Usage ......................... 71

## Chapter 7
### CLEAR REFERENCE: PRONOUNS AND ANTECEDENTS

Clear Pronoun Reference A: Ambiguous Reference, General Reference.............................. 73
Clear Pronoun Reference B: Weak Reference, Indefinite Reference ..................................... 75

# Contents


## Chapter 8

**USING VERBS CORRECTLY:**
**PRINCIPAL PARTS, TENSE, VOICE, MOOD**

Principal Parts of Verbs A: Regular Verbs ..............**77**

Principal Parts of Verbs B: Irregular Verbs ..............**79**

*Lie* and *Lay, Sit* and *Set, Rise* and *Raise* ..............**81**

Tense ..............**83**

Progressive Forms of Verbs ..............**85**

The Uses of the Tenses ..............**87**

Consistency of Tense ..............**89**

Active Voice and Passive Voice ..............**91**

## Chapter 9

**USING MODIFIERS CORRECTLY:**
**FORMS AND USES OF ADJECTIVES AND ADVERBS;**
**COMPARISON**

Troublesome Modifiers A: *bad/badly, good/well* ..........**93**

Troublesome Modifiers B: *slow/slowly, real/really* ......**95**

Degrees of Comparison ..............**97**

Use of Comparisons ..............**99**

## Chapter 10

**PLACEMENT OF MODIFIERS:**
**MISPLACED AND DANGLING MODIFIERS**

Placement of Modifiers A: Misplaced Modifiers ..**101**

Placement of Modifiers B: Dangling Modifiers ......**103**

## Chapter 11

**A GLOSSARY OF USAGE:**
**COMMON USAGE PROBLEMS**

Glossary of Usage A ..............**105**

Glossary of Usage B ..............**107**

Glossary of Usage C ..............**109**

Glossary of Usage D ..............**111**

## Chapter 12

**CAPITALIZATION:**
**STANDARD USES OF CAPITAL LETTERS**

Capitalization A: First Words; the Pronoun *I*;
Salutations and Closings ..............**113**

Capitalization B: Proper Nouns and Proper
Adjectives; Persons and Animals ..............**115**

Capitalization C: Geographical Names;
Organizations, Teams, Institutions,
and Government Bodies ..............**117**

Capitalization D: Historical Events and Periods,
Dates, Holidays; Nationalities, Races, and
Peoples; Religions, Holy Days, Holy
Writings, and Specific Deities ..............**119**

Capitalization E: Businesses and the Brand
Names of Business Products; Ships, Trains,
Aircraft, Spacecraft, and Other Vehicles;
Buildings and Other Structures ..............**121**

Capitalization F: Monuments, Memorials, and
Awards; Planets, Stars, Constellations, and
Other Heavenly Bodies; School Subjects ..........**123**

Capitalization G: Titles of Persons;
Titles of Creative Works ..............**125**

## Chapter 13

**PUNCTUATION:**
**END MARKS AND COMMAS**

End Marks ..............**127**

Abbreviations A: Personal Names; Titles;
Agencies, Organizations, and Acronyms ..........**129**

Abbreviations B: Geographical Terms; Time;
Units of Measurement ..............**131**

Commas A: Items in a Series ..............**133**

Commas B: Independent Clauses ..............**135**

Commas C: Nonessential Elements ..............**137**

Commas D: Introductory Elements ..............**139**

Commas E: Interrupters ..............**141**

Commas F: Conventional Uses ..............**143**

# Contents


## Chapter 14

**PUNCTUATION:**
**OTHER MARKS OF PUNCTUATION**

Semicolons A ....................................................145

Semicolons B....................................................147

Colons: Lists; Quotations and Explanations;
    Conventional Situations ...........................149

Italics ...............................................................151

Quotation Marks A ...........................................153

Quotation Marks B ...........................................155

Ellipsis Points ..................................................157

Apostrophes A: Forming Possessives ...................159

Apostrophes B: Contractions; Plurals .................161

Hyphens ...........................................................163

Dashes, Parentheses, and Brackets.....................165

## Chapter 15

**SPELLING:**
**IMPROVING YOUR SPELLING**

Words with *ie* and *ei* .......................................167

Prefixes and Suffixes ........................................169

Plurals of Nouns A ...........................................171

Plurals of Nouns B ...........................................173

Writing Numbers...............................................175

Words Often Confused A....................................177

Words Often Confused B....................................179

Words Often Confused C....................................181

## Chapter 16

**CORRECTING COMMON ERRORS:**
**KEY LANGUAGE SKILLS REVIEW**

Common Errors Review.......................................183

## *Using This Workbook*

The worksheets in this workbook provide instruction, practice, and reinforcement for *Elements of Language* and *Language Skills Practice*.

This workbook is designed to supplement *Language Skills Practice* by providing additional instruction and practice to students who have not yet mastered the rules and topics covered in *Elements of Language*.

You will find throughout the workbook several special features, which have been added to aid students' mastery of grammar, usage, and mechanics. The special features include notes, reminders, tips, points of instruction after instructional and exercise examples, and guided practice for the first one or two items in each exercise.

- **Notes** provide students with pertinent information related to the rule or topic covered on a given worksheet.

- **Reminders** review grammatical terms and concepts that were covered on previous worksheets.

- **Tips** provide students with tangible aids for understanding abstract concepts. These tips include mnemonic devices, identification tests, and recognition strategies.

- **Points of Instruction** explain how the rule or topic applies to the instructional and exercise examples provided.

- **Guided Practice** helps students with the first one or two items of each exercise by asking questions that guide students to the correct answer.

**Teacher's Notes** and an **Answer Key** are provided on the *Teacher One Stop*™ **DVD-ROM with ExamView® Test Generator**.

# Symbols for Revising and Proofreading

| Symbol | Example | Meaning of Symbol |
| --- | --- | --- |
| ≡ | Fifty-first street | Capitalize a lowercase letter. |
| / | Jerry's Aunt | Lowercase a capital letter. |
| ∧ | differant _(e)_ | Change a letter. |
| ∧ | The capital Ohio _(of)_ | Insert a missing word, letter, or punctuation mark. |
| ⌐ | beside the river _(lake)_ | Replace a word. |
| ℐ | Where's the the key? | Leave out a word, letter, or punctuation mark. |
| ℐ | an invisibile guest | Leave out and close up. |
| ⌒ | a close friend ship | Close up space. |
| ∿ | thier | Change the order of letters. |
| (tr) | Avoid having too many corrections of your paper in the final version. | Transfer the circled words. (Write _tr_ in nearby margin.) |
| ¶ | ¶"Hi," he smiled. | Begin a new paragraph. |
| ⊙ | Stay well | Add a period. |
| ∧ | Of course you may be wrong. | Add a comma. |
| # | icehockey | Add a space. |
| ⊙ | one of the following | Add a colon. |
| ∧ | Maria Simmons, M.D. Jim Fiorello, Ph.D. | Add a semicolon. |
| = | a great grandmother | Add a hyphen. |
| ∨ | Pauls car | Add an apostrophe. |
| (stet) | On the fifteenth of ~~July~~ | Keep the crossed-out material. (Write _stet_ in nearby margin.) |

# The Noun

**1a.**   A *noun* names a person, a place, a thing, or an idea.

|  |  |
|---|---|
| **PERSONS** | accountant, neighbor, athlete, George Washington Carver |
| **PLACES** | library, gymnasium, village, South Dakota |
| **THINGS** | calendar, shelves, streetlight, Declaration of Independence |
| **IDEAS** | truth, self-awareness, humor, belief, Confucianism |

## Common Nouns and Proper Nouns

A *common noun* names any one of a group of persons, places, things, or ideas. A common noun is capitalized only when it begins a sentence or is part of a title. A *proper noun* names a particular person, place, thing, or idea. A proper noun is always capitalized.

|  |  |
|---|---|
| **COMMON NOUNS** | monarch, state, era, treaty |
| **PROPER NOUNS** | Queen Anne, Alaska, Renaissance, Treaty of Versailles |

**EXERCISE A**  Underline all of the nouns in the following sentences. Then, write *P* above each proper noun.

**Example  1.**  The researcher, Robin Jerome, peered through the microscope at the specimen.

[*Researcher* names any one of a group of persons. *Microscope* and *specimen* name any one of a group of things. *Robin Jerome* names a particular person.]

**1.** Old Faithful, a geyser in Yellowstone National Park, erupts at fairly regular intervals.  [Which words name particular things?  Which words name any one of a group of things?]

**2.** A forerunner of jazz, ragtime is a musical style that was popular earlier in the century.

**3.** Nutritionists can help patients plan healthy meals and develop good eating habits.

**4.** Confucius was a famous teacher and philosopher from China.

**5.** The audience called for an encore after the pianist walked off the stage.

## Concrete Nouns and Abstract Nouns

A *concrete noun* names a person, a place, or a thing that can be perceived by one or more of the five senses (sight, hearing, taste, touch, and smell). An *abstract noun* names an idea, feeling, quality, or characteristic that cannot be perceived by one or more of the five senses.

|  |  |
|---|---|
| **CONCRETE NOUNS** | screen, Munich, Kobe Bryant, cactus |
| **ABSTRACT NOUNS** | dedication, courtesy, satisfaction, leisure |

**EXERCISE B**  Determine whether each of the following nouns is concrete or abstract. Then, write *C* for *concrete* or *A* for *abstract* on the line provided.

**GO ON** ➡

**Examples**   _____A_____ **1.** allegiance [*Allegiance* cannot be perceived by the senses.]

_____C_____ **2.** radio [*Radio* can be perceived by the senses.]

_______ **6.** destiny                   _______ **11.** self-sacrifice

_______ **7.** receipt                   _______ **12.** Barbara Jordan

_______ **8.** persistence               _______ **13.** joy

_______ **9.** kodiak bear               _______ **14.** birthstone

_______ **10.** loyalty                  _______ **15.** cheetah

## Collective Nouns

The singular form of a *collective noun* names a group. Some collective nouns are *family, team, council, audience,* and *herd.*

> **EXAMPLES**   The shepherd tended the **flock** that was grazing in the pasture. [*Flock* names a group of animals.]
>
> The **committee** voted for the proposal. [*Committee* names a group of people.]

## Compound Nouns

A *compound noun* is made up of two or more words that together name a person, a place, a thing, or an idea. A compound noun may be written as one word, as two or more separate words, or as a hyphenated word.

> **ONE WORD**   raindrop, flagship, playground, swordfish, Iceland
>
> **SEPARATE WORDS**   civil liberty, assistant professor, Cape Verde, rock salt
>
> **HYPHENATED WORD**   out-of-towner, make-believe, two-by-fours

**EXERCISE C** Determine whether each of the underlined nouns in the following sentences is collective or compound. Then, if the noun is collective, write *COLL* for *collective* on the line provided. If the noun is compound, write *COMP* for *compound* on the line provided.

**Example**   _COMP_ **1.** Isn't your <u>brother-in-law</u> a radio announcer? [*Brother-in-law* is a compound noun that names a single person rather than a group.]

_______ **16.** As the graduates entered the gymnasium, the <u>band</u> played a traditional march. [Does the underlined noun name one person or a group of people?]

_______ **17.** The children always ride the <u>merry-go-round</u> when they go to the carnival.

_______ **18.** In E. B. White's *Charlotte's Web*, isn't the pig Wilbur the runt of the <u>litter</u>?

_______ **19.** Using a robotic submarine, biologists watched <u>lanternfish</u> glow in the darkness.

_______ **20.** Spain and Portugal occupy the <u>Iberian Peninsula</u>.

# The Pronoun A

| **1b.** | A *pronoun* takes the place of one or more nouns or pronouns. |

An *antecedent* is the word or word group to which a pronoun refers.

**EXAMPLES**   The plate is chipped. I accidentally dropped **it** in the sink. [The pronoun *it* takes the place of *plate. Plate* is the antecedent of *it.*]

When Stephanie and Monica go hiking, **they** always follow the trails. [The pronoun *they* takes the place of the proper nouns *Stephanie* and *Monica. Stephanie* and *Monica* are the antecedents of *they.*]

## Personal Pronouns

A *personal pronoun* is a pronoun that refers to the one(s) speaking (first person), the one(s) spoken to (second person), or the one(s) spoken about (third person).

**FIRST PERSON**   I, me, my, mine, we, us, our, ours

**SECOND PERSON**   you, your, yours

**THIRD PERSON**   he, him, his, she, her, hers, it, its, they, them, their, theirs

**EXERCISE A**   Underline the personal pronouns in each of the following sentences. Then, write *1st* for *first person, 2nd* for *second person,* or *3rd* for *third person* above each personal pronoun.

**Examples  1.**   She told me a story about her youth. [*She* and *her* refer to the one spoken about. *Me* refers to the one speaking.]

**2.**   Didn't he give you my message? [*He* refers to the one spoken about. *You* refers to the one spoken to. *My* refers to the one speaking.]

**1.** Did she tell him about the emergency procedures? [Which words take the place of nouns? Do these words refer to the ones speaking, the ones spoken to, or the ones spoken about?]

**2.** We often spend our vacations with them in New England. [Which words take the place of nouns? Do these words refer to the ones speaking, the ones spoken to, or the ones spoken about?]

**3.** The teacher called out several vocabulary words and asked us to use them in a short story.

**4.** Does he know what time you will be arriving?

**5.** A snake had shed its skin, which we found lying on the ground.

**6.** Dedicating her life to the poor, Mother Teresa of Calcutta received the 1979 Nobel Peace Prize.

**7.** He wore his favorite shirt to their party.

**GO ON** ➡

**8.** I have finished the book, so you may have it now.

**9.** Robert Fulton not only made the steamboat a success, but he also designed a submarine and a

steam warship.

**10.** They bought a barn and converted it into a workshop.

---

## Reflexive and Intensive Pronouns

A *reflexive pronoun* refers to the subject of a verb. A reflexive pronoun completes the meaning
of the verb or acts as an object of a preposition. An *intensive pronoun* emphasizes its
antecedent (the noun or pronoun to which the pronoun refers). Reflexive and intensive
pronouns end in *–self* or *–selves.*

> **REFLEXIVE**  Clara let **herself** in through the front door.  [*Herself* refers to the subject
> *Clara* and completes the meaning of the verb *let.*]
> The raccoon kept the fish for **itself.**  [*Itself* refers to the subject *raccoon* and
> is the object of the preposition *for.*]
> **INTENSIVE**  The manager **himself** made the delivery.  [*Himself* emphasizes the
> antecedent *manager.*]

**TIP▶** To determine whether a pronoun is reflexive or intensive, read the sentence aloud without
the pronoun. Does the meaning of the sentence change without the pronoun? If the meaning of the sentence changes without the pronoun, the pronoun is reflexive. If the meaning
of the sentence stays the same, the pronoun is intensive.

> **EXAMPLES**  He prepared the salad **himself.**  [Without *himself,* the meaning of the
> sentence does not change. *Himself* is intensive.]
> He prepared the salad for **himself.**  [The sentence doesn't make sense
> without the pronoun. *Himself* is reflexive.]

**EXERCISE B** Determine whether the underlined pronoun in each of the following sentences is reflexive
or intensive. Then, write *REF* for *reflexive* or *INT* for *intensive* on the line provided.

**Example**  ___REF___  **1.** We laughed at <u>ourselves</u> for thinking that the tree stump was a bear.

[*Ourselves* is the object of the preposition *at.*]

_______**11.** The author <u>herself</u> gave me a copy of the book.  [Does the underlined pronoun emphasize

*author,* or does the pronoun complete the meaning of the verb *gave*?]

_______**12.** Last year, I prepared my income tax return <u>myself.</u>

_______**13.** Did you design the new kitchen <u>yourself</u>?

_______**14.** The knights of the Middle Ages pledged <u>themselves</u> to courtesy and honor.

_______**15.** As president during the Civil War, Abraham Lincoln devoted <u>himself</u> to the preserva-

tion of the Union.

**4**

# The Pronoun B

**1b.**   A ***pronoun*** takes the place of one or more nouns or pronouns.

## Demonstrative Pronouns

A ***demonstrative pronoun*** points out a noun or another pronoun. Demonstrative pronouns are *this, that, these,* and *those. This* and *that* point out singular nouns and pronouns. *These* and *those* refer to plural nouns and pronouns.

> **EXAMPLES**   Are **these** the only flavors available? [*These* points out a plural noun, *flavors.*]
> **This** is the one that I built.  [*This* points out a singular pronoun, *one.*]

**NOTE▶** The same words that are used as demonstrative pronouns can also be used as adjectives. When these words describe nouns or pronouns, they are called ***demonstrative adjectives.***

> **PRONOUN**   **This** is my favorite song. [*This* is a pronoun referring to *song.*]
> **ADJECTIVE**   **This** song is my favorite. [*This* is an adjective describing which *song.*]

**EXERCISE A**   Underline the demonstrative pronoun in parentheses that correctly completes each of the following sentences.

**Examples 1.** (*This, Those*) is the first time I have heard that story.  [*This* refers to the singular noun *time.*]

**2.** Are (*that, those*) the only scarves that the store has in stock?  [*Those* refers to the plural noun *scarves.*]

**1.** Could (*that, those*) be Lance at the door?  [Is the pronoun's antecedent singular or plural?]

**2.** (*This, These*) is a photograph of Machu Picchu, the site of ancient Incan ruins in Peru.  [Is the pronoun's antecedent singular or plural?]

**3.** Aren't (*that, those*) the sunglasses you received for your birthday?

**4.** Wow! (*That, These*) may be the largest snake I've ever seen!

**5.** (*This, Those*) will likely be our only opportunity to take a quick break.

**6.** In addition to a new type of plow, (*this, these*) is one of John Deere's inventions.

**7.** Are (*that, these*) toys the kind that require AA batteries?

**8.** (*These, This*) are letters from the Cyrillic alphabet, which is used for Russian and other similar languages.

**9.** Now part of a coffee table, (*that, those*) was once a window frame.

**10.** Do (*this, those*) vacuum cleaners come with a money-back guarantee?

**GO ON ▶**

# Interrogative Pronouns

An *interrogative pronoun* introduces a question. Interrogative pronouns are *who, whom, whose, which,* and *what*.

> **EXAMPLES**  **Whose** are these sandals?
>
> **What** is the name of your company?
>
> To **whom** should I address this letter?

**NOTE▶** Some of the words used as interrogative pronouns can also function as adjectives. Remember that a pronoun takes the place of a noun or another pronoun. An adjective makes the meaning of a noun or a pronoun more specific.

> **PRONOUN**  **Which** of these handbags belongs to her? [*Which* is an interrogative pronoun that refers to *handbags,* the object of the preposition *of.*]
>
> **ADJECTIVE**  **Which** handbag belongs to her? [*Which* is an adjective describing *handbag.*]

**EXERCISE B** Underline the demonstrative and interrogative pronouns in each of the following sentences. Then, write *DEM* for *demonstrative* or *INT* for *interrogative* above each pronoun.

**Examples**  **1.** Whose are these toys? [*Whose* is an interrogative pronoun. *These* is an adjective describing *toys.*]

**2.** This will be Naomi's last visit until next year. [*This* is a demonstrative pronoun that points out a specific noun, *visit.*]

**11.** Is that a blackberry or a dewberry? [Does the pronoun introduce a question, or does it point out another noun or pronoun?]

**12.** Whose is the abstract painting on the far wall of the gallery? [Does the pronoun introduce a question, or does it point out another noun or pronoun?]

**13.** Are those Calvin's computer magazines?

**14.** That is a model of the sphinx, a mythological creature with a human head and a lion's body.

**15.** Who are the characters in *Death of a Salesman*?

**16.** These were the least expensive tools I could find.

**17.** For whom did you write that song?

**18.** Whew! That was a near miss!

**19.** What is the name of your younger brother?

**20.** This has been a popular tourist attraction for years.

# The Pronoun C

| **1b.** | A *pronoun* takes the place of one or more nouns or pronouns. |

## Relative Pronouns

A *relative pronoun* introduces a subordinate clause. Relative pronouns include *that, which, who, whom,* and *whose.*

**EXAMPLES**   The person **who** scores the most points wins the game.  [The relative pronoun *who* introduces the subordinate clause *who scores the most points.*]

The milk **that** is in the refrigerator is fresh.  [The relative pronoun *that* introduces the subordinate clause *that is in the refrigerator.*]

Brie, **which** is a type of cheese, is made in France.  [The relative pronoun *which* introduces the subordinate clause *which is a type of cheese.*]

**REMINDER▶**   A *subordinate clause* is a group of words that contains a subject and its verb but does not express a complete thought. A subordinate clause cannot stand alone as a sentence.

**SUBORDINATE CLAUSE**   that darted under the board  [The group of words contains a subject, *that,* and a verb, *darted,* but does not express a complete thought.]

**SENTENCE**   Did you see the salamander **that darted under the board**?  [The subordinate clause is introduced by the relative pronoun *that* and is part of a complete sentence.]

**EXERCISE A**   Underline the subordinate clause introduced by the relative pronoun in each of the following sentences. Then, draw a second line under the relative pronoun.

**Examples 1.** Is the suit that is hanging in the closet made of wool?  [*That* introduces the subordinate clause *that is hanging in the closet.*]

**2.** Rachel, whom I met yesterday, knows my sister.  [*Whom* introduces the subordinate clause *whom I met yesterday.*]

**1.** The wallet that is on the table is mine.  [What relative pronoun introduces a subordinate clause?]

**2.** This cactus, which is quite large, is native to Mexico and the states of Arizona and California. [What relative pronoun introduces a subordinate clause?]

**3.** Unfortunately, the car that we bought last week already has a large dent.

**4.** The person who usually works the switchboard is on vacation.

**5.** Ms. Ross, whom I highly recommend, is an outstanding piano teacher.

**6.** Strawberries, which are Tom's favorite fruit, are not in season right now.

**GO ON ➡**

**7.** Howard Hughes, who amassed an enormous fortune over his lifetime, spent much of his life in seclusion.

**8.** The old towels that we use as rags are in the cabinet.

**9.** In small businesses, the employee who has the most seniority is often given first consideration for promotion.

**10.** Our dog, which is an Irish setter, sleeps in the laundry room.

## Indefinite Pronouns

An *indefinite pronoun* refers to a person, a place, a thing, or an idea that may or may not be specifically named. An indefinite pronoun may not have a specific antecedent.

### COMMON INDEFINITE PRONOUNS

| | | | | |
|---|---|---|---|---|
| all | both | few | nobody | several |
| another | each | many | none | some |
| any | either | more | no one | somebody |
| anybody | everybody | most | nothing | someone |
| anyone | everyone | much | one | something |
| anything | everything | neither | other | such |

> **EXAMPLES**　**Several** of our neighbors signed the petition.  [The indefinite pronoun *Several* refers to *neighbors*.]
>
> Does **anyone** have a question?  [*Anyone* has no specific antecedent.]
>
> I have received replies from **some** of the people I invited.  [*Some* refers to *people*.]

**EXERCISE B** Underline the indefinite pronouns in each of the following sentences.

**Example 1.** <u>Everyone</u> received a study guide for the course.  [*Everyone* refers to people who are not specifically named.]

**11.** The theaters usually reserve several of their best seats for important guests.  [Which pronoun refers to *seats*?]

**12.** Everything for the conference had been arranged for months.

**13.** Neither attended the family reunion.

**14.** Since no one expressed any concerns about the proposal, the committee accepted it.

**15.** Nothing is cozier than a warm fire on a chilly evening.

# The Adjective

**1c.**   An *adjective* modifies a noun or a pronoun.

Adjectives tell *what kind, which one, how many,* or *how much* about a noun or pronoun.

> **WHAT KIND**  **mountainous** landscape
>
> **WHICH ONE**  **last** chance
>
> **HOW MANY**  **three** minutes
>
> **HOW MUCH**  **enough** equipment

*Predicate adjectives* describe the subject of the sentence and appear in the predicate.

> **EXAMPLE**  The travelers felt **weary** and **uncomfortable.**  [The adjectives *weary* and *uncomfortable* appear in the predicate. Both adjectives describe *travelers*.]

**EXERCISE A** Underline the adjectives in each of the following sentences. Then, draw an arrow from each adjective to the word it modifies. Do not underline *a, an,* or *the.*

**Examples 1.** Numerous species of birds inhabit the tiny island.  [*Numerous* tells how many about *species. Tiny* tells what kind about *island.*]

**2.** What outdoor activities do we have planned for Theresa's birthday picnic? [*Outdoor* tells what kind about *activities. Theresa's* tells which one about *picnic. Birthday* tells what kind about *picnic.*]

**1.** The restaurant offers a wide selection of main dishes and free refills of beverages.  [Which words make the meanings of nouns more specific?]

**2.** The highest mountain in Washington, Mount Rainier is actually a dormant volcano.  [Which words make the meanings of nouns more specific?]

**3.** Please order fourteen new stools for the chemistry lab.

**4.** Christopher Wren, a prominent architect of the 1600s, designed the majestic St. Paul's Cathedral in London.

**5.** Scientists have made exciting and important discoveries about dinosaurs.

**6.** Did Michael make the oak bookshelves in the front hallway?

**7.** Grandmother's recipe for banana nut bread requires two cups of mashed bananas.

**8.** Rabbits and hares have long ears and long hind legs.

**9.** The flight attendants were helpful, knowledgeable, and courteous.

**10.** Last night, the full moon was beautiful.

**GO ON**

## Articles

*A*, *an*, and *the*, called *articles*, are the most frequently used adjectives. *A* and *an* refer to any member of a general group and are called *indefinite articles*. *The* is the *definite article* because it refers to a specific person, place, thing, or idea.

> **EXAMPLE**  **An** owl landed on **the** tree branch.  [*An* refers to a member of a general group, *owl*. *The* refers to a specific thing, *branch*.]

## Proper Adjectives

A *proper adjective* is an adjective that is formed from a proper noun.

> **PROPER NOUN**  Look at this satellite photograph of the **United States.**  [*United States* is a proper noun.]
>
> **PROPER ADJECTIVE**  She is going to become a **United States** citizen.  [*United States* is a proper adjective telling what kind of *citizen*.]

**EXERCISE B**  Underline all of the adjectives in the following sentences, including definite and indefinite articles. Then, draw an arrow from each adjective to the noun or pronoun it describes.

**Examples 1.** The walls are covered in bright floral wallpaper.  [*The* is an article describing *walls*. *Bright* and *floral* describe *wallpaper*.]

**2.** Certain couches have high headrests and low footrests.  [*Certain* describes *couches*, *high* describes *headrests*, and *low* describes *footrests*.]

**11.** We searched several databases but found little useful information for the project.  [Which words describe nouns or pronouns in the sentence?]

**12.** Plutonium is a radioactive chemical element.  [Which words describe nouns in the sentence?]

**13.** The divers were happy when they found the sunken ship.

**14.** The sports competition required participants to invent a new game using old equipment.

**15.** Marie, talented and dedicated, contributed to the literary magazine.

**16.** These pearls are synthetic.

**17.** Cliff crafted a large wooden table that will fit on the porch.

**18.** An urgent matter requires immediate attention.

**19.** May I borrow the blue pen and a clean sheet of paper?

**20.** Though the plant appears delicate, it is quite hardy.

# The Verb A

**1d.**   A *verb* expresses action or a state of being.

> **ACTION**   The sea often **inspires** wonder in writers and artists.
>
> **BEING**   The oceans **are** broad and deep.

## Main Verbs and Helping Verbs

A *verb phrase* is made up of at least one *main verb* and one or more *helping verbs.*

> **EXAMPLES**   **Have** we **considered** other options? [*Considered* is the main verb. *Have* is a helping verb.]
>
> The nurses **are** currently **working** at their stations. [*Working* is the main verb. *Are* is a helping verb.]
>
> Andrea **should have been sleeping.** [*Sleeping* is the main verb. *Should, have,* and *been* are helping verbs.]

Common helping verbs include forms of *be,* forms of *have,* forms of *do,* and modals.

> **BE**   am, are, be, been, being, is, was, were
>
> **HAVE**   had, has, have
>
> **DO**   do, does, did
>
> **MODALS**   can, could, may, might, must, shall, should, will, would

**REMINDER▶** A *modal* is a helping verb that is used with a main verb to express an attitude such as necessity or possibility.

> **EXAMPLES**   We **must** leave this afternoon. [*Must* expresses necessity.]
>
> If you shop carefully, you **may** find a bargain. [*May* expresses possibility.]

**EXERCISE A** Draw one line under each verb phrase in the following sentences. Then, draw two lines under each main verb.

**Examples 1.** The Barnes family has moved. [The main verb *moved* expresses an action. *Has* is a helping verb.]

**2.** Maggie should crush some ice and squeeze some lemons for her lemonade. [The main verbs *crush* and *squeeze* express actions. *Should* is a helping verb.]

**1.** Pumpkins should be harvested in the fall. [What is the main verb in the sentence? What words are helping verbs?]

**2.** Todd often has taught community education classes. [What is the main verb in the sentence? What word is a helping verb?]

**3.** Did Thomas Jefferson negotiate the Louisiana Purchase with France?

**4.** The box office will open at nine.

**5.** How does a water clock measure time?

**6.** He shall arrive soon after the press corps.

**7.** Jeannine has typed a résumé and scheduled several job interviews.

**8.** Mark and Debbie will grind their own wheat for bread.

**9.** Perhaps we should have been paying closer attention to the time.

**10.** Janice must have stumbled over that branch on the sidewalk.

---

A helping verb may be separated from the main verb.

> **EXAMPLES**   **Has** the mail **arrived** yet?
>
> **Do** you **know** the way there?

**NOTE▶** The words *never* and *not,* including the contraction *–n't,* are adverbs that tell *to what extent.* They are not part of the verb phrase.

> **EXAMPLES**   I **have** never **been** to Florida. [*Never* is an adverb that modifies *have been.* It is not part of the verb phrase.]
>
> **Does**n't that building **look** ancient? [The contraction for *not, –n't,* is an adverb that modifies *Does look.* It is not part of the verb phrase.]

**EXERCISE B** Draw one line under each verb phrase in the following sentences. Then, draw two lines under each main verb.

**Examples 1.** Have you already eaten lunch? [*Eaten* is the main verb. *Have* is a helping verb.]

    **2.** We should be starting a new unit in calculus class. [*Starting* is the main verb. *Should* and *be* are helping verbs.]

**11.** How did early Native Americans shape and hollow out logs for dugouts, a type of canoe? [What are the two main verbs in the sentence? What word is a helping verb?]

**12.** The committee isn't allotting any more money for research this year. [What is the main verb in the sentence? What word is a helping verb? Is the contraction *–n't* part of a verb phrase?]

**13.** Have you read *The Marble Faun* by Nathaniel Hawthorne?

**14.** She is hoping for a postcard from her grandparents.

**15.** In ten minutes, that puppy will have been barking for two hours.

**16.** Will they be renting an apartment or buying a house?

**17.** Isn't that picture leaning a little bit to the left?

**18.** The term *holly* can be applied to over four hundred species of red- or black-berried plants.

**19.** Hasn't the teacher assigned homework for this weekend?

**20.** This dish may be served either hot or cold.



Sixth Course

# The Verb B

**1d.**  A **verb** expresses action or a state of being.

## Action Verbs

An *action verb* expresses either physical or mental activity.

| | | | | |
|---|---|---|---|---|
| **PHYSICAL ACTIVITY** | lift | jog | listen | paint |
| **MENTAL ACTIVITY** | remember | concentrate | realize | dream |

**EXAMPLES**  Benjamin **wrote** a short story and **sold** it to a magazine.  [*Wrote* and *sold* are action verbs that describe Benjamin's physical activities.]

Dena **considered** the benefits of investing.  [*Considered* is an action verb describing Dena's mental activity.]

**EXERCISE A**  Underline the action verbs in the following sentences.  Hint: A sentence may contain more than one action verb.

**Examples  1.**  Because of the slick, wet roads, the radio announcer cautioned motorists.

[*Cautioned* expresses the announcer's physical activity.]

**2.**  Georgia dreams of the beautiful beaches in Hawaii.  [*Dreams* expresses Georgia's mental activity.]

**1.**  I finally remembered the name of the hardware store downtown.  [Which word expresses a mental activity?]

**2.**  William Caxton, a translator and publisher, printed books in England.  [Which word expresses a physical activity?]

**3.**  Please initial the first two pages and then sign the last page.

**4.**  Long vines of ivy climbed up the garden trellis.

**5.**  The ancient Romans constructed many roads, including the famous Appian Way.

**6.**  My grandfather recalls with fondness the adventures of his youth.

**7.**  Bart builds model rockets and collects *Star Wars* memorabilia.

**8.**  One steer ambled into a patch of clover and then quietly ate.

**9.**  In one of the greatest volcanic explosions in North American history, Mount Saint Helens erupted on May 18, 1980.

**10.**  The bright stadium lights illuminate the field for evening games.

**GO ON**

# Linking Verbs

A *linking verb* connects the subject to a word or word group that identifies or describes the subject. This word or word group is called a *subject complement.* Some common linking verbs are the forms of *be* as well as *appear, become, feel, grow, look, remain, seem, smell, sound, stay, taste,* and *turn.*

> **EXAMPLES**  The little boy **is** shy.  [*Is,* a form of *be,* is a linking verb that connects the subject *boy* to the subject complement *shy. Shy* describes *boy.*]
>
> Following a runoff election, she **became** mayor.  [*Became* is a linking verb that connects the subject *she* to the subject complement *mayor. Mayor* identifies *she.*]

**TIP▶** Some verbs may be used as linking verbs or as action verbs. To determine whether a verb in a sentence is a linking verb, substitute a form of the verb *be* or *seem.* If the sentence makes sense with a form of *be* or *seem,* the verb is probably a linking verb.

> **LINKING**  The apple cider **tasted** great.  [*The apple cider was great* makes sense. *Tasted* is a linking verb.]
>
> **ACTION**  Jeff **tasted** the apple cider.  [The sentence does not make sense with the verb *was* or *seemed. Tasted* is an action verb.]

**EXERCISE B**  Identify the underlined verbs in each of the following sentences as action verbs or linking verbs. Then, write *ACT* for *action verb* or *LINK* for *linking verb* on the line provided.

**Example**  ___LINK___  **1.** He <u>felt</u> uncertain about his performance on the exam.  [*Felt* connects the subject *He* to the subject complement *uncertain. Uncertain* describes *He.*]

_______ **11.** These grapes <u>taste</u> sour!  [Does *taste* connect the subject *grapes* to a subject complement that describes *grapes*?]

_______ **12.** Many builders <u>use</u> granite, a type of rock, for floors and countertops.  [Does *use* express an action performed by *builders*?]

_______ **13.** Our guests <u>stayed</u> with us for two weeks.

_______ **14.** These plants <u>grow</u> only in tropical regions.

_______ **15.** Everyone, please <u>remain</u> calm until the lights come on again.

_______ **16.** *Outback* <u>is</u> the term for the remote inland areas of Australia.

_______ **17.** We <u>felt</u> our way through the dark passageway.

_______ **18.** The camp cook <u>sounds</u> the dinner bell promptly at six o'clock.

_______ **19.** The quince, a fruit tree, <u>is</u> a native of Iran and Turkey.

_______ **20.** Rex <u>seems</u> upset to me.

# The Verb C

**1d.** A **verb** expresses action or a state of being.

## Transitive Verbs

A *transitive verb* has an *object*. An object is a word or word group that tells who or what receives the action of the verb.

> **EXAMPLES** We **built** a birdhouse.  [The object *birdhouse* receives the action of the verb *built*.]
>
> **Have** you **memorized** the poem and the name of its author?  [The objects *poem* and *name* receive the action of the verb *Have memorized*.]

**EXERCISE A**  In each of the following sentences, underline the transitive verb once and its object twice. Hint: Remember to underline all words in a verb phrase.

**Examples  1.** Shall I carry your tray to the table?  [*Shall carry* is a transitive verb whose object is *tray*.]

    **2.** We left our jackets and books in our lockers.  [*Left* is the verb, and *jackets* and *books* are its objects.]

**1.** Does Carol have a copy of the notes from history class?  [What two words form the verb phrase in this sentence?  What is the object of that verb phrase?]

**2.** Beverly Sills began her career as an opera singer at age eighteen.  [What word expresses action? What is the object of the verb in this sentence?]

**3.** The birds gathered dry grass and tufts of dog hair for their nests.

**4.** Has Frederick finished his homework yet?

**5.** An impressive structure, the Sears Tower in Chicago has 110 floors.

**6.** The copy machine needs toner and paper.

**7.** Felicia chooses her vehicles for their safety features and style.

**8.** Will you be sending the package first class?

**9.** The Mughal emperor Shah Jahan built the Taj Mahal in honor of his wife.

**10.** That company awards scholarships to children of employees.

## Intransitive Verbs

An *intransitive verb* does not have an object.

> **EXAMPLES** The baby **drew** clumsily.  [*Drew* does not have an object. *Clumsily* is an adverb describing how the baby drew.]
>
> Everyone **shouted** and **jumped** for joy.  [*Shouted* and *jumped* do not have objects. *Joy* is the object of the preposition *for*.]

**GO ON**

**NOTE▸** Although action verbs may be transitive or intransitive, linking verbs and state-of-being verbs are always intransitive. Linking verbs and state-of-being verbs never have direct objects.

> **EXAMPLES**  The basket **is** in the kitchen.
> The bear **became** slightly agitated.
> I **feel** much better now.
> That **sounds** like fun.

Many verbs can be either transitive or intransitive, depending on how they are used in a sentence.

> **TRANSITIVE**  The candidate **won** the election.  [*Election* is the object receiving the action of the verb *won*.]
> **INTRANSITIVE**  The candidate **won** by a landslide.  [*Won* does not have an object. *Landslide* is the object of the preposition *by*.]

**TIP▸** Most dictionaries indicate whether verbs are used transitively or intransitively. To determine whether a verb is transitive or intransitive, find the definition of the verb as you intend to use it. Then, look for one of these symbols: *vt* for *verb transitive* or *vi* for *verb intransitive*.

**EXERCISE B**  Identify the underlined words in each of the following sentences as transitive verbs or intransitive verbs. Then, write *TRANS* for *transitive verb* or *INT* for *intransitive verb* on the line provided. Hint: If the verb has an object, the verb is transitive.

**Examples**  __INT__  **1.** Cattle grazed in the green fields.  [*Grazed* does not have an object.]

__TRANS__  **2.** Brenda planted geraniums in large pots.  [*Planted* has an object, *geraniums*.]

_______ **11.** My father plays the hammered dulcimer, which is an instrument with strings that are beaten with hammers rather than plucked.  [Does the verb *plays* have an object?]

_______ **12.** The coach talked with the athletic director.  [Does the verb *talked* have an object?]

_______ **13.** Born in Germany, Henry Kissinger became a political scientist in the United States.

_______ **14.** Last night, lightning struck a tree near our home.

_______ **15.** Glowing brightly, the moon lit the path for the campers.

_______ **16.** We strolled leisurely through the park.

_______ **17.** According to legend, Betsy Ross made the first flag of the United States.

_______ **18.** Hurry! The train stops for only a few minutes!

_______ **19.** The post office sells stamps as well as boxes.

_______ **20.** Each of the performers impressed the audience.

# The Adverb

**1e.**    An *adverb* modifies a verb, an adjective, or another adverb.

An adverb tells *how, when, where,* or *to what extent* (*how much, how often,* or *how long*).

> **EXAMPLES**   The surgeon proceeded **cautiously.** [how]
>
> They work **here.** [where]
>
> She understood the instructions **entirely.** [to what extent]

## Adverbs Modifying Verbs

Adverbs are used most often to modify verbs. An adverb makes the meaning of a verb more specific.

> **EXAMPLE**   She did **not** explain the instructions **clearly.** [The adverbs *not* and *clearly* describe the verb phrase *did explain* by telling *how.*]

**EXERCISE A**   Underline the adverb in each of the following sentences. Then, draw an arrow from each adverb to the verb it modifies. Hint: Remember to include all parts of the verb phrase.

**Example**   **1.** He is carefully proofreading the documents for errors. [*Carefully* modifies the verb phrase *is proofreading* by telling *how.*]

**1.** The superintendent dealt with the situation fairly. [Which word makes the meaning of the verb *dealt* more specific?]

**2.** During the trial, the attorney presented her case effectively.

**3.** My hiking boots were completely covered with mud.

**4.** I looked everywhere for the lost library book.

**5.** American folklorist Carl Sandburg wrote poetically about the strength of people.

## Adverbs Modifying Adjectives

An adverb makes the meaning of an adjective more specific.

> **EXAMPLES**   The students were **quite** inventive with their projects. [The adverb *quite* describes the adjective *inventive* by telling *to what extent.*]
>
> An **exceptionally** musical child, Dinah played the piano at an early age. [The adverb *exceptionally* describes the adjective *musical* by telling *to what extent.*]

**GO ON** ➡

**EXERCISE B** Underline the adverb in each of the following sentences. Then, draw an arrow from the adverb to the adjective it modifies.

**Example  1.** The political debate seemed rather awkward for the candidates.  [*Rather* describes the adjective *awkward* by telling *to what extent.*]

**6.** The virus is entirely new, and researchers are trying to understand how it spreads.  [Which word makes the meaning of an adjective in this sentence more specific?]

**7.** Karl Marx's socialist philosophies were quite controversial in many circles.

**8.** The students, unusually attentive during the presentation, applauded when the lecture ended.

**9.** The hundred-year-old house was in remarkably good condition.

**10.** The special effects in the film are truly amazing.

## Adverbs Modifying Other Adverbs

An adverb makes the meaning of another adverb more specific.

**EXAMPLES**  Is it **too** late to sign up for tryouts?  [The adverb *too* modifies the adverb *late* by telling *to what extent.*]

A beginner, he plays the guitar **remarkably** well.  [The adverb *remarkably* modifies the adverb *well* by telling *to what extent.*]

**EXERCISE C** Underline the two adverbs in each of the following sentences. Then, draw an arrow from the modifying adverb to the adverb it modifies.

**Example  1.** The children were disguised very cleverly, but I recognized each of them.  [The adverb *very* modifies the adverb *cleverly* by telling *to what extent.*]

**11.** Only rarely have sailors spotted giant squid.  [Which adverb makes the meaning of the other adverb more specific?]

**12.** Our cousins arrived too late for the first song.

**13.** After a strong gust of wind, paper and leaves were scattered nearly everywhere.

**14.** We entered the dark cave somewhat reluctantly.

**15.** Although she feels nervous in a crisis, Sandra reacts quite calmly.

# The Preposition

**1f.**   A *preposition* shows the relationship of a noun or pronoun, called the *object of the preposition,* to another word.

Some common prepositions are *about, above, across, at, before, behind, between, by, down, during, for, from, in, like, near, of, on, out, past, throughout, under, upon, with,* and *without.*

The preposition in each of the following sentences shows the relationship between *plants* and *greenhouse. Greenhouse* is the object of each preposition.

> **EXAMPLES**   The plants **inside** the greenhouse are on sale.
>
> The plants **behind** the greenhouse are on sale.
>
> The plants **near** the greenhouse are on sale.

A preposition that consists of two or more words is a *compound preposition.* Some common compound prepositions are *according to, along with, apart from, aside from, as of, because of, in addition to, in front of, in place of, instead of, next to, on account of,* and *out of.*

> **EXAMPLES**   I sat **next to** the window.
>
> **In front of** the store are several parking spaces.

The *object of a preposition* is a noun, a pronoun, or a word group that functions as a noun. A preposition, its object, and any modifiers of the object form a *prepositional phrase.*

> **EXAMPLES**   Did you put the flowers **in cold water**? [*In cold water* is a prepositional phrase. *In* is the preposition, *water* is the object of the preposition, and *cold* is an adjective modifying *water.*]
>
> Maybe the car is parked **next to it.** [*Next to it* is a prepositional phrase. *Next to* is the compound preposition, and *it* is the object of the preposition.]

**EXERCISE A**  Underline the prepositions in each of the following sentences. Then, draw two lines under the object of each preposition. Hint: Some prepositions may be compound. Some sentences may contain more than one preposition.

**Examples 1.**  Eve and Lou rescued a cat that was stuck in a tree. [*In* is a preposition. *Tree* is the object of the preposition.]

**2.**  Out of nowhere swooped a large, black bird with a yellow beak. [*Out of* is a compound preposition. *Nowhere* is the object of *Out of. With* is a preposition. *Beak* is the object of *with.*]

**1.**  Before his career with the Yankees, baseball great Lou Gehrig attended Columbia University. [Which words are prepositions? Which words are objects of prepositions?]

**2.**  We rode the elevator to the top of the Empire State Building. [Which words are prepositions? Which words are objects of prepositions?]

**GO ON** ➡

**3.** With no moving parts, solar cells are an ideal power supply in space.

**4.** Ms. Stapleton brought us a basket of vegetables from her garden.

**5.** All of the tools are in the garage.

**6.** The commission has changed its strategy for the future.

**7.** My cat's favorite toy is a sock filled with catnip.

**8.** The park ranger walked slowly toward the bear cub.

**9.** Near the subway station there's an old newspaper stand.

**10.** Nearly 80 percent of the shipment was damaged by the storm.

## Adverb or Preposition?

Some words that can be used as prepositions may also be used as adverbs. Remember that an adverb is a modifier and does not have an object. Prepositions always have objects.

> **PREPOSITION**  I stood **outside** my house.  [*Outside* has an object, *house*.]
>
> **ADVERB**  I stood **outside.**  [*Outside* is an adverb describing *stood*.]
>
> **PREPOSITION**  We walked **around** the airport.  [*Around* has an object, *airport*.]
>
> **ADVERB**  We walked **around.**  [*Around* is an adverb describing *walked*.]

**EXERCISE B**  Determine whether the underlined word in each of the following sentences is a preposition or adverb. Then, write *PREP* for *preposition* or *ADV* for *adverb* on the line provided.

**Example**  _PREP_  **1.** Before the concert, we rode through the park.  [*Before* introduces a

prepositional phrase and has an object, *concert*.]

_______ **11.** Some of the members of our tour group were lagging <u>behind</u>.  [Does the underlined

word have an object?]

_______ **12.** Areas <u>outside</u> a defined boundary are said to be "beyond the pale."

_______ **13.** He stood <u>by</u> and watched from the sidelines.

_______ **14.** Jewelry and sculptures made <u>from</u> jade are very valuable.

_______ **15.** An emergency medical technician, Eddie is prepared <u>for</u> nearly any situation.

# The Conjunction and the Interjection

**1g.**   A *conjunction* joins words or word groups.

## Coordinating and Correlative Conjunctions

A *coordinating conjunction* joins words or word groups that are used in the same way. The coordinating conjunctions are *and, but, for, nor, or, so,* and *yet.*

> **EXAMPLES**   In the morning, the team jogs **and** does sit-ups.  [*And* joins two verbs, *jogs* and *does.*]
>
> Your keys are in your purse **or** on the table.  [*Or* joins two phrases, *in your purse* and *on the table.*]
>
> It's raining, **so** the seats are wet.  [*So* joins two clauses, *It's raining* and *the seats are wet.*]

*Correlative conjunctions* are pairs of conjunctions that join words or word groups that are used in the same way. The correlative conjunctions are *both . . . and, either . . . or, neither . . . nor, not only . . . but also,* and *whether . . . or.*

> **EXAMPLES**   **Both** Tiffany **and** Russell are from Denver.  [*Both . . . and* joins two nouns, *Tiffany* and *Russell.*]
>
> **Not only** did we discover a boat, **but** we **also** found oars and a life preserver.  [*Not only . . . but also* joins two clauses, *did we discover a boat* and *we found oars and a life preserver.*]

**EXERCISE A**   Underline the conjunctions in each of the following sentences.

**Example  1.**  Marshall joined us for lunch, <u>and</u> then we all went to the mall.  [*And* joins two clauses, *Marshall joined us for lunch* and *then we all went to the mall.*]

**1.** All of the books had been sold, so I checked out a copy from the library.  [Which word is used to join two clauses?]

**2.** The rehearsal was brief, but the director was happy with her actors' performances.

**3.** Langston Hughes wrote not only poetry but also plays.

**4.** Neither Lauren nor Ted knows of a solution to the problem.

**5.** Is bronze an alloy of copper and tin?

## Subordinating Conjunctions

A *subordinating conjunction* begins a subordinate clause and connects that clause to an independent clause. Some commonly used subordinating conjunctions are *after, although, because, before, how, if, in order that, so that, unless, until, whenever, whether,* and *while.*

**GO ON**

> **EXAMPLES**   We left early **because** the weather was bad.  [*Because* begins the
> subordinate clause *because the weather was bad* and connects it to the
> independent clause.]
>
> **If** the weather is bad, we'll leave early.  [*If* introduces the subordinate clause
> *If the weather is bad.* The subordinate clause is connected to the
> independent clause.]

**EXERCISE B**   Underline the subordinating conjunction in each of the following sentences.

**Example  1.**   While we searched for shells, he built a sand castle.  [The subordinating conjunction
*While* introduces a subordinate clause.]

**6.** If we hurry, we'll miss the traffic.  [Which word introduces a subordinate clause?]

**7.** Ethan took a detour because the main road was closed.

**8.** Unless the outfit goes on sale, I will not buy it.

**9.** Though the refrigerator was somewhat expensive, it should last for a long time.

**10.** We printed extra copies so that we would have enough for everyone.

## Interjections

**1h.**   An *interjection* expresses emotion and has no grammatical relation to the rest of the sentence.

Some interjections are *ah, alas, hey, oh, oops, ouch, well, whew,* and *yeah.*

An interjection is often set off from the rest of the sentence by an exclamation point or by one
or more commas. An exclamation point indicates strong emotion. A comma indicates mild
emotion.

> **EXAMPLES**   **Oh, no!** I locked my keys in the car!  [*Oh, no* expresses strong emotion.]
> **Well,** we can always get tickets later.  [*Well* expresses mild emotion.]

**EXERCISE C**   Underline the interjection in each of the following sentences. Then, on the line provided,
write *strong* if the interjection indicates strong emotion or *mild* if the interjection indicates mild
emotion.

**Example** ___mild___ **1.**   Oh, I thought that Sandra's appointment was before mine.  [*Oh* is set off by a
comma and expresses mild emotion.]

________**11.** Aha! The mystery is solved!  [What type of emotion does an exclamation point indicate?]

________**12.** Whew! That was a close call!

________**13.** Well, there's always next season.

________**14.** Ah, isn't the warm ocean breeze relaxing?

________**15.** Hey! That dog is running away with the newspaper!

# Subjects

**2b.**  Sentences consist of two basic parts: *subjects* and *predicates.* The **subject** is a word or word group that tells whom or what the sentence is about. The **predicate** is a word or word group that tells something about the subject.

| SUBJECT | PREDICATE |
| --- | --- |
| The dance routine | amazed everyone. |

## The Simple Subject and the Complete Subject

**2c.**  The **simple subject** is the main word or word group that tells whom or what the sentence is about.

The simple subject may consist of a noun, a pronoun, or a word group that functions as a noun. The *complete subject* includes the simple subject as well as any words that modify the simple subject.

> **SIMPLE SUBJECT**  The **author** of this children's series lives in Vermont. [*Author* is the main word that tells *whom* the sentence is about.]
>
> **COMPLETE SUBJECT**  **The author of this children's series** lives in Vermont. [The complete subject includes the simple subject *author* and all modifiers of the simple subject.]

Remember the following guidelines when you are trying to find the subject of a sentence.

- In a sentence that expresses a command or a request, the subject is always understood to be *you,* even though the word *you* may not appear in the sentence.
- The subject of a sentence is never the object of a prepositional phrase.
- In a question, the subject usually follows the verb or comes between parts of the verb phrase.
- The word *here* or *there* is almost never the subject of the sentence.

**TIP▶** To help find the subject of a sentence that expresses a question, turn the question into a statement. The subject of the statement will probably be the subject of the question.

> **QUESTION**  Has the sidewalk been repaired?
>
> **STATEMENT**  The sidewalk has been repaired. [What has been repaired? The *sidewalk* has been repaired. *Sidewalk* is the subject of both the statement and the question.]

**EXERCISE A**  Draw two lines under the simple subject of each of the following sentences. Then, underline the rest of the complete subject.

**Examples 1.**  Several of the players ran onto the field. [*Several* is the simple subject. *Several* is modified by the prepositional phrase *of the players.*]

**2.**  Are the suitcases stored in the closet or under the bed? [When you turn the question into a statement, you get *The suitcases are stored in the closet or under the bed.* What are stored? *Suitcases* are stored. *Suitcases* is the simple subject. The article *the* modifies *suitcases.*]

**GO ON ▶**

1. Two of the judges agreed to hear the case. [Can the object of a preposition be part of a simple subject? What prepositional phrase modifies the simple subject?]

2. Glowing brightly against the night sky was the light from the old lighthouse. [What was glowing brightly? What phrase is part of the complete subject?]

3. Are all of the autographs authentic?

4. Here are the plans for the new addition to the house.

5. The chemists were wearing safety glasses and protective clothing.

6. At the end of the street lives a family from the Netherlands.

7. Was that map created by a famous explorer?

8. Members of the club will meet next Friday at four o'clock.

9. Pittsburgh was built at the intersection of two rivers that become the Ohio River.

10. Did everyone at the reception sign the guest book?

## Compound Subjects

Subjects can be compound. A *compound subject* consists of two or more subjects that are joined by a conjunction such as *and* or *or*. The parts of a compound subject have the same verb.

> **EXAMPLES**  **Alaska** and **Hawaii** do not border any other states. [*Alaska* and *Hawaii* are joined by the conjunction *and* and have the same verb, *do border*.]
>
> Did **Alyssa** or **Janelle** write this note? [*Alyssa* and *Janelle* are joined by the conjunction *or* and have the same verb, *Did write*.]

**EXERCISE B**  Underline the parts of the compound subject in each of the following sentences.

**Example  1.** Are <u>tomato</u>, <u>onion</u> and <u>oregano</u> used in this recipe? [*Tomato, onion,* and *oregano* are parts of a compound subject that have the same verb, *Are used.*]

11. Did Cecilia or Lawrence find Ms. Clay's car keys? [Who *did find*?]

12. Haiku and tanka are both forms of Japanese poetry.

13. At the career fair, an oceanographer, an actor, and a cartoonist gave the most interesting presentations.

14. Sopranos, altos, tenors, and basses sing together in our community choir.

15. Exceptional hitters, Hank Aaron and Ty Cobb set many records in professional baseball.

# Predicates

**2b.**  Sentences consist of two basic parts: *subjects* and *predicates*.  The *subject* is a word or word group that tells whom or what the sentence is about. The *predicate* is a word or word group that tells something about the subject.

| SUBJECT | PREDICATE |
|---|---|
| Several birds | perched on the fence. |

| PREDICATE | SUBJECT | PREDICATE |
|---|---|---|
| Where did | you | put the mail? |

## The Simple Predicate and the Complete Predicate

**2d.**  The *simple predicate,* or verb, is the main word or word group that tells something about the subject.

The simple predicate may be a one-word verb or a *verb phrase.* A verb phrase is a main verb with one or more helping verbs. The *complete predicate* includes the simple predicate and all words that modify the simple predicate and complete its meaning.

**SIMPLE PREDICATE (VERB)**  To warm them up, the coach **gave** the team a pep talk.

**COMPLETE PREDICATE**  **To warm them up,** the coach **gave the team a pep talk.**  [*To warm them up* tells *why* the coach gave the pep talk. *The team* and *a pep talk* are objects that complete the meaning of the verb.]

**SIMPLE PREDICATE (VERB)**  **Has** the mail **been sorted** today?

**COMPLETE PREDICATE**  **Has** the mail **been sorted today?**  [*Today* tells *when* the mail has been sorted.]

**SIMPLE PREDICATE (VERB)**  The tide **was rising.**

**COMPLETE PREDICATE**  The tide **was rising.**  [If no words modify or complete the meaning of the simple predicate, the simple predicate and the complete predicate are the same.]

**EXERCISE A**  Draw two lines under the simple predicate in each of the following sentences. Then, underline the rest of the complete predicate. [Hint: The simple predicate may contain more than one word.]

**Examples 1.**  At the end of the month, I will have lived here for a year.  [*Will have lived* is the simple predicate that tells something about the subject *I.* *At the end of the month* and *here for a year* modify *will have lived* by telling *when* and *where* I will have lived.]

**2.**  Do these plants thrive in cooler climates? [*Do thrive* is the simple predicate that tells something about the subject *plants.* *In cooler climates* modifies *Do thrive* by telling *where* the plants thrive.]

**GO ON** ➡

1. Has the game schedule been posted on the bulletin board? [Which three words form the verb phrase that is the simple predicate? Which prepositional phrase modifies the predicate by telling where?]

2. A Norse explorer, Leif Ericson is often considered the first European on North American shores. [Which two words form the simple predicate? What adverb modifies the simple predicate? What words complete the meaning of the simple predicate?]

3. During peak traffic hours, we usually ride the subway.

4. During the night, a gust of wind blew a large branch onto the roof of the house.

5. Will the Russian ballet company perform at the local theater this weekend?

6. Most folk songs have survived through an oral tradition rather than a written one.

7. Ralph, the winner of the door prize, presented his ticket to the store manager.

8. Does the manufacturer's warranty cover labor costs?

9. Kung fu, a martial art, combines exercise with concentration and self-discipline.

10. Should the government preserve more land for national parks?

## Compound Verbs

Some sentences contain two or more verbs that share the same subject. These verbs are called *compound verbs.* The parts of a compound verb are usually joined by the conjunction *and, but,* or *or.*

> **EXAMPLES**  The clerk **has** already **opened** the cash register and **counted** the money. [The verbs *has opened* and *counted* have the same subject, *clerk.*]
> Isabella **bought** a gift but **forgot** to bring it to the party. [The verbs *bought* and *forgot* have the same subject, *Isabella.*]

**EXERCISE B**  Underline the compound verbs in each of the following sentences. Be sure to underline all parts of any verb phrases.

**Example 1.** Did W.E.B. DuBois share in the creation of the NAACP and edit its magazine? [*Did share* and *edit* have the same subject, *W.E.B. DuBois.*]

11. Did anyone call or leave a message for me today? [Which verbs have the same subject, *anyone*?]

12. A noted scientist, Alfred Nobel invented dynamite and founded the Nobel Prizes.

13. Should we recycle these boxes or store them in the attic?

14. As his first project, Val sanded the wood and primed it.

15. During autumn, leaves turn bright colors and fall from the trees.

# Direct Objects

**2h.**   A **direct object** is a complement that tells who or what receives the action of a verb or shows the result of the action.

**REMINDER** A *complement* is a word or word group that completes the meaning of a verb.

A direct object may be a noun, a pronoun, or a word group that functions as a noun. To identify a direct object, ask *Whom?* or *What?* after a transitive verb.

| | |
|---|---|
| **NOUN** | The accountant usually hires an **assistant** during tax season. [*Whom* does the accountant hire? The accountant hires an *assistant*.] |
| **PRONOUN** | Did the dog bury **it**? [The dog did bury *what*? It buried *it*.] |
| **WORD GROUP** | I will take **whatever is available.** [I will take *what*? I will take *whatever is available*.] |

A direct object may be compound.

| | |
|---|---|
| **EXAMPLE** | We drove **Mary** and **Sam** to school. [*Mary* and *Sam* tell *who* receives the action of the verb *drove*.] |

**EXERCISE A** Underline the direct object(s) in each of the following sentences.

**Examples 1.** Do you remember the <u>combination</u> to the safe? [*Combination* receives the action of the verb *Do remember*.]

      **2.** Without her glasses, she can see only <u>what is right in front of her</u>. [*What is right in front of her* tells *what* she can see.]

**1.** We need some bread and milk from the grocery store. [What do we need?]

**2.** Has the rain washed the mud off the sidewalk? [What has the rain washed?]

**3.** The famous architect Frank Lloyd Wright popularized certain home designs in the early twentieth century.

**4.** They pitched their tents close to the lake.

**5.** The actor performed an amazing stunt!

**6.** Haven't you already received information and an application?

**7.** For the quilt, Sidney arranged the strips of fabric in a "log cabin" pattern.

**8.** An early advocate for women's rights, Mary Wollstonecraft wrote *A Vindication of the Rights of Woman* in 1792.

**9.** After the yard sale, Chandra will donate whatever is left to the thrift store.

**10.** The English sport of rugby requires an oval ball similar to an American football.

**GO ON**

# Objective Complements

**2j.**    An ***objective complement*** is a complement that helps complete the meaning of a transitive verb by identifying or modifying the direct object.

A sentence can have an objective complement only if the sentence has a direct object. An objective complement may be a noun, a pronoun, an adjective, or a word group that functions as a noun or an adjective.

> **EXAMPLES**   Many people consider Tiger Woods a positive **role model** for youth. [The compound noun *role model* identifies the direct object *Tiger Woods*.]
> We painted the shutters **green.** [The adjective *green* describes the direct object *shutters*.]

**NOTE▶** Only a few verbs take objective complements. These verbs include *consider, make,* and any verbs that can be replaced by *consider* or *make.* Verbs that can be replaced by *consider* or *make* include *appoint, believe, call, choose, color, cut, dye, elect, find, keep, name, paint, render,* and *sweep.*

An objective complement may be compound.

> **EXAMPLE**   Competition in business often makes products more **affordable** and **available.** [*Affordable* and *available* form a compound objective complement describing the direct object *products.*]

**EXERCISE B**   Underline the objective complement(s) in each of the following sentences. [Hint: First, identify the direct object. Then, determine which word or words identify or modify the direct object.]

**Example 1.** Did recent rock slides make some roads <u>impassable</u> and <u>dangerous</u>? [*Impassable* and *dangerous* describe the direct object *roads.*]

**11.** The gardener clipped the hedges straight and even. [What words describe the direct object *hedges*?]

**12.** City employees decorated the city hall red, white, and blue in honor of Independence Day.

**13.** Does the Food and Drug Administration consider these chemicals safe?

**14.** The Morrises named their children Ramón and Isabel.

**15.** You have made our visit pleasant!

           Sixth Course

# Indirect Objects

**2i.**    An *indirect object* is a complement that often appears in sentences containing direct objects and that tells *to whom* or *to what* or *for whom* or *for what* the action of a transitive verb is done.

A sentence must have a direct object in order to have an indirect object. Indirect objects usually come between the verb and the direct object. An indirect object may be a noun, a pronoun, or a word group that functions as a noun.

> **EXAMPLES**    Our grandparents brought **us** some peaches from Georgia. [The direct object *peaches* receives the action of the verb *brought* and tells *what* was brought. The indirect object *us* tells *to whom* the peaches were brought. The indirect object *us* comes between the verb *brought* and the direct object *peaches*.]
>
> Our math teacher allows **whoever has been absent** two days for make-up work. [The direct object *days* receives the action of the verb *allows* and tells *what* is allowed. The indirect object *whoever has been absent* tells *for whom* the teacher allows two days. The indirect object *whoever has been absent* comes between the verb *allows* and the direct object *days*.]

**EXERCISE A**   Underline the indirect object in each of the following sentences.

**Examples 1.** The golf pro gave my <u>boss</u> some tips on improving her swing. [*Boss* tells *to whom* the pro gave tips.]

**2.** Did this corporation send the relief <u>organization</u> a donation? [*Organization* tells *to what* the corporation did send a donation.]

**1.** A guest artist taught the class a lesson on perspective art. [Which word tells *to whom* the artist taught a lesson?]

**2.** Through much of history, parents awarded whichever son was born first most of the family's property. [Which group of words tells *to whom* the property was awarded?]

**3.** The new store owner handed the first several customers gift certificates.

**4.** At the end of our baseball season, the former champions present the new champions the trophy.

**5.** Before a car leaves the factory, employees give it a thorough inspection.

**6.** Would you please save me a seat in the front row?

**7.** Juanita's teacher wrote her an excellent letter of recommendation.

**8.** King George V gave his son a home called Fort Belvedere.

**9.** The auctioneer sold the buyers the rest of the cars from the lot.

**10.** The mayor's presence lent the event an air of formality.

**GO ON** ➡

**NOTE▶** Be careful not to confuse an indirect object with an object of the preposition *to* or *for*.

    **INDIRECT OBJECT**    The officer read the **suspects** their rights. [The indirect object *suspects* tells *to whom* the officer read the rights.]

**OBJECT OF A PREPOSITION**    The officer read the rights to the **suspects.** [*Suspects* is the object of the preposition *to*.]

An indirect object may be compound.

    **EXAMPLE**    I always bring my **brother** and **sister** souvenirs from camp. [*Brother* and *sister* tell *to whom* I bring souvenirs.]

**EXERCISE B**   In each of the following sentences, underline the direct object once and the indirect object(s) twice.

**Examples 1.** Sheila sent her aunt and uncle a graduation picture. [*Picture* is the direct object that tells *what* Sheila sent. *Aunt* and *uncle* are indirect objects that tell *to whom* a picture was sent.]

        **2.** Did Colleen give him or her the key to the trunk? [*Key* tells *what* was given. *Him* and *her* tell *to whom* the key was given.]

**11.** According to legend, a Greek soldier ran from Marathon to Athens and delivered the citizens news of an Athenian military victory. [*What* did the soldier deliver? *To whom* did he deliver it?]

**12.** The judges will present whoever finishes first and whoever makes a perfect score blue ribbons. [What word tells *what* the judges will present? What two word groups tell *to whom* the judges will present it?]

**13.** During baseball practice, the coach hit the players several ground balls.

**14.** Did you give Jenny and Ted directions to the house?

**15.** Did the Egyptian queen Cleopatra pledge Marc Antony her loyalty?

**16.** Every evening, Mr. Shelton reads his children a bedtime story.

**17.** My mother knitted my sister and me wool sweaters.

**18.** Has the teacher allowed Stan and Ian extra time for their reports?

**19.** Show Lori and Dale your wildlife sketches.

**20.** The supervisor assigned Gail and Shane the first two projects.

for **CHAPTER 2: PARTS OF A SENTENCE**   `page 95`

# Predicate Nominatives

**2k.**   A *subject complement* is a complement that identifies or modifies the subject of a linking verb.

**REMINDER** Some common linking verbs include forms of *be* (such as *am, is, was, were, being, will be,* and *have been*), *appear, become, feel, grow, look, remain, seem, smell, sound, stay, taste,* and *turn.*

A *predicate nominative* is a type of subject complement that identifies or refers to the subject of a linking verb. A predicate nominative may be a noun, a pronoun, or a word group that functions as a noun.

> **EXAMPLES**   The Grangers were the first **settlers** in the region. [The noun *settlers* identifies the subject *Grangers.*]
>
> **Who** is the woman in the back row? [The pronoun *Who* refers to the subject *woman.*]
>
> The goal of the architects is **to restore the building to its original condition.** [The infinitive phrase *to restore the building to its original condition* functions as a noun and identifies the subject *goal.*]

**NOTE** For emphasis, a writer sometimes places a subject complement before the subject and the verb.

> **EXAMPLE**   What an interesting **sculpture** that is! [The noun *sculpture* identifies the subject *that.*]

**EXERCISE A** Underline the predicate nominative in each of the following sentences.

**Examples 1.** In my childhood, I became an avid <u>reader</u> of suspense novels. [*Reader* refers to the subject *I.*]

    **2.** Sunscreen and a hat are <u>what Stacey brings to the beach</u>. [*What Stacey brings to the beach* identifies the compound subject *Sunscreen* and *hat.*]

**1.** The purpose of the press conference was to clarify the senator's position on the issue. [What group of words identifies the subject *purpose*?]

**2.** For over a thousand years, Kyoto was the capital of Japan. [What word follows the linking verb and refers to the subject *Kyoto*?]

**3.** With his coach's encouragement, Evan has become a competitive swimmer.

**4.** Aren't the Burnetts good friends of yours?

**5.** What an entertaining speaker he is!

**6.** My parents are active volunteers in several service organizations.

**7.** Idaho did not become a state until 1890.

**8.** Charles will remain vice president until the end of March.

**9.** *The Federalist* papers were essays in support of the U.S. Constitution.

**10.** Gloves and a scarf are what I put on in cold weather.

---

A predicate nominative may be compound.

> **EXAMPLES**   The colors of the rainbow are **violet, indigo, blue, green, yellow, orange,**
> and **red.** [*Violet, indigo, blue, green, yellow, orange,* and *red* identify the
> subject *colors.*]
>
> The top salespeople for the month were **Brady** and **Ramona.** [*Brady* and
> *Ramona* refer to the subject *salespeople.*]

---

**EXERCISE B**   Underline the compound predicate nominatives in the following sentences.

**Examples 1.** Important employee benefits are health <u>insurance</u> and a retirement <u>plan</u>. [*Insurance*

and *plan* refer to the subject *benefits.*]

**2.** This fall, Felicia will become <u>editor</u> and business <u>manager</u> of the student journal.

[*Editor* and *manager* identify the subject *Felicia.*]

**11.** The only businesses in the neighborhood are the corner market and a small convenience store.

[Which words follow the linking verb and refer to the subject *businesses*?]

**12.** Two of the highest-paid teachers in the school are Ms. Robinson and Mr. Floyd. [Which words

in the predicate identify the subject *Two*?]

**13.** Mr. Carson's favorite types of programs are sports events and nature shows.

**14.** Two of the smallest countries in Europe are Luxembourg and Belgium.

**15.** The first guests at the reception were Cheryl and I.

**16.** A pioneer in higher education for women, Mary Lyon was the founder and first principal of

Mount Holyoke Female Seminary.

**17.** Did Tyrone become a computer programmer or a psychologist?

**18.** The earliest of Jane Austen's novels were *Sense and Sensibility* and *Pride and Prejudice.*

**19.** After a successful singing career, Sonny Bono became a mayor and later a U.S. representative.

**20.** The assistant band directors are Ms. Lawson and Mr. Samuelson.

# Predicate Adjectives

**2k.**   A *subject complement* is a complement that identifies or modifies the subject of a linking verb.

A *predicate adjective* is a type of subject complement. A predicate adjective is an adjective that is in the predicate and that modifies or describes the subject of a linking verb.

> **EXAMPLES**   The puppy seemed **energetic** after its bath.  [The predicate adjective *energetic* describes the subject *puppy*.]
>
> Is this set of antique dishes **complete?**  [The predicate adjective *complete* describes the subject *set*.]

**NOTE▶** Sometimes writers place a predicate adjective before the subject and the verb for emphasis.

> **EXAMPLE**   **Hot** and **muggy** was our hike through the woods.  [The predicate adjectives *Hot* and *muggy* modify the subject *hike*.]

**EXERCISE A**  Underline the predicate adjective in each of the following sentences.

**Examples 1.**  Does this soup taste too <u>spicy</u> to you?  [The adjective *spicy* refers to the subject *soup*.]

**2.**  The customers became <u>impatient</u> after the long wait.  [The adjective *impatient* refers to the subject *customers*.]

**1.** The fresh blueberries were delicious in my oatmeal.  [What word completes the meaning of the linking verb *were* and describes the subject *blueberries*?]

**2.** The air always smells fresh after a summer shower.  [What word completes the meaning of the linking verb *smells* and describes the subject *air*?]

**3.** The crowd became restless in the third quarter.

**4.** Even in a hot desert, temperatures can turn cold at night.

**5.** After the meeting, everyone seemed confident about the chairperson's budget proposal.

**6.** Is this table narrow enough for the space beside the couch?

**7.** After learning more about chess, Nancy became more enthusiastic about the game.

**8.** Powerful were the speeches of Dr. Martin Luther King, Jr.

**9.** The novels of French writer and political activist Émile Zola were often controversial.

**10.** Does this outfit seem appropriate for the wedding reception?

**GO ON ➡**

**NOTE** ▶ Not all adjectives that are in the predicate are predicate adjectives. Remember that a predicate adjective describes only the subject.

> **EXAMPLES**   *The Pirates of Penzance* is probably **popular** among fans of musicals. [*Popular* is a predicate adjective because it completes the meaning of the linking verb *is* and describes the subject *The Pirates of Penzance*.]
>
> *The Pirates of Penzance* is probably a **popular** production among fans of musicals. [The adjective *popular* describes *production*, not the subject *The Pirates of Penzance*. *Popular* is not a predicate adjective.]

A predicate adjective may be compound.

> **EXAMPLE**   These porcelain vases are **rare** and **expensive**. [The predicate adjectives *rare* and *expensive* describe the subject *vases*.]

**EXERCISE B**   Underline the compound predicate adjectives in each of the following sentences.

**Examples 1.** Isn't that actor usually <u>funny</u> and often <u>sensitive</u>? [The predicate adjectives *funny* and *sensitive* describe the subject *actor*.]

**2.** The city's centennial celebration was <u>memorable</u> and <u>historic</u>. [The predicate adjectives *memorable* and *historic* describe the subject *celebration*.]

**11.** Were your grandmother's parents Puerto Rican or Italian? [Which predicate adjectives identify the subject *parents*?]

**12.** The holidays were brief but restful. [Which adjectives complete the meaning of the linking verb and describe the subject *holidays*?]

**13.** During the debate, both teams remained calm and attentive.

**14.** The old house looks fresh and bright in its new coat of paint.

**15.** The Guggenheim Museum's art collection is extensive and diverse.

**16.** Thorough and informative were Dr. Jacobson's lectures on genetics.

**17.** The personnel at the hospital are always compassionate and sympathetic.

**18.** Sometimes the moon appears yellow or even orange in the night sky.

**19.** Cautious and deliberate were the scientists during the dinosaur fossil's excavation.

**20.** This type of essay is argumentative or persuasive.

# The Prepositional Phrase

**3b.**   A *prepositional phrase* includes a preposition, the object of the preposition, and any modifiers of that object.

Common prepositions include *to, with, before, off, next to,* and *in spite of.*

> **EXAMPLES**   **In the brightly lit room,** Eric and Amy practiced the waltz step.  [The prepositional phrase tells where the waltz step was practiced. The phrase begins with the preposition *In.*]
>
> The rhythm **of waltz music** swings along happily.  [The prepositional phrase tells which rhythm the sentence describes. The phrase begins with the preposition *of.*]

**REMINDER▶** A phrase is a group of related words that is used as a single part of speech. A phrase will not have both a verb and its subject.

The object of a preposition may be compound.

> **EXAMPLE**   The book I'm reading is about an old **man** and the **sea.**  [*Man* and *sea* are objects of the preposition *about.*]

## The Adjective Phrase

There are two types of prepositional phrases: adjective phrases and adverb phrases.

**3c.**   A prepositional phrase that modifies a noun or a pronoun is called an *adjective phrase.*

Like single-word adjectives, adjective phrases modify nouns or pronouns and often follow the word or words they modify. Adjective phrases answer the questions *What kind(s)?* and *Which one(s)?*

> **EXAMPLES**   Micah likes movies **about real-life heroes.**  [The adjective phrase *about real-life heroes* modifies the noun *movies.* It tells *what kind* of movies Micah likes to watch.]
>
> One movie starred a hero **in a red, white, and blue costume with stars.** [The adjective phrase *with stars* modifies *costume,* telling *what kind* of costume. The adjective phrase *in a red, white, and blue costume* tells *which one* about the noun *hero.*]

**EXERCISE A**  Find and underline the adjective phrase in each sentence. Then, draw an arrow from the phrase to the word or words it modifies.

**Example  1.**  The library books on the counter are due Wednesday.  [The preposition *on* begins the adjective phrase *on the counter.* The entire phrase tells which books are due.]

**1.**  Water the plants on the back patio every day.  [Which word group includes a preposition, its object, and modifiers of that object?  What does the adjective phrase describe?]

**2.**  Next, we'll paint the shelves next to the stove.

**GO ON ➡**

**3.** Does the cat with the stripes need its shots?

**4.** Trees near rivers usually have a good water supply.

**5.** The children behind the stage curtain practiced their lines once again.

## The Adverb Phrase

**3d.**   A prepositional phrase that modifies a verb, an adjective, or an adverb is called an ***adverb phrase.***

Like single-word adverbs, adverb phrases modify verbs, adjectives, or other adverbs. They answer these questions: *How? When? Where? Why? To what extent? How far? How long?* More than one adverb phrase may be used to add specific information to a sentence.

> **EXAMPLES**   Janette sprinkled dried basil **into the sauce** and stirred it.  [The prepositional phrase *into the sauce* tells where Janette sprinkled the basil. The phrase modifies the verb *sprinkled.*]
>
> **In her garden,** she grows basil **from seeds.**  [The prepositional phrase *In her garden* tells where the basil grows, and the phrase *from seeds* tells how the basil is grown. Both phrases modify the verb *grows.*]
>
> Which of these ties is most appropriate **for the occasion**?  [The prepositional phrase *for the occasion* tells how the tie is appropriate. The phrase modifies the adjective *appropriate.*]

**EXERCISE B**   Find and underline the adverb phrase in each sentence. Then, draw an arrow from each phrase to the word or words it modifies.

**Example  1.**  I chose this novel because of its suspenseful plot.  [The compound preposition *because of* begins the phrase *because of its suspenseful plot.* The phrase modifies the verb *chose.*]

**6.** Tim poured turpentine on the paintbrush.  [Which word group includes a preposition, its object, and modifiers of that object?  Which verb does the adverb phrase modify?]

**7.** Coach Winters wears her whistle during basketball games.

**8.** My grandmother, active in volunteer organizations, is often quite busy.

**9.** Dash to the front door and unlock it.

**10.** The old moose moved quickly for its age.

# The Participle and the Participial Phrase

**3e.**   A ***participle*** is a verb form that can be used as an adjective.

There are two kinds of participles: present participles, which always end in *–ing*, and past participles. Regular verbs have past participles that end in *–d* or *–ed*. Irregular verbs have irregularly formed past participles.

**PRESENT PARTICIPLES**   the **exciting** news      a **surprising** outcome  [Adding *–ing* to the verbs *excite* and *surprise* makes them present participles that function as adjectives.]

**PAST PARTICIPLES**   a **welcomed** guest      **polished** windows      the **worn** book  [Adding *–d* to the verb *welcome* and *–ed* to the verb *polish* makes them regular past participles. *Worn* is the irregular past participle of the verb *wear*. All three past participles function as adjectives.]

**REMINDER**▶ You will often see participles in verb phrases, such as *have been welcoming* or *is worn*. If a participle appears with these helping verbs, it is not an adjective. It is part of the verb phrase.

**EXERCISE A**  Underline the participle in each sentence below. Then, draw an arrow to the word or words the participle modifies.

**Example  1.**  The shining harp gleamed with jewels.  [*Shining* is the present participle of the verb *shine* and modifies *harp*. Note that *gleamed*, which also ends in *–ed*, is not a modifier; it is the verb of the sentence.]

**1.**  The balanced rock was precisely perched on the cliff's edge.  [Is there a participle in the sentence? Does it modify a noun or pronoun?]

**2.**  Quick! Get out of this pouring rain!

**3.**  Laughing, the children played tag in the park.

**4.**  Everyone's attention was on the ringing phone.

**5.**  Did you see that well-researched report on the news last night?

## The Participial Phrase

**3f.**   A ***participial phrase*** consists of a participle and any modifiers or complements the participle has. The entire phrase is used as an adjective.

Like single-word adjectives, participial phrases modify nouns and pronouns.

**EXAMPLES**   **Watching thoughtfully,** Kent noticed a change in the solution's temperature. [The present participle *Watching* is modified by *thoughtfully.* The whole phrase modifies the proper noun *Kent.*]

**GO ON** ▶

The moviegoers, **concerned for the hero's safety,** sat on the edges of their seats.  [The past participle *concerned* is modified by the prepositional phrase *for the hero's safety.* The whole phrase modifies the noun *moviegoers.*]

**REMINDER** If you are unsure of how the past participle of an irregular verb is formed, look the verb up in a current dictionary or handbook.

**EXERCISE B** Underline each of the participial phrases in the sentences below. Then, draw an arrow to the word or words the phrase modifies.

**Example 1.** Whistling a tune, Dusty strolled along.  [The present participle *Whistling* has an object, *tune.* The whole phrase modifies the proper noun *Dusty.*]

**6.** Plugging in the toaster, Marsha wondered if there were any bagels.  [Is there a participle in the sentence?  Does the participial phrase modify a noun or pronoun?]

**7.** The travelers, arriving at the airport in the nick of time, sighed with relief.

**8.** How long will the meeting rescheduled for this afternoon last?

**9.** Pushing snow to either side of the road, the snowplows pressed on.

**10.** The fan, bought at a flea market, did little to cool the room.

**EXERCISE C** Using the verb suggested in the parentheses, add a participle to create a participial phrase. Hint: If you are not sure whether to use a present participle (*–ing*) or a past participle (*–d, –ed*), try both forms and choose the one that makes sense in the sentence.

**Example 1.** (Open) ____*Opening*____ her present, Mom smiled at us.  [*Open* is a regular verb, and its present participle, *opening,* describes *Mom.*]

**11.** (puff)    The steam engine rounded the corner, ____________ into the station on time.  [Is *puff* a regular or irregular verb?  Does a present or a past participle make sense in the sentence?]

**12.** (force)    The stoplight turned red, ____________ the cars to wait.

**13.** (blow)    The beach ball, ____________ too full, popped when Jamie caught it.

**14.** (laugh)    The audience, ____________ at the lead comic, began to applaud.

**15.** (Tap)    ____________ on the door, I called out, "Is anybody home?"

                                                                 Sixth Course

# The Gerund and the Gerund Phrase

**3g.**   A *gerund* is a verb form ending in *–ing* that is used as a noun.

The *–ing* form of a verb can be used as its present participle, functioning as an adjective. The *–ing* form can also be part of a verb phrase.

**–*ING* FORM AS PART OF A VERB PHRASE**   Lonnie has been **cleaning** house all day.  [*Cleaning* is part of the verb phrase *has been cleaning*.]

**–*ING* FORM AS A PRESENT PARTICIPLE**   These **cleaning** brushes work well on many surfaces. [*Cleaning* is a participle and functions as an adjective describing *brushes*.]

**–*ING* FORM AS A GERUND**   Lonnie doesn't mind **cleaning** if the rest of his family will pitch in, too.  [*Cleaning* is a gerund and functions as the direct object of the verb phrase *does mind*.]

A gerund can function in all the ways a noun can function: as a subject, predicate nominative, direct object, indirect object, or object of a preposition.

**EXERCISE A**   In each sentence, an *–ing* form of a verb is underlined. If the *–ing* form is part of a verb phrase, write *V* on the line provided. If it is a participle, write *P* on the line.  If it is a gerund, write *G* on the line.

**Examples**   ___*P*___  **1.** This folding chair is made of maple.  [The participle *folding* describes *chair*.]

___*G*___  **2.** Suzi likes humming while she works.  [The gerund *humming* is the direct object of the verb *likes*.]

______  **1.** Who is rocking the baby to sleep?  [Is the underlined word modifying a noun, functioning as a noun, or acting as part of a verb phrase?]

______  **2.** Members of the band enjoyed marching. [Is the underlined word modifying a noun, functioning as a noun, or acting as part of a verb phrase?]

______  **3.** Focusing, the students started the next step of the project.

______  **4.** Plowing should be part of this field's preparation.

______  **5.** If you want to study fossils, be prepared for a lot of digging!

______  **6.** To reduce office wastes, we're going to give recycling a try.

______  **7.** The backhoe has been digging a hole for the house's foundation.

______  **8.** The loudest sound in the gymnasium was Latrice's clapping.

______  **9.** Debating inspired Juan to become a lawyer.

______  **10.** The rising moon lit up the landscape.

**GO ON**

**3h.** A ***gerund phrase*** consists of a gerund and any modifiers or complements the gerund has. The entire phrase is used as a noun.

As with nouns, gerund phrases can function as subjects, predicate nominatives, direct and indirect objects, and objects of prepositions.

**EXAMPLES**  Janet earns top scores for **solving math problems quickly.** [The gerund *solving* has a complement, *math problems*, and is modified by the adverb *quickly*. The whole phrase acts as the object of the preposition *for*.]

**Riding in the parade** was a fun experience. [The gerund *Riding* is modified by a prepositional phrase, *in the parade*. The whole phrase acts as the subject of the sentence.]

**EXERCISE B**  Underline the gerund phrase in each sentence. Then, underline the gerund a second time.

**Examples 1.** Lounging on the couch is a pleasant way to spend a rainy afternoon. [The gerund *Lounging* is modified by the prepositional phrase *on the couch*. The whole phrase functions as the subject of the sentence.]

**2.** I heard a loud buzzing. [The gerund *buzzing* is modified by *a* and *loud*. The whole phrase functions as the direct object of the sentence.]

**11.** Nell is practicing her math by memorizing geometry theorems. [Is there an *–ing* form of a verb that functions as a noun in the sentence? Does it have a complement?]

**12.** Measuring carefully is important in carpentry. [Is there an *–ing* form of a verb that functions as a noun in the sentence? Does it have a modifier?]

**13.** The dog enjoys chewing on the twigs from the pecan tree.

**14.** Raising livestock is hard work.

**15.** This crab moves by scuttling sideways.

**16.** Let's go dancing at that new club.

**17.** Running a marathon takes months of preparation.

**18.** Don't make the mistake of promising what you can't deliver.

**19.** Feeding the fish is one of Josh's daily chores.

**20.** He gives winning the match his full attention.

# The Infinitive and the Infinitive Phrase

**3i.** An *infinitive* is a verb form that can be used as a noun, an adjective, or an adverb. Most infinitives begin with *to*, but occasionally the word *to* is omitted.

> **EXAMPLES** Is it time **to go?** [The infinitive *to go* is used as an adjective to modify *time.*]
>
> Try **to exercise** daily. [The infinitive *to exercise* is used as a noun. The infinitive phrase is the direct object of the verb *Try.*]
>
> Your next task is **to lift** this crate. [The infinitive *to lift* is used as a noun. The infinitive phrase is the predicate nominative of the verb *is.*]

**TIP▶** Remember that the word *to* is often used as a preposition. If *to* is followed by a noun or pronoun, *to* is a preposition. If *to* is followed by a verb, *to* is the sign of the infinitive.

| | | | |
|---|---|---|---|
| **INFINITIVES** | to permit | to count | to observe |
| **PREPOSITIONAL PHRASES** | to you | to the house | to New York |

**EXERCISE A** Underline the infinitive in each sentence. Be sure to underline both the sign of the infinitive, the word *to,* and the verb itself.

**Examples 1.** Get ready <u>to go</u> to the park, please. [The word *to* comes before the verb *go*, making an infinitive. The word *to* that comes before the noun *park* is a preposition.]

    **2.** How fast will the race car drivers try <u>to drive</u>? [The word *to* comes before the verb *drive*, making an infinitive.]

**1.** In front of the fireplace is a warm place to sit. [Is the word *to* used in the sentence? Does *to* come before a verb?]

**2.** After a good performance, it's polite to applaud. [Is the word *to* used in the sentence? Does *to* come before a verb?]

**3.** The tired child managed to smile.

**4.** To finish is my only concern at this point!

**5.** On a warm, breezy day, it's fun to sail.

**6.** Shane told us that he had finally learned to draw.

**7.** To win tonight would really improve the team's record.

**8.** The best course to take is the one proposed by the commission.

**9.** Once the water began filling the canoe, it began to sink.

**10.** This pair of slacks is sure to fit.

**GO ON ▶**

**3j.** An ***infinitive phrase*** consists of an infinitive and any modifiers or complements the infinitive has. The entire phrase can be used as a noun, an adjective, or an adverb.

> **EXAMPLES**  **To apply a good coat of paint,** sand and clean the surface first. [The infinitive *To apply* has a direct object, *coat. Coat* is modified by *a* and *good* and by the prepositional phrase *of paint.* The whole infinitive phrase functions as an adverb modifying the verbs *sand* and *clean.*]
>
> My little brother is easy **to put to bed.** [The infinitive *to put* is modified by the prepositional phrase *to bed.* The whole phrase functions as an adverb modifying the adjective *easy.*]

**NOTE▶** In formal speech and writing it is best to avoid "splitting infinitives." An infinitive is "split" if a modifying word or words come between the sign of the infinitive, *to,* and the verb.

> **SPLIT INFINITIVE**  My parents plan **to** soon **buy** a new computer.
> **REVISED**  My parents plan **to buy** a new computer soon.

**EXERCISE B** Underline the infinitive phrase in each of the following sentences. Then, underline the infinitive a second time.

**Examples 1.** It's hard to remain patient. [The infinitive phrase *to remain patient* functions as an adverb modifying the adjective *hard.*]

**2.** Does Daniel want to join us for lunch? [The infinitive phrase *to join us for lunch* functions as a noun and is the direct object of the verb *Does want.*]

**11.** Thunder began to boom loudly. [Is the word *to* followed by a verb? Does the infinitive have any complements or modifiers?]

**12.** Do you have anything to say about this situation? [Is the word *to* followed by a verb? Does the infinitive have any complements or modifiers?]

**13.** To lose herself in a good mystery novel is Gina's wish right now.

**14.** To reach the harbor, turn right at the light and drive two miles.

**15.** Has Kayla ever been tempted to tell your secret?

**16.** You need to lift this barbell slowly and steadily ten times.

**17.** How to cross the river safely was the question.

**18.** It's important to be really honest with your friends.

**19.** The next step is to ventilate the room thoroughly.

**20.** To resolve this issue permanently will require time and effort.

# The Appositive and the Appositive Phrase

**3k.**  An ***appositive*** is a noun or a pronoun placed beside another noun or pronoun to identify or describe it.

Appositives add specific details that the sentence would otherwise lack. An appositive may be a single noun or pronoun, or it may be a compound noun or pronoun.

> **EXAMPLES**  Their cat **Frost** has a silver coat.  [*Cat* is a general noun, but the appositive *Frost* tells which cat.]
>
> Our earliest crops, **carrots** and **radishes,** were almost ready for harvesting. [*Crops* is a general noun, but the appositive nouns, *carrots* and *radishes,* tell what specific crops.]
>
> **Vegetables,** these plants are good for our health.  [The appositive *Vegetables* comes before the more general noun *plants* for emphasis. Usually, an appositive follows the noun or pronoun it identifies.]

**TIP** ▶ Very often, single-word or compound appositives are set off from the main sentence by commas. Sometimes, the commas can help you locate appositives.

> **EXAMPLE**  These plants, fresh corn and prickly okra, will be harvested soon.

**EXERCISE A**  Underline the appositive in each of the following sentences. Then, draw an arrow to the noun or pronoun it identifies or describes.

**Examples 1.** Tom's favorite food, pasta, is easy to make.  [The appositive *pasta* identifies the more general noun *food.*]

**2.** He likes the long pasta shapes, linguine and spaghetti, most of all.  [The compound appositive nouns *linguine* and *spaghetti* identify the more general noun *shapes.*]

**1.** That man, Dr. Nathan Bedford, has already testified in court.  [Does the sentence contain a general noun that is made more specific by an appositive?]

**2.** This book, *Walden,* is a favorite in our English class.  [Does the sentence contain a general noun that is made more specific by an appositive?]

**3.** Which boy is your brother Jason?

**4.** That store, Dollar-and-Dime, sells paper goods and other items.

**5.** Do you play her favorite instrument, guitar?

**6.** This Thursday, we volunteers will begin our final fund-raising campaign.

**7.** The museum's latest acquisitions, sculptures, are now on display.

**GO ON** ▶

**8.** One of her friends, Jerome, will be helping us build the float.

**9.** The yard sale begins tomorrow, Wednesday, unless it rains.

**10.** The dog is learning a new skill, obedience.

---

**3l.** An ***appositive phrase*** consists of an appositive and any modifiers the appositive has.

Like appositives, the appositive phrase adds detail and interest to the main sentence.

> **EXAMPLE**   The two machines, **an off-balance washer and a dryer with a frayed belt,** made a lot of noise.  [The appositive phrase identifies the more general noun *machines*.]

**EXERCISE B**  Underline the appositive phrase in each of the following sentences.

**Examples 1.** John's favorite movie, the classic *Casablanca*, is a favorite of mine, too.  [The appositive phrase *the classic Casablanca* identifies the noun *movie*.]

**2.** Mammals like us, white whales sometimes swim in rivers.  [The appositive phrase *Mammals like us* describes *white whales*.]

**11.** Flour, an important ingredient in baking, comes in several varieties.  [What phrase identifies or describes a more general noun?]

**12.** Sit and watch this show, a suspenseful science fiction drama, with me.  [What phrase identifies or describes a more general noun?]

**13.** A chore I don't mind at all, mowing the lawn actually relaxes me.

**14.** The long train, loaded freight cars and beat-up boxcars, blocked traffic for at least ten minutes.

**15.** Ficus, tropical plants with shiny leaves, are sometimes grown as ornamentals.

**16.** Beaches and ski slopes, popular vacation destinations, are always crowded in season.

**17.** The clean laundry, freshly washed jeans and socks, lay stacked on the kitchen table.

**18.** Hawks and eagles, both birds of prey, have hook-tipped beaks.

**19.** The advisor, attorney Mavis Newton of Dallas, is an expert in medical legal issues.

**20.** The clouds, streaks of pink against the sky, reflected the sunset.

# The Adjective Clause

A clause is a group of words that contains a verb and its subject. Clauses may be independent and stand on their own, or subordinate, functioning as part of a sentence. A subordinate clause cannot stand alone as a sentence.

**4d.**   An *adjective clause* is a subordinate clause that modifies a noun or a pronoun.

Adjective clauses usually follow the noun or pronoun they modify. They describe nouns or pronouns, adding interesting details to sentences by telling *what kind* or *which one.*

> **EXAMPLES**   Felicia's house, **which is the red brick one on the corner,** is shaded by pine trees.  [The adjective clause follows the noun it modifies, *house,* and describes it, telling which house it is.]
>
> The shade **that moves across her yard each day** allows her little brothers to play outside comfortably.  [The adjective clause follows the noun it modifies, *shade,* telling what kind of shade.]

**NOTE▶**   An adjective clause usually begins with a *relative pronoun,* which shows the relationship of the clause to the word or words it modifies. Common relative pronouns include *that, which, who, whom,* and *whose.* An adjective clause may also begin with a *relative adverb,* such as *when* or *where.*

**EXERCISE A**   Find and underline the adjective clause in each sentence below. Then, circle the noun or pronoun that the adjective clause modifies.

**Example  1.**  A snowy egret stalked among the (reeds) that fringed the lake.  [The adjective clause *that fringed the lake* modifies the noun *reeds.*]

**1.**  Please wind the clock that sits on the mantel.  [What relative pronoun or relative adverb begins a clause?  What word does the clause modify?]

**2.**  Is the Scott family looking for a car that has lots of legroom?

**3.**  The chairperson, to whom the committee listened closely, outlined the proposal.

**4.**  Where is the trophy that Samantha won at the tennis match?

**5.**  Do you remember the time when Aunt Emma taught us to fish?

Adjective clauses come in two types, depending on what they do in a sentence. An *essential* (or *restrictive*) *clause* is critical to the meaning of the sentence. An essential clause restricts the meaning of the noun or pronoun it modifies. If you remove an essential adjective clause from the sentence, the sentence loses part of its basic message and may not make sense at all.

> **ESSENTIAL**   Avoid exercises **that cause you pain.**  [Without the essential clause, the sentence would read, "Avoid exercises." The essential clause restricts the meaning of *exercises.* Not all exercises should be avoided, only those *that cause you pain.*]

**GO ON ➡**

A *nonessential* (or *nonrestrictive*) *clause,* on the other hand, adds additional information to a sentence. Removing a nonessential clause from a sentence makes the sentence less specific or less interesting, but it does not change the basic meaning of the sentence. Because nonessential clauses can be removed from the sentence in this way, these clauses are separated from the sentence by commas.

> **NONESSENTIAL**   A weight bar**,** **to which weights can be added,** should carry just enough weight to challenge your muscles. [The adjective clause adds a detail about a weight bar that is interesting. However, if you remove the clause, the sentence's basic meaning stays the same: "A weight bar should carry just enough weight to challenge your muscles."]

**EXERCISE B**   Underline the adjective clause in each of the following sentences. Then, on the line before the sentence, write **E** if the clause is essential or **NE** if the clause if nonessential. Hint: Remember that nonessential clauses are set off by one or more commas.

**Example**     _E_     **1.** Children <u>who are finishing kindergarten</u> probably know their alphabet.

[Without the essential adjective clause, the sentence inaccurately reads, "Children probably know their alphabet." Note that the clause is **not** set off from the sentence by commas.]

______ **6.** Many kindergarten teachers keep healthful snacks handy for their students, who get hungry often. [What clause begins with a relative pronoun or a relative adverb? Is the clause essential to the meaning of the sentence?]

______ **7.** On the bulletin board, the teacher displayed art that the children had made. [What clause begins with a relative pronoun or a relative adverb? Is the clause essential to the meaning of the sentence?]

______ **8.** Letters and numbers, which are the building blocks of writing and math, are taught to these children.

______ **9.** The children also play finger games, which improve motor skills and hand-eye coordination.

______ **10.** Their teachers must be people who enjoy the company of small children.

______ **11.** My best friend, whom I have known since kindergarten, is in my math class.

______ **12.** Is that the book that you've been looking for?

______ **13.** Those pictures remind me of a time when I didn't worry about anything.

______ **14.** Isn't the site where the old elementary school stood being turned into a park?

______ **15.** The new elementary school, which my youngest brother will attend, was just completed last year.

# The Noun Clause

**4e.** A *noun clause* is a subordinate clause that is used as a noun. A noun clause can function in any way that a single noun can function.

|  |  |
|---|---|
| **SUBJECT** | **Whoever leaves last** should turn off the lights. [The noun clause is the subject of the verb phrase *should turn.*] |
| **PREDICATE NOMINATIVE** | My hope is **that the bees will not sting him.** [The noun clause is the predicate nominative, following the verb *is.*] |
| **DIRECT OBJECT** | Does someone know **where we pick up the tickets**? [The noun clause is the direct object of the verb *Does know.*] |
| **INDIRECT OBJECT** | Give **whoever is thirsty** a bottle of cold water. [The noun clause is the indirect object of the verb *give* (*bottle* is the direct object).] |
| **OBJECT OF A PREPOSITION** | Please hand a blank form to **whoever does not have one.** [The noun clause is the object of the preposition *to.*] |

**EXERCISE A** Identify the function of the noun clause in each of the following sentences. On the line provided, write **S** for subject, **PN** for predicate nominative, **DO** for direct object, **IO** for indirect object, or **OP** for object of a preposition. The noun clauses have been underlined for you.

**Example** _**DO**_ **1.** No one knows what the coach will say next. [The noun clause follows the verb *knows* and is its direct object.]

_______ **1.** Show whoever hasn't yet signed them these documents. [Does the noun clause come after a verb or before a verb? Does it follow a preposition?]

_______ **2.** Kelly suddenly realized what might happen next.

_______ **3.** What Mel learned is how he can be successful in math.

_______ **4.** That horses are intelligent animals is a well-known fact to their trainers.

_______ **5.** The judges awarded prizes to whoever had done well.

**NOTE▶** Noun clauses are usually introduced by a word such as *how, that, what, when, which, who, whom,* or *whose.* The introductory word often has a function within the noun clause, such as serving as the subject, direct object, or predicate nominative. When *who/whom* and *whoever/whomever* are part of a noun clause, their function in that clause determines which form to use, not the word that comes before the pronoun.

        **EXAMPLE** Concert seating is free to **whoever wants to attend.** [In the noun clause, *whoever* is the subject of the verb *wants.* The entire noun clause is the object of the preposition *to.*]

**GO ON ▶**

**EXERCISE B**  Underline the noun clause in each of the following sentences. Hint: If you are having trouble finding the whole clause, look first for one of the words that commonly introduce noun clauses.

**Example  1.**  Naomi said <u>that there is a message for you.</u>  [This noun clause, *that there is a message for you,* is the direct object of the verb *said.*]

**6.**  Only his mother knew why the child was laughing.  [What word group functions as the direct object of the verb *knew*?]

**7.**  Where the treasure is buried remains a mystery to this very day.

**8.**  Will each student conduct an interview with whoever has inspired him or her?

**9.**  The final decision is whether we should travel by car or by train.

**10.**  Notify whichever teacher is closest if a problem occurs.

> **TIP** Adjective clauses and noun clauses can both begin with *that, which, who, whom,* or *whose.* Remember that an adjective clause **describes** a noun or a pronoun, while a noun clause performs the function of a noun in the sentence.

**EXERCISE C**  Underline the noun clause in each of the following sentences. Then, tell how the noun clause functions in the sentence by writing **S** for subject, **PN** for predicate nominative, **DO** for direct object, **IO** for indirect object, or **OP** for object of a preposition on the line provided.

**Example  __S__  1.**  <u>Whoever is finished</u> may help another student.  [The noun clause is introduced by *Whoever* and serves as the subject of the verb *may help.*]

______**11.**  Careful consideration is what is required now.  [Which word commonly introduces noun clauses? Does the noun clause follow an action verb or a linking verb?]

______**12.**  Kevin asked when the movie starts.

______**13.**  Let's get in line at whichever cash register has the fewest people waiting.

______**14.**  The stadium is where all the excitement is happening.

______**15.**  That the kitten attacked its own reflection amused all of us.

# The Adverb Clause

**4f.**  An ***adverb clause*** is a subordinate clause that modifies a verb, an adjective, or an adverb.

Like single-word adverbs, adverb clauses tell *how, when, where, why, to what extent,* or *under what conditions.* Unlike adjective clauses, which follow the words they modify, adverb clauses can appear at the beginning, in the middle, or at the end of sentences. However, they are easy to identify because they begin with a subordinating conjunction. Common subordinating conjunctions include *after, although, as if, as long as, because, before, since, so that, unless, whenever,* and *while.*

> **EXAMPLES**   **Before the biologist sampled the water,** she dropped a dye tablet into the test tube.  [The adverb clause tells *when* the action of the sentence occurred. The adverb clause begins with the subordinating conjunction *Before.*]
>
> She scooped up a few tablespoons of water **so that she could examine it in the lab.**  [This adverb clause begins with the subordinating conjunction *so that* and tells *why* she collected the water.]

**EXERCISE A**  Find and underline the adverb clause in each sentence. The word or words the adverb clause modifies have been underlined already. Hint: If you are having trouble finding the adverb clause, look first for the subordinating conjunction that begins the clause.

**Example  1.**  David reads nonfiction <u>more</u> <u>than he reads fiction</u>.  [The subordinating conjunction *than* begins the clause *than he reads fiction,* which modifies the adverb *more.*]

**1.** As long as Michelle keeps practicing, her abilities <u>will grow</u>.  [Which subordinating conjunction begins the adverb clause?]

**2.** <u>Relieved</u> because the hard rain had stopped, Nicholas steered the car back out onto the road.

**3.** Please <u>continue</u> working on the test until time is called.

**4.** Since the store's inventory sold more quickly than expected, employees <u>may go</u> home early.

**5.** When the curtain had risen completely, Susan <u>walked</u> onto the stage.

> **NOTE**  You may have noticed that when an adverb clause begins a sentence, it is followed by a comma. The comma marks the end of the adverb clause and the beginning of an independent (or main) clause.

**GO ON**

**EXERCISE B**  Underline the adverb clause in each of the following sentences. Then, underline twice the verb, adverb, or adjective that the clause modifies.

**Example**  **1.**  Exhausted because she had weeded and planted all day, Felicia welcomed a rest in the hammock and a cold glass of tea.  [The clause modifies the adjective *Exhausted* by telling *why* Felicia was exhausted.]

**6.**  George should study anatomy carefully if he wants to be a personal trainer for athletes.  [What clause tells *under what conditions* about a word group in the sentence?  What word group does it modify?]

**7.**  Will Nell help her brother with his homework so that he will complete it on time?

**8.**  Sam must kick the ball harder than he has so far, or he will not be able to score.

**9.**  Please put another coat of paint on the wall because the old color is showing through.

**10.**  When we take our dog Pepper to the dog park, she always comes home tired but happy.

**4g.**  Part of a clause may be left out when its meaning can be clearly understood from the context of the sentence.  Such a clause is called an ***elliptical clause.***

As long as the meaning of the sentence remains clear, certain words—often the subject, the verb, or both—can be omitted from the adverb clause.

> **COMPLETE CLAUSE**  Frances runs more often **than Mike runs.**
>
> **ELLIPTICAL CLAUSE**  Frances runs more often **than Mike.**  [Both sentences and both adverb clauses mean the same thing. In the second sentence, the verb *runs* is understood, though not expressed.]

**EXERCISE C**  Underline the elliptical clause in each of the following sentences.

**Example  1.**  I enjoy a good game of chess as much as the next person.  [The words *enjoys a good game of chess* are understood in this elliptical clause.]

**11.**  When building a campfire, start with small pieces of dry wood.  [What group of words leaves out the words *you are?*]

**12.**  Adrienne sings more loudly than Janet.

**13.**  The painter carefully mixed new paint while waiting for the canvas to dry.

**14.**  When revising their writing, some students choose to read aloud to a friend.

**15.**  Marta received as many notes of congratulations as her sister.

**for CHAPTER 4: THE CLAUSE**     pages 140–141

# Sentence Structure A

## Simple Sentences and Compound Sentences

**REMINDER▶** An independent clause expresses a complete thought. It can stand by itself as a sentence. A subordinate clause has a verb and its subject but does not express a complete thought. It cannot stand by itself as a sentence.

> **SUBORDINATE**    when the doorbell rang   [This thought leaves the reader asking, "What happened when the doorbell rang?" The thought is not complete.]
>
> **INDEPENDENT**   The doorbell rang.   [This thought is complete by itself.]

**4h.**    Depending on its structure, a sentence can be classified as simple, compound, complex, or compound-complex.

**(1)**   A *simple sentence* has one independent clause and no subordinate clauses.

A simple sentence may have a compound subject or verb, or both a compound subject and compound verb.

> **EXAMPLES**    The water sparkled in the bright sun.   [one independent clause]
>
> The reeds by the lake rustled and whispered in the wind.   [one independent clause with a compound verb: *rustled* and *whispered*]

**EXERCISE A**   Underline the subject once in each of the following sentences. Then, underline the verb twice. Hint: Remember to underline all parts of a compound subject or a compound verb and all parts of a verb phrase.

**Example 1.** Do you have a favorite hobby?   [The subject is *you,* and the verb is *Do have.*]

**1.** Hal and I carve wood into sculptures.   [Who is the sentence about? What are they doing?]

**2.** Some people prefer quieter hobbies.

**3.** For example, my brother spends many hours watching birds.

**4.** Did he see a new species of bird for the first time yesterday?

**5.** Almost everyone has some sort of hobby or collects something.

**(2)**   A *compound sentence* has two or more independent clauses and no subordinate clauses.

Like simple sentences, compound sentences do not have any subordinate clauses.

> **EXAMPLES**    We fished during the morning, we napped during the afternoon, and we hiked around the lake during the evening.   [Three independent clauses—*we fished, we napped, we hiked*—with their modifiers form one compound sentence.]
>
> Later, clouds gathered, and a storm seemed likely.   [Two independent clauses—*clouds gathered* and *a storm seemed likely*—form a compound sentence. Each independent clause could be a sentence by itself.]

**GO ON ▶**

**EXERCISE B** Underline each independent clause in the sentences below. If a sentence has only one independent clause, write **S** for *simple sentence* on the line before the sentence. If the sentence has more than one independent clause, write **C** for *compound sentence*.

**Example** _____*C*_____ **1.** The fire burned down slowly, the moon rose, and the campers looked

forward to sleep. [Three independent clauses make this a compound sentence.

Each clause could stand alone as a sentence.]

_____ **6.** It took only minutes to douse the fire completely. [How many complete thoughts are

expressed in this sentence?]

_____ **7.** Not even an ember glowed in the ashes; as a result, the stars seemed to shine more

brightly than before.

_____ **8.** The campers looked at the stars in awe; after all, most of the boys were used to bright

city lights and dim stars.

_____ **9.** In the distance, a coyote yowled, paused, and then yipped.

_____ **10.** The campers called goodnight to one another; then they zipped their tents up and slept.

---

**NOTE▶** Simple sentences can be joined to form compound sentences in one of three ways:

- Use a comma followed by one of the seven coordinating conjunctions (*and, but, for, nor, or, so, yet*). Example: Seth was tired**,** **but** he kept working anyway.
- Use a semicolon. Example: I'm having some juice**;** would you like a glass?
- Use a semicolon followed by a conjunctive adverb or transitional expression. Example: Water the hanging plants daily**;** **otherwise,** they will dry out and wilt.

---

**EXERCISE C** Identify each of the following sentences as *simple* or *compound*. On the line provided, write **S** if the sentence is *simple* or **C** if the sentence is *compound*. Hint: If you are not sure, first underline each independent clause.

**Example** _____*S*_____ **1.** Does your city have a public library? [Only one complete thought is

expressed in this sentence.]

_____ **11.** At one time, libraries were only for books, but they are not any more. [How many

complete thoughts are expressed in this sentence?]

_____ **12.** For instance, many libraries have computers with Internet access; patrons can spend

hours surfing the World Wide Web.

_____ **13.** Most libraries also have DVDs and CDs available for checkout.

_____ **14.** Borrowing a movie from your library is free, and you get to keep it for a whole week.

_____ **15.** Just don't forget to bring it back on time!

# Sentence Structure B

## Complex Sentences and Compound-Complex Sentences

**REMINDER** An independent clause expresses a complete thought. It can stand by itself as a sentence. A subordinate clause has a verb and its subject but does not express a complete thought. It cannot stand by itself as a sentence.

**SUBORDINATE** if the shop is already closed [This thought leaves the reader asking, "What will happen if the shop is already closed?" The thought is not complete.]

**INDEPENDENT** The shop is already closed. [This thought is complete by itself.]

**4h.** Depending on its structure, a sentence can be classified as simple, compound, complex, or compound-complex.

You have already studied simple and compound sentences.

**(3)** A ***complex sentence*** has one independent clause and at least one subordinate clause.

The subordinate clauses may be an adjective, a noun, or an adverb clause. A complex sentence may also have other modifiers or phrases.

**EXAMPLE** Unless we use the avocados today, we will have to throw them away because they will go bad. [A subordinate clause, *Unless we use the avocados today,* introduces the independent clause, *we will have to throw them away.* The complex sentence ends with a second subordinate clause, *because they will go bad.*]

**EXERCISE A** Underline each independent clause in the sentences below; then underline each subordinate clause twice.

**Example 1.** Have you ever muted the television volume because an ad came on? [The subordinating conjunction *because* begins the subordinate clause *because an ad came on;* the rest of the sentence, *Have you ever muted the television volume,* is an independent clause.]

**1.** Composers spend time composing catchy jingles so that people will walk around whistling and humming them. [Which word group expresses a complete thought? Which word group does not?]

**2.** Because the images in ads are so important, sometimes there are no words at all.

**3.** Although there are quiet ads, many ads scream at viewers to get their attention.

**4.** Have you ever enjoyed an ad but forgotten what product it was for right away?

**GO ON**

**5.** Because so many people watch the Super Bowl, it costs millions of dollars to run an ad during that event.

---

**(4)** A *compound-complex sentence* contains two or more independent clauses and at least one subordinate clause.

> **EXAMPLES** Place the paper, which has already been used, in the recycle bin, but leave the other art supplies out. [Two independent clauses—*Place the paper in the recycle bin* and *leave the other art supplies out*—combine with the subordinate adjective clause *which has already been used* to make a compound-complex sentence.]
>
> Until the entire art area is cleaned up, the students may not leave; therefore, everyone works quickly to get the job, which no one particularly likes, done. [This complicated sentence combines two independent clauses—*the students may not leave* and *everyone works quickly to get the job done*—and two subordinate clauses, an adverb clause—*Until the entire art area is cleaned up*—and an adjective clause—*which no one particularly likes*.]

---

**EXERCISE B** Underline the independent clause or clauses in each of the following sentences. Then, underline any subordinate clauses twice. If a sentence has one independent clause, write **Cx** for *complex* on the line provided. If a sentence has two or more independent clauses, write **Cd-Cx** for *compound-complex*.

**Example** _Cd-Cx_ **1.** While reading is important in the workplace, it also offers us recreation; after all, a good book can take us away from our hectic lives. [This sentence has two independent clauses and one subordinate clause.]

______ **6.** Some people like to read history, while others prefer romance. [Which word group expresses a complete thought? Which word group does not?]

______ **7.** Have you ever been swept up in a book, even though you knew it was only a story, and have you ever been sorry when you reached the last page?

______ **8.** Magazines, which cover every possible interest, have many readers as well; in fact, our family currently subscribes to seven magazines because everyone in the family wants to read something different.

______ **9.** If you want to keep up with the daily news, there's still no beating a good city newspaper, which has coverage of local, national, and global events and issues.

______ **10.** However, some people like to get their news from the Internet, or they listen to news radio programs while they do chores around the house.

# Subject-Verb Agreement A

## Singular and Plural Subjects

**5b.**   A verb should agree in number with its subject.

Singular subjects take singular verbs.

> **EXAMPLE**   **Taylor draws** designs for robots.  [The singular subject *Taylor* agrees with the singular verb *draws*.]

Plural subjects take plural verbs.

> **EXAMPLE**   **Are** those **robots** products of his designs?  [The plural subject *robots* agrees with the plural verb *Are*.]

> **NOTE▶** Verb phrases also agree with their subjects. A verb phrase is made up of a main verb and one or more helping verbs. The first helping verb in the verb phrase agrees with the subject.

> **EXAMPLE**   **Has he been designing** robots for long?  [*Has been designing* is the verb phrase. The singular helping verb *has* agrees with the singular subject *he*.]

**EXERCISE A**   Underline the subject in each of the following sentences. Then, draw two lines under the verb in parentheses that agrees in number with the subject.

**Example  1.** *(Do, Does)* factories sometimes use robots?  [The subject of the sentence is *factories*. *Do use* is the verb phrase. The plural helping verb *Do* agrees with the plural subject *factories*.]

**1.** Many industries *(rely, relies)* on the work of robots.  [Is the subject singular or plural? Which verb form agrees with the subject?]

**2.** For example, the automotive industry *(uses, use)* robots on assembly lines.

**3.** Certain robots *(welds, weld)* vehicle bodies.

**4.** At a different stage of the process, another robot *(paints, paint)* the vehicles.

**5.** *(Do, Does)* an engineer design a different robot for each specific task?

## Compound Subjects

Two or more subjects joined together form a *compound subject.* The words in a compound subject take the same verb.

**5e.**   Subjects joined by *and* usually take a plural verb.

> **EXAMPLES**   **Basil** and **thyme are** herbs.  [The subjects *Basil* and *thyme* are joined by *and,* so the compound subject agrees with the plural verb *are*.]
>
> **Michelle** and the **others swim** for the school team.  [The subjects *Michelle* and *others* are joined by *and,* so the compound subject agrees with the plural verb *swim*.]

**GO ON ▶**

**5f.** Singular subjects joined by *or* or *nor* take a singular verb.

> **EXAMPLE** **Was** the **speech** or the **poster** Grant's idea?  [*Speech* and *poster* are singular
> subjects joined by *or*. The compound subject agrees with the singular
> verb *Was*.]

**5g.** When a singular subject and a plural subject are joined by *or* or *nor*, the verb agrees with the
subject nearer the verb.

> **EXAMPLES** The **speech** or the **posters were** Grant's idea.  [*Or* joins *speech*, a singular
> subject, to *posters*, a plural subject. The plural verb *were* agrees with
> *posters*, the subject nearer the verb.]
> Neither the campaign **buttons** nor the **Web site is** ready.  [*Nor* joins *buttons*,
> a plural subject, to *Web site*, a singular subject. The singular verb *is* agrees
> with *Web site*, the subject nearer the verb.]

**EXERCISE B** Underline the compound subject in each of the following sentences. Then, draw two lines
under the verb in parentheses that agrees with the compound subject.

**Examples 1.** *(Is, Are)* Marsha and Ted watching the debate on television?  [Joined by *and*, the

compound subject *Marsha* and *Ted* agrees with the plural verb phrase *Are watching*.]

**2.** Neither Frank nor his opponents *(has, have)* run for office before.  [Joined by *nor*, the

compound subject is formed from a singular subject, *Frank,* and a plural subject,

*opponents*.  The plural verb phrase *have run* agrees with the compound subject because

the subject nearer the verb, *opponents,* is plural.]

**6.** *(Does, Do)* the president and the vice-president meet each day?  [Does a compound subject

joined by *and* take a singular or plural verb?]

**7.** The refrigerator, the dishwasher, or the disposal *(hum, hums)* rather loudly.  [Does a compound

subject joined by *or* take a singular or plural verb?]

**8.** Leon and Lana *(love, loves)* being on the debate team.

**9.** Neither the planet nor its moon *(sustain, sustains)* life.

**10.** In their jobs, lawyers and politicians *(debates, debate)* many issues.

**11.** After high school he and I *(am, are)* going to college.

**12.** The chairs or the coffee table *(fit, fits)* next to the sofa.

**13.** *(Has, Have)* you and she chosen careers in the legal profession?

**14.** The principal or the teachers *(counts, count)* the votes.

**15.** Rachel, Phil, or the editor *(writes, write)* about every election.

# Subject-Verb Agreement B

## Intervening Phrases and Clauses

**5c.**   The number of a subject is not changed by a word in a phrase or a clause following the subject.

**EXAMPLES**   The **bread** with walnuts **is** homemade.  [The phrase *with walnuts* comes between the subject *bread* and its verb *is*. Although the plural noun *walnuts* comes between the subject and verb, *bread* and *is* still agree.]

**Bread,** when we bake it, **smells** delicious.  [The adverb clause *when we bake it* comes between the subject *Bread* and its verb *smells*. Although the plural pronoun *we* comes between the subject and verb, *Bread* and *smells* still agree.]

**EXERCISE A**   Underline the subject in each of the following sentences. Then, draw two lines under the verb in parentheses that agrees with the subject.

**Example  1.**   The story about the space aliens *(was, were)* inventive.  [The singular subject *story* agrees with the singular verb *was*.]

**1.**  Strange lights across the lake *(flashes, flash)* along the shore every night.  [Is the subject singular or plural?  Which verb agrees with the subject?]

**2.**  Each morning, a delivery truck that carries packages *(stops, stop)* at the corner.

**3.**  A banana, together with those berries, *(makes, make)* a tasty smoothie.

**4.**  The artists who own this studio *(has, have)* filled it with their own art.

**5.**  His property, which includes a house and a barn, *(is, are)* for sale.

## Indefinite Pronouns

**5d.**   Some indefinite pronouns are singular, some are plural, and some can be singular or plural, depending on how they are used.

*Anybody, anyone, anything, each, either, everybody, everyone, everything, neither, nobody, no one, nothing, one, somebody, someone,* and *something* are always singular.

**EXAMPLE**   **Everybody likes** the building's new look.  [The singular indefinite pronoun *Everybody* agrees with the singular verb *likes*.]

*Both, few, many,* and *several* are always plural.

**EXAMPLES**   **Several** of those birds **have built** nests.  [The plural indefinite pronoun *Several* agrees with the plural verb phrase *have built*.]

When **are both arriving**?  [The plural indefinite pronoun *both* agrees with the plural verb phrase *are arriving*.]

**EXERCISE B**   Underline the subject in each of the following sentences. Then, draw two lines under the verb in parentheses that agrees with the subject.

**GO ON**

for **CHAPTER 5: AGREEMENT**   pages 153–156  *continued*

**Examples**  **1.** *(Is, Are)* each of them ready?  [*Each* is singular, so the verb should be singular.]

        **2.** In winter, few *(attend, attends)* the games.  [*Few* is plural, so the verb should be plural.]

**6.** After lunch someone always *(feeds, feed)* the parakeet.  [Is the subject singular or plural? Which verb agrees with the subject?]

**7.** *(Is, Are)* many in the stands cheering for my brother?  [Is the subject singular or plural? Which verb agrees with the subject?]

**8.** *(Has, Have)* anybody seen my beach towel and sunscreen lotion?

**9.** One of the scientists *(have, has)* discovered a new vaccine.

**10.** At the same moment, both *(jumps, jump)* for the basketball.

**11.** Once underwater, each quickly *(swim, swims)* toward the school of fish.

**12.** *(Is, Are)* something in that large blue bag for you?

**13.** Luckily, nothing on that buffet table *(tempt, tempts)* me to overeat tonight.

**14.** Every evening, several *(gather, gathers)* near the edge of the clearing.

**15.** Neither *(run, runs)* faster than that little bird can fly.

---

The indefinite pronouns *all, any, more, most, none,* and *some* may be singular or plural, depending on their meaning in a sentence. If the indefinite pronoun refers to a singular word, it is singular. If the indefinite pronoun refers to a plural word, it is plural.

    **EXAMPLES**  **Some** of the mail **goes** to Horace.  [*Some* refers to the singular noun *mail. Some* agrees with the singular verb *goes.*]

              **Some** of the letters **go** to Horace.  [*Some* refers to the plural noun *letters. Some* agrees with the plural verb *go.*]

---

**EXERCISE C**  Underline the subject in each of the following sentences. Then, draw two lines under the verb in parentheses that agrees with the subject.

**Example**  **1.** None of the recycling bins *(has, have)* been emptied yet.  [The subject *None* refers to the plural noun *bins,* so the verb should be plural.]

**16.** Most of the movie *(has, have)* been very suspenseful.  [Does the indefinite pronoun refer to a singular or plural word? Which verb agrees with the subject?]

**17.** *(Are, Is)* any of the apartments on the list already furnished?

**18.** More of the proposals under discussion *(sound, sounds)* sensible now.

**19.** None of the other players *(score, scores)* as well as Rosa.

**20.** By the end of the game, all of his uniform *(was, were)* drenched with sweat.

# Subject-Verb Agreement C

## *Don't* and *Doesn't*

The contraction *don't* stands for the words *do not*. The helping verb *do* is plural. The contraction *doesn't* stands for the words *does not*. The helping verb *does* is singular.

**5h.**   The contractions *don't* and *doesn't* should agree with their subjects.

Use *don't* with plural subjects and with the pronouns *I* and *you*. Use *doesn't* with singular subjects, except for the pronouns *I* and *you*.

> **EXAMPLES**   Those **beetles do**n't **scare** me!  [Both subject and verb are plural.]
>
> **I do**n't **fear** beetles.  [*I* is the subject, so *don't* agrees.]
>
> That **beetle does**n't **scare** me!  [Both subject and verb are singular.]

## Collective Nouns

*Collective nouns* name a group of people or things. Common collective nouns include *army, assembly, audience, band, club, crowd, family, flock, group, herd, jury, staff, swarm,* and *team.*

**5j.**   A collective noun may be either singular or plural, depending on its meaning in a sentence.

A collective noun is singular when it refers to the group as a whole. A collective noun is plural when it refers to the individual parts or members of the group.

> **SINGULAR**   The **committee is** meeting at four o'clock.  [The group as a unit is meeting, so the noun is singular. The singular verb *is* agrees in number.]
>
> **PLURAL**   The **committee are** preparing their notes.  [Individual members of the committee are preparing their notes, so the noun is plural. The plural verb *are* agrees in number.]

**EXERCISE A**   Underline the verb in parentheses that agrees with the underlined subject in each of the following sentences.

**Examples  1.** (*Doesn't, Don't*) his jokes make you laugh?  [The subject *jokes* is plural, so the verb should be plural.]

**2.** After the show, the crowd (*claps, clap*) their hands.  [Individual members of the crowd clap, so the verb should be plural.]

**1.** This volleyball (*doesn't, don't*) have enough air in it.  [Which contraction agrees with the singular subject?]

**2.** (*Is, Are*) a group going to the new action movie tonight?  [Is the collective noun referring to the whole group or individual members of the group?]

**3.** (*Doesn't, Don't*) you work at the YMCA each summer?

**4.** A swarm of bees (*lives, live*) in that hollow tree!

**5.** The <u>flock</u> (*fly, flies*) toward their nests in the forest.

**6.** In science class the <u>experiments</u> (*doesn't, don't*) seem difficult.

**7.** Once a month, the <u>club</u> (*brings, bring*) their own guests to the meeting.

**8.** The <u>army</u> (*recruit, recruits*) at a booth at the career fair.

**9.** Because of my allergies, <u>I</u> (*doesn't, don't*) eat dairy foods.

**10.** (*Was, Were*) the <u>team</u> in the dugout when the rain began?

## Expressions of Amount

**5k.**  An expression of an amount (a measurement, a percentage, or a fraction, for example) may be singular or plural, depending on how it is used.

When an expression of an amount refers to a unit, it is singular. When an expression of an amount refers to separate units, it is plural.

> **SINGULAR**  **Ten minutes is** the length of my speech.  [The expression is of one unit of time, so it agrees with the singular verb *is*.]

> **PLURAL**  **Ten minutes are** slowly ticking by on the clock.  [The expression is of individual minutes, so it agrees with the plural verb *are*.]

A fraction or a percentage is singular when it refers to a singular word. A fraction or a percentage is plural when it refers to a plural word.

> **SINGULAR**  **One third** of the barn **needs** paint.  [The fraction refers to the singular word *barn*, so it agrees with the singular verb *needs*.]

> **PLURAL**  **One third** of the boards **need** paint.  [The fraction refers to the plural word *boards*, so it agrees with the plural verb *need*.]

An expression of measurement such as length, weight, capacity, and area is usually singular.

> **EXAMPLE**  **Two acres is** the size of Ty's homestead.  [The expression of measurement refers to an area, so it agrees with the singular verb *is*.]

**EXERCISE B**  Underline the verb in parentheses that agrees in number with the underlined subject in each of the following sentences.

**Example  1.** (<u>*Has*</u>, *Have*) fifty <u>percent</u> of your paycheck been spent?  [*Fifty percent* refers to the singular word *paycheck*, so the verb should be singular.]

**11.** At this thrift store, eight <u>dollars</u> (*is, are*) enough to buy a shirt.  [Is *eight dollars* used as a single unit of amount or as separate units?  Which verb agrees with the subject?]

**12.** (*Do, Does*) two <u>pounds</u> of flour fill this bin?

**13.** Forty-six <u>cents</u> (*was, were*) scattered across Mandy's dresser.

**14.** At the shelter seventy-five <u>percent</u> of the cats (*lives, live*) in the outdoor yard.

**15.** As quick as a wink, two <u>thirds</u> of the omelet (*was, were*) eaten.

# Subject-Verb Agreement D
## Nouns Plural in Form

**5l.** Some nouns that are plural in form take singular verbs.

Some of these nouns are *civics, economics, electronics, gymnastics, mathematics, measles, molasses, news,* and *physics.*

> **EXAMPLE**  **Gymnastics demands** time and dedication.  [The noun *Gymnastics* agrees with the singular verb *demands.* Even though *Gymnastics* is plural in form, it is treated as one thing, a sport.]

Some plural nouns that refer to single items take plural verbs. Some of these nouns are *binoculars, eyeglasses, pliers, scissors, shears,* and *trousers.*

> **EXAMPLE**  **Are** the **pliers** in Jessie's toolbox?  [The noun *pliers* agrees with the plural verb *Are.* Although *pliers* refers to one thing, it is treated as a plural noun.]

**EXERCISE A**  Underline the subject in each of the following sentences. Then, draw two lines under the verb in parentheses that agrees with the subject.

**Example  1.**  The gray trousers *(has, have)* a rip in one knee.  [*Trousers* refers to a single item, but it agrees with a plural verb.]

**1.** *(Is, Are)* mathematics your favorite subject in school?  [Is the subject of the sentence treated as one or more than one thing?]

**2.** For durability, the eyeglasses *(has, have)* spring-loaded hinges.

**3.** According to Aunt Leigh, molasses *(adds, add)* a good flavor to bread.

**4.** Usually, the local news *(features, feature)* at least one human-interest story.

**5.** Binoculars *(magnifies, magnify)* an object in the distance.

## Titles and Names

**5m.** Even when plural in form, the titles of creative works (such as books, songs, movies, or paintings) and the names of countries, cities, and organizations generally take singular verbs.

> **EXAMPLES**  *The Martian Chronicles* **describes** the colonization of Mars.  [Although the title is plural in form, it represents one book, so the verb is singular.]
>
> **Los Alamos** in New Mexico **has been** the site of an atomic energy facility.  [The name of a city usually takes a singular verb.]

**GO ON**

**EXERCISE B** Decide whether the underlined subject agrees with the verb in each of the following sentences. If the subject and verb agree, write *C* for *correct* on the line provided. If the subject and verb do not agree, write the correct verb form on the line provided.

**Example** _Was_ **1.** Were *Domino Players* painted in oil in 1943? [*Domino Players* is the name of one painting and takes the singular verb phrase *Was painted*.]

_______ **6.** The United States share the North American continent with Canada and Mexico. [Does the name of a country take a plural or singular verb?]

_______ **7.** Once a month, Friends of the Homeless meets in a room at the library.

_______ **8.** *Hard Times* by Charles Dickens tell the story of Louisa Gradgrind and her father.

_______ **9.** In my opinion, *101 Dalmatians* have a fun and inventive plot.

_______ **10.** Do "The Bells" by Edgar Allan Poe have an intricate rhyme scheme?

## Relative Pronouns

**5p.** When the relative pronoun *that, which,* or *who* is the subject of an adjective clause, the verb in the clause agrees with the word to which the relative pronoun refers.

    **EXAMPLES** These dolls, **which are** handmade, sell rapidly. [*Which* refers to the plural noun *dolls,* so the plural verb *are* agrees.]

           This doll, **which is** handmade, belongs to Nina. [*Which* refers to the singular noun *doll,* so the singular verb *is* agrees.]

**EXERCISE C** Underline the verb in parentheses that agrees with the underlined relative pronoun in each of the following sentences.

**Example 1.** Hurricanes that *(cause, causes)* great damage are long remembered. [The relative pronoun *that* refers to the plural word *Hurricanes,* so *that* agrees with a plural verb.]

**11.** In 1998, a hurricane that *(was, were)* powerful was Hurricane Mitch. [Does *that* refer to a plural word or to a singular word?]

**12.** The Caribbean Sea, which *(is, are)* south of Cuba, was the site of Mitch's damage.

**13.** Of the people who *(was, were)* affected, most lived in Nicaragua and Honduras.

**14.** Did these two countries, which *(is, are)* very poor, take the brunt of the hurricane?

**15.** Sadly, thousands who *(was, were)* living in the capital of Honduras suffered.

# Pronoun-Antecedent Agreement A

## Number, Gender, and Person

**5q.**  A pronoun should agree in number, gender, and person with its antecedent.

**REMINDER** A pronoun is a word that takes the place of a noun or another pronoun. An *antecedent* is the noun or pronoun to which a pronoun refers.

> **EXAMPLE**   The **shrub** grew a new branch to replace the one **it** lost.  [*Shrub* is the antecedent of the pronoun *it*.]

Singular pronouns refer to singular antecedents. Plural pronouns refer to plural antecedents.

> **SINGULAR**   The **snake** shed **its** skin.  [*Its* refers to the singular antecedent *snake*.]

> **PLURAL**   **They** raised **their** hands.  [*Their* refers to the plural antecedent *They*.]

Some singular pronouns indicate gender and may be masculine, feminine, or neuter, depending on the gender of the antecedent.

> **MASCULINE**   **Carl**'s notes are in **his** locker.  [The masculine pronoun *his* refers to the masculine antecedent *Carl*.]

> **FEMININE**   Tell the uniformed **woman** because **she** is in charge.  [The feminine pronoun *she* refers to the feminine antecedent *woman*.]

> **NEUTER**   Is the **camera itself** also voice activated?  [The neuter pronoun *itself* refers to the neuter antecedent *camera*.]

*Person* indicates whether a pronoun refers to the one(s) speaking *(first person)*, the one(s) spoken to *(second person)*, or the one(s) spoken of *(third person)*.

> **FIRST PERSON**   I, me, my, mine, myself, we, us, our, ourselves
> **SECOND PERSON**   you, your, yours, yourself, yourselves
> **THIRD PERSON**   he, she, it, they, him, her, them, his, hers, its, their, theirs, himself, herself, itself, themselves

**EXERCISE A** Underline the pronoun in parentheses that agrees with the underlined antecedent in each of the following sentences.

**Example 1.** Are the ice cubes in *(its, his, their)* bucket in the freezer?  [*Ice cubes* is a plural antecedent, so the pronoun should be plural.]

**1.** Is the order on *(its, his, their)* way to the customers?  [Which pronoun is both singular and neuter?]

**2.** In the afternoons, several students volunteer *(his, their, its)* time to tutor others.

**3.** The boy rolled off *(his, its, their)* inner tube and into the pool.

**GO ON**

**4.** At the young age of eight, <u>Sylvia Plath</u> published *(her, its, their)* first poem.

**5.** White <u>daisies</u> gripped the thin layer of soil with *(its, their, his)* roots.

## Compound Antecedents

**5s.**  Use a plural pronoun to refer to two or more antecedents joined by *and*.

> **EXAMPLE**  The **lizard** and the **snake** flicked **their** tongues in the breeze.  [*Lizard* and *snake* form a compound antecedent joined by *and*. The plural pronoun *their* refers to the nouns in the compound antecedent.]

**5t.**  Use a singular pronoun to refer to two or more singular antecedents joined by *or* or *nor*.

> **EXAMPLES**  **Grandma** or **she** brought **her** notebook along.  [*Grandma* and *she* form a compound antecedent joined by *or*. The singular pronoun *her* refers to the nouns in the compound antecedent.]
>
> Neither **Paul** nor **Willie** left **his** umbrella in the car.  [*Paul* and *Willie* form a compound antecedent joined by *nor*. The singular pronoun *his* refers to the nouns in the compound antecedent.]

**EXERCISE B**  Underline the compound antecedent in each of the following sentences. Then, draw two lines under the pronoun in parentheses that agrees with the compound antecedent.

**Examples 1.** Will the <u>book</u> and <u>magazine</u> have mystery stories in *(it, them)*?  [The singular antecedents are joined by *and*, so the pronoun should be plural.]

**2.** Neither this <u>book</u> nor that <u>magazine</u> has a mystery story in *(it, them)*.  [The singular antecedents are joined by *nor*, so the pronoun should be singular.]

**6.** On summer days Michelle and Felicia spend *(her, their)* afternoons together.  [Should a pronoun referring to antecedents joined by *and* be singular or plural?]

**7.** Ella or Sue Ann will bring an ice chest full of cold fruit drinks with *(her, them)*.  [Should a pronoun referring to singular antecedents joined by *or* be singular or plural?]

**8.** Neither the deck nor the table has *(its, their)* surface sealed against rain.

**9.** A book, a magazine, and good food provide *(its, their)* own kind of entertainment.

**10.** This card and that envelope have familiar handwriting on *(it, them)*.

**11.** In the backyard a tree or an umbrella is useful because *(it, they)* provides shade.

**12.** Dad or Joe sometimes offers sandwiches when *(he, they)* makes lunch.

**13.** Often our cat and dog treat *(itself, themselves)* to a swim in our backyard pool.

**14.** Is Ken or Vern famous in the neighborhood for *(his, their)* "backyard banquets"?

**15.** Are the books and magazines in *(its, their)* usual place next to the reclining chair?

# Pronoun-Antecedent Agreement B

## Indefinite Pronouns

Pronouns must agree in number, gender, and person with their antecedents.

**5r.**  Some indefinite pronouns are singular, some are plural, and some can be either singular or plural, depending on how they are used in the sentence.

The following antecedents are singular: *anybody, anyone, anything, each, either, everybody, everyone, everything, neither, nobody, no one, nothing, one, somebody, someone,* and *something.*

> **EXAMPLE**   **No one** brought a lunch with **him or her.**  [The singular antecedent *No one* may be either masculine or feminine, so both masculine and feminine singular pronouns are used.]

Clues in the sentence often reveal whether these singular antecedents are masculine, feminine, or neuter.

> **EXAMPLE**   **Each** of the **girls** brought **her** ballet slippers.  [*Each* is the singular antecedent of *her. Girls* shows that *Each* is feminine.]

**EXERCISE A**  Underline the pronoun in parentheses that agrees with the underlined antecedent in each of the following sentences.

**Example  1.**  Neither of the bus drivers has a map with *(them, him or her).*  [The singular antecedent *Neither* may be either masculine or feminine, so *him or her* is the correct choice.]

**1.**  Everyone who entered the girls' tennis competition should bring *(her, their)* racket.  [Which pronoun agrees with *Everyone* in number and gender?]

**2.**  Did either of those students lose *(their, his or her)* trigonometry book?

**3.**  For the presentation, one of the men brought slides with *(them, him).*

**4.**  Might anyone improve *(himself or herself, themselves)* on this exercise equipment?

**5.**  Everything in this attic has a thick layer of dust on *(it, them)!*

The following antecedents are plural: *both, few, many,* and *several.*

> **EXAMPLE**   **Few** brought lunches with **them.**  [The plural pronoun *them* refers to *Few.*]

Use a singular or a plural pronoun, depending on the meaning of the sentence, to refer to any of the following indefinite pronouns: *all, any, more, most, none,* and *some.*

> **EXAMPLES**   **All** of the pages have corrections. Please revise **them.**  [*All* refers to the plural noun *pages.* Therefore, the plural pronoun *them* agrees.]
>
> **All** of the report has corrections. Please revise **it.**  [*All* refers to the singular noun *report.* Therefore, the singular pronoun *it* agrees.]

**GO ON**

**EXERCISE B**   Underline the antecedent in each of the following sentences. Then, draw two lines under the pronoun in parentheses that agrees with the antecedent.

**Example 1.** Meg can't find <u>any</u> of the green pencils. (*It,* <u><u>*They*</u></u>) were here yesterday. [The antecedent *any* refers to the plural word *pencils,* so the pronoun should be plural.]

**6.** Does most of the road to your house have asphalt on (*its, their*) surface? [Does *most* refer to a singular or a plural word?]

**7.** Chad talked with both of the mechanics about (*his or her, their*) estimates.

**8.** Several of the watches are broken. Can (*it, they*) be fixed?

**9.** None of the truck drivers are tired. Will (*he or she, they*) drive another hour?

**10.** All of the fence has been painted. Please don't touch (*it, them*).

## Relative Pronouns

**5x.**   The gender and number of the relative pronoun *that, which,* or *who* are determined by the gender and number of the word to which it refers—its antecedent.

> **EXAMPLES**   **Cedric, who** rebuilt **his** car, will drive there.   [*Who* refers to a singular, masculine antecedent, *Cedric.* Therefore, the masculine pronoun *his* agrees with *who.*]
>
> The **chairs that** have had **their** cushions cleaned are in the dining room. [*That* refers to a plural antecedent, *chairs.* Therefore, the plural pronoun *their* agrees with *that.*]

**EXERCISE C**   Underline the pronoun in parentheses that agrees in number and gender with the underlined pronoun in each of the following sentences.

**Example 1.** The young girl <u>who</u> has freckles on (*their,* <u>*her*</u>) nose is Brenda. [*Who* refers to a singular, feminine antecedent, *girl.* Therefore, the pronoun should be both feminine and singular.]

**11.** Please pass me the platter <u>that</u> has the fruit on (*it, them*). [Does *that* refer to a singular antecedent or to a plural antecedent?]

**12.** Rosa, <u>who</u> submitted (*their, her*) application yesterday, will probably get the job.

**13.** Does the kangaroo, <u>which</u> carries (*its, their*) young in a pouch, live in Australia?

**14.** Do you know the boys <u>who</u> brought the skateboard with (*him, them*)?

**15.** Is the river <u>that</u> overflowed (*its, their*) banks the Mississippi River?

# Personal Pronouns A

## The Nominative Case

Pronouns are grouped into three cases, depending on how they are used. *Nominative case* pronouns include *I, you, he, she, it, we,* and *they.*

**6a.**   The subject of a verb should be in the nominative case.

> **EXAMPLES**   **We** are paddling the boat.  [*We* is the subject of the verb *are paddling.*]
>
> **She** or **I** will wash the car.  [*She* and *I* are the compound subject of the verb *will wash.*]

**6b.**   A predicate nominative should be in the nominative case.

A *predicate nominative* is a word or word group in the predicate that identifies or refers to the subject.

**TIP▶** The predicate nominative identifies the subject by completing the meaning of a linking verb. Some common linking verbs are *am, is, are, was, were, be,* and *been.*

> **EXAMPLES**   The winner of the race is **she.**  [The predicate nominative *she* identifies the subject *winner* and completes the meaning of the linking verb *is.*]
>
> My parents are **she** and **he.**  [The compound predicate nominative *she* and *he* identifies the subject *parents* and completes the meaning of the linking verb *are.*]

**EXERCISE A**   Underline the correct form of the pronoun in parentheses in each of the following sentences.

**Examples  1.**  Were the coauthors of the article your brother and *(they, them)*?  [The predicate nominative *they* identifies the subject *coauthors.*]

**2.**  Jason and *(I, me)* will help put up decorations.  [The subject *I* is in the nominative case.]

**1.**  Will the Andersons and *(they, them)* be at the council meeting?  [Which pronoun should be used as a subject?]

**2.**  Last summer, Josh's camp counselors were Lane and *(him, he).*  [Which pronoun should be used as a predicate nominative?]

**3.**  Was it *(she, her)* at the front door?

**4.**  The judges and *(he, him)* will decide the winners.

**5.**  The seniors on the drama team are *(they, them).*

**6.**  *(Her, She)* and her sisters have formed a band.

**7.**  What kind of trees were *(them, they)*?

**8.**  The mother of those kittens is *(she, her).*

**GO ON ➡**

**9.** The Washingtons and *(we, us)* are organizing a neighborhood cleanup.

**10.** Julia and *(I, me)* have finished our project.

## The Possessive Case

Possessive pronouns show ownership. Some possessive pronouns, such as *mine, yours, his, hers, its, ours,* and *theirs,* may be used as subjects, predicate nominatives, and objects.

**SUBJECT**   **Theirs** is the poodle with pink toenails.  [*Theirs* is the subject of the verb *is.*]

**PREDICATE NOMINATIVE**   Was the tie-breaking touchdown **his**?  [*His* completes the meaning of the linking verb *Was* and identifies the subject *touchdown.*]

**OBJECT**   Recently, Tana gave **hers** to charity.  [*Hers* is the direct object of the verb *gave.*]

Other possessive pronouns, such as *my, our, your, his, her, its,* and *their,* are used to modify, or describe, nouns.

**EXAMPLES**   **My** car is in the garage.  [*My* modifies *car.*]

Cleaning the tables will be **your** job.  [*Your* modifies *job.*]

Pronouns that come before a gerund should be in the possessive case.

**EXAMPLES**   **Your** volunteering for the fair was a surprise.  [The possessive pronoun *your* comes before the gerund *volunteering.* The gerund *volunteering* is the subject of the sentence.]

Stella was fascinated by **its** ringing.  [The possessive pronoun *its* comes before the gerund *ringing.* The gerund *ringing* is the object of the preposition *by.*]

**REMINDER▶**  A *gerund* is a verb form that ends in *–ing* and is used as a noun.

**VERB**   She **is training** for a marathon.  [*Training* is part of the verb phrase *is training.*]

**GERUND**   Her **training** is very time consuming.  [The gerund *training* is the subject of the sentence.]

**EXERCISE B**   Underline the correct form of the pronoun in parentheses in each of the following sentences.

**Example   1.** Was the noise I heard *(their, them)* arriving home?  [The possessive pronoun *their* is used before the gerund *arriving.*]

**11.** Is your foot the same size as *(hers, she)*?  [Which pronoun is in the possessive case?]

**12.** No one knew that the Nat King Cole CD was *(you, yours)*.

**13.** *(Your, You)* laughing woke the children from their nap.

**14.** We'll have to take your car; *(my, mine)* is in the repair shop.

**15.** As always, the audience was charmed by *(him, his)* singing.

# Personal Pronouns B

## The Objective Case

*Objective case* pronouns are used as direct objects, indirect objects, and objects of prepositions. Objective case pronouns include *me, us, you, him, her, it,* and *them.*

**6c.**   A direct object should be in the objective case.

A *direct object* tells who or what receives the action of a transitive verb.

> **EXAMPLE**   Joel's e-mails amuse **her.**  [Amuse whom? Amuse her. *Her* receives the action of the verb *amuse.*]

**6d.**   An indirect object should be in the objective case.

You will often find an indirect object in a sentence with a direct object. An *indirect object* tells to whom, for whom, to what, or for what the action of a transitive verb is done.

>            **IO**     **DO**
> **EXAMPLE**   Will Joel send **me** an e-mail?  [Will send an e-mail to whom? The indirect object *me* tells *to whom* Joel will send an e-mail. The direct object *e-mail* receives the action of *Will send.*]

**EXERCISE A**   Underline the correct form of the pronoun in parentheses in each of the following sentences.

**Examples 1.** In the runoff election, the citizens elected *(her, she)*.  [The pronoun is the direct object

of the verb *elected,* so the objective form, *her,* is correct.]

**2.** The interview went well, and the manager offered *(he, him)* a job.  [The pronoun is

the indirect object of the verb *offered,* so the objective form, *him,* is correct.]

**1.** That comedian can imitate *(them, they)* with incredible accuracy!  [Which pronoun is in the

objective case?]

**2.** Please hand *(I, me)* that map of Chicago.  [Which pronoun is in the objective case?]

**3.** After a short pause, the audience gave *(him, he)* an enthusiastic round of applause.

**4.** Will Mr. Volney present *(her, she)* the MVP trophy at the banquet tonight?

**5.** Call *(me, I)* this weekend if you need help with the garage sale.

**6.** A large wave crashed on the rocks and gave *(they, them)* a darker appearance.

**7.** Did the results of the student-opinion poll surprise *(he, him)*?

**8.** Every time she gives a tour of the capitol, a tourist asks *(her, she)* that very question.

**9.** The actor and the actress both thanked *(them, they)* for the award.

**10.** Coach Sandoval gave *(them, they)* an encouraging speech at halftime.

**GO ON** ➡

**6e.** An object of a preposition should be in the objective case.

An *object of a preposition* is the noun or pronoun that follows a preposition.

> **EXAMPLE**   Joel sent e-mails to **us.**   [*Us* is the object of the preposition *to.*]

**TIP** To choose the correct form of a pronoun in a sentence with a compound object, cross out any objects before the pronoun. Then, choose the pronoun that sounds correct.

> **EXAMPLE**   These flowers are from ~~Mom and~~ *(he, him).*  [Which sounds correct? *These flowers are from he* or *These flowers are from him*? The correct pronoun is *him.*]

**EXERCISE B**   Underline the correct form of the pronoun in parentheses in each of the following sentences. Hint: For help choosing the correct pronoun when there is a compound object, you can cross out one object.

**Examples 1.** Ms. Ruiz sent the neighbors and *(we, <u>us</u>)* homemade tortillas.  [The pronoun is part of the compound indirect object, so the objective form, *us,* is correct.]

**2.** Have you read that article about Glen and *(I, <u>me</u>)*?  [The pronoun is part of the compound object of a preposition, so the objective form, *me,* is correct.]

**11.** That roller coaster ride is thrilling for Justin and *(I, me).*  [Which pronoun is in the objective case?]

**12.** When did Uncle Bart make Holly and *(them, they)* that tire swing?  [Which pronoun is in the objective case?]

**13.** Grandpa showed the neighbors and *(us, we)* some old photographs.

**14.** Will this secret stay between you and *(I, me)*?

**15.** Where did you find Chi and *(him, he)* those unusual Christmas gifts?

**16.** Coach McIntire sent the pitcher and *(her, she)* a secret signal.

**17.** Please give Mr. Tatum or *(I, me)* your permission slips for the field trip.

**18.** These plates of chicken and biscuits are for you and *(they, them).*

**19.** There was a safety railing between the edge of the cliff and *(we, us).*

**20.** I wish you and *(she, her)* many happy times together.

# Special Problems in Pronoun Usage

## Appositives

An *appositive* is a word or word group that is placed near a noun or a pronoun to identify or describe it.

**6i.** A pronoun used as an appositive should be in the same case as the word to which it refers.

  **EXAMPLE** My best friends, Chris and **she,** are applying to the same colleges. [The appositive *she* identifies the subject *friends.* It is in the nominative case.]

**TIP** To decide which form of a pronoun to use as an appositive, substitute the pronoun for the word to which it refers. The pronoun that is correct in this position will also be correct as the appositive.

  **EXAMPLE** I helped my friends, Chris and *(they, them),* with their applications. [Which sounds correct? *I helped they with their applications* or *I helped them with their applications*? The correct form of the appositive is *them.*]

Sometimes the pronoun *we* or *us* is followed by an appositive.

  **EXAMPLE** **We seniors** are excited about college. [The subject *We* is followed by the appositive *seniors.*]

**TIP** To decide whether to use *we* or *us* before an appositive, cross out the appositive. Whichever pronoun form is correct without the appositive will be correct with the appositive.

  **EXAMPLE** Which college is a good choice for *(we, us)* musicians? [Which sounds correct? *Which college is a good choice for we* or *Which college is a good choice for us*? The correct pronoun is *us.*]

**EXERCISE A** Underline the correct form of the pronoun in parentheses in each of the following sentences.

**Example 1.** Have you given our assistants, Zack and *(them, they),* a call? [*Them* is an appositive that identifies the indirect object *assistants. Have you given them a call?* sounds correct.]

**1.** The editors of the school newspaper are those students, Marta and *(her, she).* [Which pronoun is in the same case as the predicate nominative, *students*?]

**2.** *(Us, We)* editors are looking for an interesting story to publish in next week's edition.

**3.** Are you writing an article about the all-star players, Kelsey and *(they, them)*?

**4.** All details about school pictures should be sent to *(we, us),* the writers.

**5.** The newspaper gives my friends, Tia and *(he, him),* something to discuss at lunch.

GO ON

## *Who* and *Whom*

The pronoun *who* is used as a subject of a verb or as a predicate nominative. The pronoun *whom* is used as a direct object, an indirect object, or an object of a preposition.

    **NOMINATIVE CASE**   **Who** wrote this note? [subject of the verb *wrote*]

                   **Whoever** wrote this note should speak up. [subject of the subordinate clause *Whoever wrote this note*]

                   **Who** was the author of this note? [predicate nominative identifying the subject *author*]

    **OBJECTIVE CASE**   To **whom** is the note addressed? [object of the preposition *To*]

                   Give it to **whomever** you see first. [*Whomever* is a direct object in the subordinate clause *whomever you see first.*]

**TIP▶** To decide whether to use *who* or *whom* in a subordinate clause, follow these steps: (1) First, decide how the pronoun is used in the clause. Is the pronoun being used as a subject or predicate nominative, or is the pronoun being used as an object? (2) Then, decide which case form is correct for this use. If the pronoun is being used as a subject or a predicate nominative, use *who.* If the pronoun is being used as an object, use *whom.*

        **EXAMPLE**   Joe DiMaggio, *(who, whom)* Marilyn Monroe married, played baseball. [In the subordinate clause, the pronoun is used as the direct object of the verb *married.* Marilyn Monroe married *whom? Whom* is in the objective case, so it is the correct pronoun.]

**EXERCISE B**   Underline the correct form of the pronoun in parentheses in each of the following sentences.

**Example 1.** Arthur Conan Doyle, (<u>who</u>, whom) wrote the Sherlock Holmes stories, was British.

        [*Who* is the subject of the subordinate clause *who wrote the Sherlock Holmes stories.*]

**6.** *(Who, Whom)* gave Doyle inspiration for the Holmes character? [Which pronoun is in the nominative case?]

**7.** The person upon *(who, whom)* Doyle partially modeled Holmes was Doyle's teacher, Dr. Joseph Bell.

**8.** Doyle, *(who, whom)* was interested in medicine, worked as a doctor until 1891.

**9.** He wrote about Holmes and Dr. Watson, *(who, whom)* shared many adventures.

**10.** *(Who, Whom)* do readers love more, Holmes or Dr. Watson?

# Clear Pronoun Reference A

A pronoun stands for a word or word group called its *antecedent.* The antecedent to which a pronoun refers must be clear in order for readers to understand a pronoun's meaning.

> **EXAMPLE**    After Leslie painted the old dresser, **it** looked much better.  [The pronoun *it* clearly refers to its antecedent, *dresser.*]

## Ambiguous Reference

**7b.**    Avoid an ***ambiguous reference,*** which occurs when any one of two or more words could be a pronoun's antecedent.

To revise an ambiguous reference, replace the pronoun with a specific noun or rewrite the sentence to eliminate the ambiguous reference.

> **AMBIGUOUS**    When Tammy saw Joy at the wedding, she was dancing.  [The antecedent of *she* is unclear. Is Tammy or Joy dancing?]
>
> **CLEAR**    When Tammy saw Joy at the wedding, **Tammy** was dancing.  [The ambiguous pronoun *she* is replaced with the specific noun *Tammy.*]
>
> **CLEAR**    When Joy was dancing at the wedding, **she** saw Tammy.  [The sentence is rewritten to eliminate the ambiguous reference. Now, the pronoun *she* clearly refers to its antecedent, *Joy.*]

**EXERCISE A**  Decide whether each sentence below has an ambiguous pronoun reference or a clear pronoun reference. On the line provided, write *A* for *ambiguous reference* or *C* for *clear reference.*  Hint: Draw an arrow from the pronoun to the antecedent. If you can draw one arrow, the pronoun reference is clear. If you can draw more than one arrow, the pronoun reference is ambiguous.

**Example**  ___A___  **1.** After the dress was placed in the display, it attracted shoppers.  [What attracted shoppers, the dress or the display?]

_______  **1.** Megan met Sonia at the movies, and she offered to buy some popcorn.  [Does *she* refer to Megan or to Sonia?]

_______  **2.** Wayne eats a nutritious snack before he baby-sits Tommy for the afternoon.

_______  **3.** When the bowling ball hit the pin, it fell into the gutter.

_______  **4.** When the teacher talks to the student, does he make eye contact?

_______  **5.** Greg repaired an old sailboat, and he went sailing yesterday.

**GO ON**

# General Reference

A pronoun must refer to a specific antecedent, not a general idea.

**7c.** Avoid a ***general reference,*** which is the use of a pronoun that refers to a general idea rather than to a specific antecedent.

The pronouns *it, that, this,* and *which* are often used in general references. To revise a general reference, use a specific noun or rewrite the sentence to eliminate the general reference.

> **GENERAL**  I once found an arrowhead. That was exciting.  [*That* does not have a specific antecedent. Instead, it refers to the general idea of finding an arrowhead.]
>
> **CLEAR**  I once found an arrowhead. **That find** was exciting.  [The word group *That find* is clearer and more specific.]
>
> **CLEAR**  **Finding an arrowhead** was exciting.  [The sentence is rewritten to avoid the general reference.]

**EXERCISE B**  Each of the following items contains an unclear pronoun reference. On the lines provided, revise each sentence to correct the ambiguous pronoun reference error or the general pronoun reference error.  Hint: There is more than one way to revise each sentence. The unclear pronoun has been underlined.

**Example**  **1.**  Before you put the figurine back on the shelf, will you dust <u>it</u>?  [The sentence has an ambiguous pronoun reference error. *It* could refer either to *figurine* or to *shelf.* The sentence has been rewritten to correct the error.]

    **Will you dust the shelf before you put the figurine back?**

**6.** The tornado uprooted a tree near our house. <u>That</u> really scared me.  [Can the sentence be rewritten to eliminate the general reference?]

_________________________________________________

**7.** When the leaves on the trees turn red, <u>they</u> look beautiful.

_________________________________________________

**8.** Suddenly the cat pounced on the box. <u>That</u> was amusing.

_________________________________________________

**9.** The horses raced around the field, <u>which</u> was a beautiful sight.

_________________________________________________

**10.** Did Melanie find Amy in the mall? Did <u>she</u> have the car keys?

_________________________________________________

# Clear Pronoun Reference B

A pronoun stands for a word or word group called its *antecedent.* The antecedent to which a pronoun refers must be clear in order for readers to understand a pronoun's meaning.

> **EXAMPLE** Charles and Alex think **their** design for a catapult will win first prize in the physics contest. [The pronoun *their* clearly refers to its antecedents, *Charles* and *Alex.*]

## Weak Reference

**7d.** Avoid a *weak reference,* which occurs when a pronoun refers to an antecedent that has been suggested but not expressed.

To revise a weak reference, replace the pronoun with a specific noun or rewrite the sentence to eliminate the weak reference.

> **WEAK** Nate's brother plays professional basketball, but I haven't met any. [What is the antecedent of *any?* It is not stated.]
>
> **CLEAR** Nate's brother plays professional basketball, but I haven't met **his teammates.** [*His teammates* replaces the pronoun *any.*]
>
> **CLEAR** Nate's brother plays professional basketball with his **teammates,** but I haven't met **any.** [The sentence was rewritten to eliminate the weak reference. Now *any* clearly refers to *teammates.*]

**EXERCISE A** Decide whether each item below has a weak pronoun reference or a clear pronoun reference. On the line provided, write *W* for *weak reference* or *C* for *clear reference.* Hint: If you can draw an arrow from the pronoun to a specific antecedent, the pronoun reference is clear. If you cannot draw such an arrow, the pronoun reference is weak.

**Example** _W_ **1.** When the convention was held, they stayed at Hotel Regalia. [The antecedent of *they* is not stated.]

______ **1.** Jennifer enrolled in the journalism class because she wants to be a professional one. [Can you draw an arrow from *one* to an antecedent?]

______ **2.** Although I believe that friends should be honest with each other, it is not always easy.

______ **3.** Did Grace open her sister's closet and try several on?

______ **4.** The statistics surprised the professor. Are they accurate?

______ **5.** I couldn't make photocopies of the worksheets because it was out of order.

**GO ON**

## Indefinite Reference

**7e.**  Avoid an *indefinite reference*—the use of a pronoun that refers to no particular person or thing and that is unnecessary to the structure and meaning of a sentence.

The pronouns *it*, *they*, and *you* are often used in indefinite references. To revise a sentence with an indefinite reference, remove the unnecessary pronoun and rewrite the sentence.

| | |
|---|---|
| **INDEFINITE** | On the radio it said that a new high school will open next year. [*It* does not refer to a particular person or thing. *It* is not needed in the sentence.] |
| **CLEAR** | **The radio announcer said** that a new high school will open next year. [*It* is removed, and the sentence is rewritten.] |
| **INDEFINITE** | In Elizabethan England, they valued a knowledge of Latin. [*They* does not have a clear antecedent.] |
| **CLEAR** | In Elizabethan England, **a knowledge of Latin was valued.** [*They* is removed, and the sentence is rewritten.] |

**EXERCISE B**  Each of the following items contains an unclear pronoun reference. On the lines provided, revise each sentence to correct the weak pronoun reference error or the indefinite pronoun reference error. Hint: There is more than one way to revise each sentence. The unclear pronoun has been underlined.

**Example  1.**  Keisha spent an hour in the clothing store but didn't buy one. [The sentence has a

weak pronoun reference. *One* does not refer to a specific antecedent.]

Keisha spent an hour in the clothing store but didn't buy a dress.

**6.** In the army, you learn discipline, stamina, and obedience. [Can *you* be replaced with a specific

noun to eliminate the indefinite reference?]

_________________________________________________________________

**7.** My grandparents own a bakery, and they make them fresh every morning.

_________________________________________________________________

**8.** Find the number for the fire department! We need them now!

_________________________________________________________________

**9.** In the comic strip, it shows an argument between Charlie Brown and Lucy.

_________________________________________________________________

**10.** The class spent several hours in the museum and studied one in particular.

_________________________________________________________________

# Principal Parts of Verbs A

## The Principal Parts of Verbs

Every verb can take different forms to show when the verb's action or state of being happened. The main forms of a verb are called its *principal parts.*

**8a.** The ***principal parts*** of a verb are the *base form,* the *present participle,* the *past,* and the *past participle.* All other verb forms are formed from these principal parts.

In the following chart, all helping verbs are shown in brackets because present participles and past participles cannot be used as verbs unless accompanied by helping verbs.

| BASE FORM | PRESENT PARTICIPLE | PAST | PAST PARTICIPLE |
|---|---|---|---|
| trick | [is] tricking | tricked | [have] tricked |
| marry | [is] marrying | married | [have] married |
| go | [is] going | went | [have] gone |

**EXERCISE A**  Label the form of each of the following verbs. Write *base form, present participle, past,* or *past participle* on the line provided.

**Examples**  __*past participle*__  **1.** [has] spoken  [*Spoken* is the past participle form of *speak.* Past participles are used with a helping verb.]

__*past*__  **2.** popped  [*Popped* is the past form of *pop.*]

______________  **1.** [are] flashing  [Which verb form ends in *–ing* and is used with a form of *be?*]

______________  **2.** [have] found  [Which verb form is used with a form of *have?*]

______________  **3.** taste

______________  **4.** managed

______________  **5.** [had] counseled

______________  **6.** encourage

______________  **7.** [is] studying

______________  **8.** showed

______________  **9.** [has] proven

______________  **10.** [are] practicing

## Regular Verbs

All verbs form the ***present participle*** by adding *–ing* to the base form.

| BASE FORM | PRESENT PARTICIPLE |
|---|---|
| spray | [is] spray**ing** |
| organize | [is] organiz**ing** |
| swing | [is] swing**ing** |

**GO ON**

**8b.** A *regular verb* forms its past and past participle by adding *–d* or *–ed* to its base form.

| BASE FORM | PAST | PAST PARTICIPLE |
|---|---|---|
| prepare | prepare**d** | [have] prepare**d** |
| follow | follow**ed** | [have] follow**ed** |

**REMINDER** Do not leave off the *–d* or *–ed* from the past or past participle forms of a regular verb.

**NONSTANDARD** Betty use to put her toys away when she was suppose to do so.

**STANDARD** Betty **used** to put her toys away when she was **supposed** to do so.

**EXERCISE B** Complete the following chart by writing the base form, present participle, past, and past participle of each verb that has been provided.

**Examples 1.** bake  [is] _____baking_____  _____baked_____  [have] _____baked_____

[The present participle of *bake* is *[is] baking,* the past is *baked,* and the past participle is *[have] baked.*]

**2.** _____trot_____  [is] _____trotting_____  trotted  [have] _____trotted_____

[The base form of the past verb form *trotted* is *trot,* the present participle is *[is] trotting,* and the past participle is *[have] trotted.*]

| BASE FORM | PRESENT PARTICIPLE | PAST | PAST PARTICIPLE |
|---|---|---|---|
| **11.** print | [is] _____________ | _____________ | [have] _____________ |

[What needs to be added to *print* to make each of the other three forms?]

| BASE FORM | PRESENT PARTICIPLE | PAST | PAST PARTICIPLE |
|---|---|---|---|
| **12.** _____________ | [is] _____________ | proposed | [have] _____________ |

[To what verb has *–d* been added to make a past form? What needs to be added to make each of the other two forms?]

| BASE FORM | PRESENT PARTICIPLE | PAST | PAST PARTICIPLE |
|---|---|---|---|
| **13.** _____________ | [is] _____________ | _____________ | [have] chased |
| **14.** _____________ | [is] _____________ | giggled | [have] _____________ |
| **15.** borrow | [is] _____________ | _____________ | [have] _____________ |
| **16.** snare | [is] _____________ | _____________ | [have] _____________ |
| **17.** _____________ | [is] _____________ | _____________ | [have] unpacked |
| **18.** stop | [is] _____________ | _____________ | [have] _____________ |
| **19.** _____________ | [is] dribbling | _____________ | [have] _____________ |
| **20.** call | [is] _____________ | _____________ | [have] _____________ |

**78**

# Principal Parts of Verbs B

## Irregular Verbs

**8c.** An ***irregular verb*** forms its past and past participle in some way other than by adding *–d* or *–ed* to its base form.

Irregular verbs form their past and past participle forms in one of the following ways:

- changing vowels
- changing consonants
- changing vowels and consonants
- making no change

| BASE FORM | PAST | PAST PARTICIPLE |
|---|---|---|
| win | won | [have] won [The *i* in *win* changes to *o*.] |
| build | built | [have] built [The *d* in *build* changes to *t*.] |
| do | did | [have] done [Vowels and consonants in *do* change.] |
| spread | spread | [have] spread [There is no change to *spread*.] |

**REMINDER** All verbs form the present participle by adding *–ing* to the base form of the verb.

| VERB | begin | forsake |
|---|---|---|
| PRESENT PARTICIPLE | [is] beginning | [is] forsaking |

**EXERCISE A** Complete the following chart by writing the base form, present participle, past, and past participle of each verb that is provided. Hint: You may look in a dictionary to find the correct spellings of any past or past participle verb forms.

**Examples** 1. weave  [is] ___weaving___  ___wove___  [have] ___woven___

[The present participle of *weave* is *[is] weaving*, the past is *wove*, and the past participle is *[have] woven*.]

2. ___swing___  [is] swinging  ___swung___  [have] ___swung___

[The base form of the present participle *[is] swinging* is *swing*, the past is *swung*, and the past participle is *[have] swung*.]

| BASE FORM | PRESENT PARTICIPLE | PAST | PAST PARTICIPLE |
|---|---|---|---|
| 1. ________________ | [is] ________________ | ________________ | [have] sunk |

[What is the base form of the past participle *[have] sunk*? How are the present participle and past forms of the verb formed?]

| 2. ________________ | [is] ________________ | took | [have] ________________ |

[What is the base form of the past verb *took*? How are the present participle and past participle of the verb formed?]

**GO ON** ➡

**3.** cost    [is] ________________    ________________    [have] ________________

**4.** ________________    [is] ________________    torn    [have] ________________

**5.** ________________    [is] losing    ________________    [have] ________________

**6.** sing    [is] ________________    ________________    [have] ________________

**7.** ________________    [is] ________________    ________________    [have] eaten

**8.** ________________    [is] ________________    set    [have] ________________

**9.** hide    [is] ________________    ________________    [have] ________________

**10.** ________________    [is] spending    ________________    [have] ________________

---

Avoid the following common errors:

- Using the past form of an irregular verb with a helping verb

  **NONSTANDARD**   Todd has broke your record.
  **STANDARD**   Todd **broke** your record.

- Using the past participle of a verb without a helping verb

  **NONSTANDARD**   We seen the races between you.
  **STANDARD**   We **have seen** the races between you.

- Adding *–d*, *–ed*, or *–t* to the base form of an irregular verb

  **NONSTANDARD**   Todd breaked your record.
  **STANDARD**   Todd **broke** your record.

---

**EXERCISE B**   Underline the correct verb form in parentheses in each of the following sentences.

**Example 1.** Yuck! The pickup's tires (<u>flung</u>, *flinged*) mud on us. [*Fling* forms its past form by changing the *i* to *u*.]

**11.** Every night this week, your friends have (*came, come*) over to study. [Is a helping verb used with the past (*came*) or the past participle (*come*)?]

**12.** Fireworks (*burst, bursted*) brightly in the night sky.

**13.** Before the rain, the coyote (*woked, woke*) to loud crashes of thunder.

**14.** Someone has (*stole, stolen*) the camp counselor's whistle.

**15.** As a Girl Scout, I (*have rung, rung*) many doorbells for the fund-raiser.

# Lie and Lay, Sit and Set, Rise and Raise

## Lie and Lay

The verb **lie** means "to rest," "to recline," or "to be in a certain place." *Lie* does not take a direct object. The verb **lay** means "to put [something] in a place." *Lay* generally takes a direct object.

| BASE FORM | PRESENT PARTICIPLE | PAST | PAST PARTICIPLE |
|---|---|---|---|
| lie | [is] lying | lay | [have] lain |
| lay | [is] laying | laid | [have] laid |

**EXAMPLES**   Fran's scrapbook **lay** on her desk.  [The verb *lay* means "rested" and does not have a direct object.]

Fran **laid** the scrapbook on her desk.  [The verb *laid* means "put" and has a direct object, *scrapbook*.]

**EXERCISE A**  Underline the correct form of *lie* or *lay* in parentheses in each of the following sentences. Hint: If the verb has a direct object, the verb must be a form of *lay*.

**Example  1.**  The puppy had (*lain, laid*) down for a nap, so the veterinarian (*lay, laid*) a blanket

over it.  [*Lain* does not have a direct object.  *Laid* has a direct object, *blanket*.]

**1.**  A white carnation (*lay, laid*) on the table; I (*lay, laid*) the flower there for Jessica.  [Which verb

takes a direct object?]

**2.**  If you (*lay, lie*) a rug before the fire, our dog, King, will (*lay, lie*) on it.

**3.**  The teenager had (*laid, lain*) his towel on the sand and had (*laid, lain*) on it.

**4.**  Dirty laundry is (*lying, laying*) on the floor. Did you (*lay, lie*) it there?

**5.**  Please (*lie, lay*) these tools near the mechanic who is (*lying, laying*) beneath the brown car.

## Sit and Set

The verb **sit** means "to be in a seated, upright position" or "to be in a place." *Sit* seldom takes a direct object. The verb **set** means "to put [something] in a place." *Set* usually takes a direct object.

| BASE FORM | PRESENT PARTICIPLE | PAST | PAST PARTICIPLE |
|---|---|---|---|
| sit | [is] sitting | sat | [have] sat |
| set | [is] setting | set | [have] set |

**EXAMPLES**   A small gift **sat** on the table.  [*Sat* means "was in a place" and has no direct object.]

Morgan **set** a gift nearby.  [*Set* means "put" and has a direct object, *gift*.]

**EXERCISE B**   Underline the correct form of *sit* or *set* in parentheses in each of the following sentences. Hint: If the verb has a direct object, the verb is a form of *set*.

**Example 1.** Mark had (*set*, *sat*) an apple on his tray; it (*set*, *sat*) next to his soup.  [*Set* has a direct object, *apple*, and means "put." *Sat* has no direct object and means "was in a place."]

**6.** A cafeteria employee (*sits*, *sets*) rolls on plates, and the plates (*sit*, *set*) on large trays.  [Which verb takes a direct object?]

**7.** This milk was (*sitting*, *setting*) here when I arrived. Did you (*sit*, *set*) it here?

**8.** First, his lunch tray was (*set*, *sat*) on the table, and then he (*set*, *sat*) down.

**9.** Are Mark's friends (*sitting*, *setting*) nearby? Their books are (*sitting*, *setting*) by Mark.

**10.** The boys will (*sit*, *set*) with Mark in a moment. They had (*sat*, *set*) their books there earlier.

---

## *Rise* and *Raise*

The verb *rise* means "to go up" or "to get up." *Rise* does not take a direct object. The verb *raise* means "to lift up" or "to cause [something] to rise." *Raise* usually takes a direct object.

| BASE FORM | PRESENT PARTICIPLE | PAST | PAST PARTICIPLE |
| --- | --- | --- | --- |
| rise | [is] rising | rose | [have] risen |
| raise | [is] raising | raised | [have] raised |

**EXAMPLES**   A heron **rose** into the air.  [*Rose* has no direct object and means "went up."]
It **raised** its wings.  [*Raised* means "lifted up" and has a direct object, *wings*.]

---

**EXERCISE C**   Underline the correct form of *rise* or *raise* in parentheses in each of the following items. Hint: If the verb has a direct object, the verb is a form of *raise*.

**Example 1.** Did you (*raise*, *rise*) the alarm? The river has (*risen*, *raised*).  [*Raise* has a direct object, *alarm*, and means "to lift up." *Risen* has no direct object and means "gone up."]

**11.** I (*raise*, *rise*) the blinds on the windows when I (*raise*, *rise*) each morning.  [Which verb takes a direct object?]

**12.** After the helicopter (*rose*, *raised*) into the sky, the general (*rose*, *raised*) a hand in farewell.

**13.** Inflation is (*rising*, *raising*), and stores are (*rising*, *raising*) their prices.

**14.** The tires had (*risen*, *raised*) a cloud of dust, which (*rose*, *raised*) into the summer air.

**15.** During our hike, temperatures had (*risen*, *raised*), so we (*rose*, *raised*) a shelter.

# Tense

**8d.** The *tense* of a verb indicates the time of the action or of the state of being expressed by the verb.

Each verb in English has six tenses: *present, past, future, present perfect, past perfect,* and *future perfect.* These six tenses are formed from the four principal parts of each verb.

**PRESENT**  We **are** artists. We **paint.**  [existing or happening now]

**PAST**  We **were** artists. We **painted.**  [existing or happening in the past]

**FUTURE**  We **will be** artists. We **will paint.**  [existing or happening in the future]

**PRESENT PERFECT**  We **have been** artists. We **have painted.**  [existing or happening sometime before now; may be continuing now]

**PAST PERFECT**  We **had been** artists. We **had painted.**  [existing or happening before a specific time in the past]

**FUTURE PERFECT**  We **will have been** artists. We **will have painted.**  [existing or happening before a specific time in the future]

**EXERCISE A** Identify the tense of the underlined verb in each of the following sentences. On the line provided, write *present, past, future, present perfect, past perfect,* or *future perfect.*

**Examples** _____future perfect_____ **1.** In May, Lily <u>will have been</u> our pitcher for two years. [The verb phrase *will have been* indicates a state of being that will have existed before a specific time in the future, May, so the verb phrase is in the future perfect tense.]

_____present_____ **2.** Pam <u>hits</u> home runs often. [The verb *hits* indicates an action that is happening now, so the verb is in the present tense.]

____________ **1.** Will Pilar <u>catch</u> during Friday's game? [Does this action happen in the present or in the future?]

____________ **2.** Maria <u>pitches</u> skillful fastballs. [Does this action happen in the present or in the past?]

____________ **3.** That summer, Kimi <u>had batted</u> really well!

____________ **4.** Every day last season, Marion <u>practiced</u> diligently.

____________ **5.** Has Maria <u>pitched</u> to you before?

____________ **6.** This <u>is</u> the most important game of the season.

____________ **7.** Our team <u>has been</u> district champions twice.

____________ **8.** In June, Mrs. Lewis <u>will have coached</u> the team for five years.

____________ **9.** Lilac's Florist <u>was</u> our sponsor last year.

____________ **10.** Will they <u>be</u> our sponsor again this year?

**GO ON**

Listing the forms of a verb according to tense is called *conjugating* the verb.

| | | | |
|---|---|---|---|
| **PRESENT** | I paint. | **PRESENT PERFECT** | I have painted. |
| **PAST** | I painted. | **PAST PERFECT** | I had painted. |
| **FUTURE** | I will paint. | **FUTURE PERFECT** | I will have painted. |

Notice that helping verbs are used with four of the tenses: the future, present perfect, past perfect, and future perfect tenses.

**EXERCISE B** Conjugate the verbs in the following items according to the given instructions. Write the correct tense on the line provided.

**Examples 1.** Past perfect tense of *know:* We _____**had known**_____. [The past perfect tense of *know* is

formed by adding *had* to the past participle *known.*]

**2.** Future tense of *know:* We _____**will know**_____. [The future tense of *know* is formed by

adding *will* to the base form.]

**11.** Past tense of *believe:* We ________________. [How is the past tense of *believe* formed?]

**12.** Future tense of *believe:* We ________________. [Which helping verb is used with *believe* to form

the future tense?]

**13.** Present perfect tense of *believe:* We ________________.

**14.** Present tense of *believe:* We ________________.

**15.** Future perfect tense of *believe:* We ________________.

**16.** Past tense of *study:* We ________________.

**17.** Future tense of *study:* We ________________.

**18.** Present perfect tense of *study:* We ________________.

**19.** Past perfect tense of *study:* We ________________.

**20.** Future perfect tense of *study:* We ________________.

# Progressive Forms of Verbs

Each of the six verb tenses has a form called the *progressive form,* which expresses continuing action or state of being. Each progressive form consists of a form of the verb *be* and the present participle (*–ing* form) of the verb.

**PRESENT PROGRESSIVE**   am creating, is creating, are creating  [continuous action in the present]

**PAST PROGRESSIVE**   was creating, were creating  [continuous action in the past]

**FUTURE PROGRESSIVE**   will be creating  [continuous action in the future]

**EXERCISE A** Complete each of the following sentences by writing the verb tense in parentheses on the line provided.

**Example  1.** That movie _______*is showing*_______ at several theaters. (present progressive tense of

*show*)  [The present progressive tense of *show* is formed by adding the appropriate form

of the helping verb *be* to the present participle *showing.*]

**1.** The orchestra _______________ when the blizzard struck. (past progressive form of *per-*

*form*)  [How is the past progressive form of a verb formed?]

**2.** That artist _______________ portraits of us. (future progressive form of *paint*)

**3.** Outside of the convenience store, a phone _______________. (past progressive form of *ring*)

**4.** A spider _______________ on the keys of the piano. (present progressive form of *crawl*)

**5.** That song _______________ on the radio when we left for our date last week, too. (past

progressive form of *play*)

**PRESENT PERFECT PROGRESSIVE**   has been creating, have been creating  [continuous action that happens before and up to the present]

**PAST PERFECT PROGRESSIVE**   had been creating  [continuous action that happened before a specific time in the past]

**FUTURE PERFECT PROGRESSIVE**   will have been creating  [continuous action that will happen before a specific time in the future]

**EXERCISE B** Complete each of the following sentences by writing the verb tense in parentheses on the line provided.

**Example  1.** They _______*have been applying*_______ to vocational schools. (present perfect progressive

form of *apply*)  [The present perfect progressive form of *apply* is formed by adding

appropriate forms of the helping verbs *have* and *be* to the present participle *applying.*]

`GO ON` ▶

**6.** The class _______________________ some new welding techniques. (past perfect progressive

form of *learn*)  [What helping verbs are added to form the past perfect progressive form of a verb?]

**7.** Construction crews _______________________ several streets in our neighborhood. (present

perfect progressive form of *pave*)

**8.** These hummingbirds _______________________ for several days. (future perfect progressive

form of *migrate*)

**9.** We _______________________ in our new apartment for three months in July. (future perfect

progressive form of *live*)

**10.** Her brother _______________________ his money diligently. (past perfect progressive form

of *save*)

---

**TIP▶** To tell the difference between the *progressive* form and the *perfect progressive* form, compare
their structures. The perfect progressive form requires an extra word.

> **PROGRESSIVE**    a form of *be* **plus** the *–ing* verb
> **PERFECT PROGRESSIVE**    a form of *have* **plus** a form of *be* **plus** the *–ing* verb

---

**EXERCISE C** Identify the form of the underlined verb in each of the following sentences. Then, write
*present progressive, past progressive, future progressive, present perfect progressive, past perfect progressive,*
or *future perfect progressive* on the line provided.

**Example** __*past perfect progressive*__    **1.** Had Rita <u>been sleeping</u> well before school started?

[Rita's continuous action in the past has happened before

a specific time, so the verb phrase is a past perfect progres-

sive form.]

_______________________**11.** By ten o'clock, the rain <u>will have been falling</u> for four hours.

[Does this verb express a continuous action in the future or does it

express a continuous action that will happen before a specific time in

the future?]

_______________________**12.** The wind <u>has been blowing</u> a lot lately.

_______________________**13.** In her cool, quiet room, Alma <u>is reading</u> a magazine.

_______________________**14.** Last week the phones <u>were ringing</u> constantly.

_______________________**15.** In the winter, these animals <u>will be sleeping</u> in their dens.

# The Uses of Tenses

## The Present, Past, and Future Tenses

**8e.** Each of the six tenses has its own uses.

The *present tense* is used to express an action or a state of being that is occurring now, to show habitual or customary action, to convey a general truth, to create a literary present, to make historical events seem current, and to express future time.

| | |
|---|---|
| **OCCURRING NOW** | Detective Dane **solves** another mystery. [Present tense is used to show that the action happens now.] |
| **HABITUAL ACTION** | Doug Dane **works** as a detective. [Present tense is used to show that the action occurs on a regular basis.] |
| **GENERAL TRUTH** | In Dane's town, criminals never **win.** [Present tense is used to show that something is always true.] |
| **LITERARY PRESENT** | In this chapter, Dane **finds** a new clue. [Present tense is used to summarize the plot or subject matter of a literary work.] |
| **HISTORICAL PRESENT** | In 1861, the Pinkerton National Detective Agency **stops** a plot to kill President-elect Lincoln and **saves** his life. [Present tense is used to make a historical event seem current.] |
| **FUTURE TIME** | The new book **comes** out tomorrow. [Present tense is used, but the word *tomorrow* indicates that the action will occur in the future.] |

The *past tense* is used to express an action or a state of being that occurred in the past and does not continue into the present.

    **EXAMPLE**  Last year Detective Dane **solved** many mysteries.

The *future tense* is used to express an action or a state of being that will occur. The future tense is formed with the helping verb *will* or *shall* and the base form of the verb.

    **EXAMPLES**  Detective Dane **will solve** many more mysteries.
               Detective Dane **shall work** for many years to come.

---

**EXERCISE A** Identify the tense of the underlined verb in each of the following sentences. Write *present, past,* or *future* on the line provided.

**Example** ___*future*___ **1.** Will Kim enter an act in the talent show? [Kim *Will enter* in the future.]

__________ **1.** In the auditorium, the audience waits for the show to begin. [Does this action occur in the present or in the future?]

__________ **2.** Nick and Christina usually work the sound system from a special booth.

__________ **3.** During the previous week, rehearsals went well.

__________ **4.** Will the newspaper send reporters to the performance?

__________ **5.** The article says, "Last night's show pleased a huge crowd of happy spectators."

**GO ON** ➡

# The Present Perfect, Past Perfect, and Future Perfect Tenses

The *present perfect tense* expresses an action or a state of being that occurred at some indefinite time in the past and may be continuing into the present. The present perfect tense is formed with the helping verb *have* or *has* and the past participle of a verb.

> **EXAMPLE**   The report **has undergone** many changes.  [*Has undergone* shows an action that occurred at an indefinite time in the past.]

The *past perfect tense* expresses an action or a state of being that ended before some other past action or state of being. The past perfect tense is formed with the helping verb *had* and the past participle of a verb.

> **EXAMPLE**   **Had** the computer network **crashed** before the lightning struck?  [*Had crashed* shows that the network's action ended before another past action occurred.]

The *future perfect tense* expresses an action or a state of being that will end before some other future action or state of being. The future perfect tense is formed with the helping verbs *will have* or *shall have* and the past participle of a verb.

> **EXAMPLE**   By Friday, the council **will have determined** their next course of action.  [*Will have determined* shows that the council's action will end before a specific future time.]

**EXERCISE B**   Identify the tense of the underlined verb in each of the following sentences. Write *present perfect, past perfect,* or *future perfect* on the line provided.

**Example**   _____future perfect_____   **1.** By noon, will everyone have begun lunch?  [*Will have begun* shows that the action will end before a specific future time; therefore, the verb phrase is in the future perfect tense.]

_________________   **6.** Most of the seniors eagerly have prepared for graduation.  [Does this action continue into the present or did the action end in the past?]

_________________   **7.** Soon, Shawna will have completed her graduation speech.

_________________   **8.** Had the principal expected so many family members to attend the ceremony?

_________________   **9.** Over two hundred students will have graduated this year.

_________________   **10.** Our class has become famous for its wealth of talent and promise.

# Consistency of Tense

**8f.**   Use tense forms correctly to show relationships between verbs in a sentence.

## Events That Occur at the Same Time

When describing events that occur at the same time, use verbs in the same tense.

**PRESENT**   The pitcher **throws** the ball, and the batter **swings** at it.

**PAST**   The pitcher **threw** the ball, and the batter **swung** at it.

**FUTURE**   The pitcher **will throw** the ball, and the batter **will swing** at it.

**EXERCISE A** Underline the verb in parentheses that is in the same tense as the underlined verb in each of the following sentences.

**Example 1.** An army of ants has invaded our picnic and (*ate, has eaten*) some of our food.. [*Has invaded* is in the present perfect tense, so the correct verb choice should also be in the present perfect tense.]

**1.** Yesterday afternoon I wanted privacy, so I (*will retreat, retreated*) to my room.  [Which verb is in the same tense as the past tense verb *wanted*?]

**2.** The trip (*will go, goes*) smoothly and we will arrive on time.

**3.** Did William Wordsworth write this poem, or (*does, did*) John Keats write it?

**4.** Mike enjoys yardwork, so he happily (*maintains, maintained*) his family's lawn.

**5.** The cat (*has returned, had returned*) from its wandering and has fallen asleep on the sofa.

## Events That Occur at Different Times

When describing events that occur at different times, use verbs in different tenses to show the order of events.

**EXAMPLES**   Lynn **attends** the state university now, but she **went** to a community college last year.  [In the present, Lynn goes to the state university, so *attends* is in the present tense. At a specific time in the past, before she began attending the university, Lynn attended a community college, so *went* is in the past tense.]

Lynn **has decided** that she **will become** a speech therapist.  [Lynn made her decision at some indefinite time in the past, so *has decided* is in the present perfect tense. In the future Lynn will become a speech therapist, so *will become* is in the future tense.]

**GO ON** ➡

*Developmental Language Skills*

The tense used depends on the writer's desired meaning.

> **EXAMPLES**   Jesse **says** that he **is taking** some nursing classes. [Both verbs are in the present tense. Both actions are occurring now.]
>
> Jesse **says** that he **will take** some nursing classes. [*Says* is in the present tense, so this action is happening now. *Will take* is in the future tense, so this action will happen in the future.]

**EXERCISE B**   In each of the following sentences, underline the correct form of the verb in parentheses to show the order of events.

**Example 1.** Terry forgot that he (*had promised, will promise*) you a ride to school. [Terry's promise happened before he forgot. Therefore, *forgot* is in the past tense and *had promised* is in the past perfect tense.]

**6.** Darla and Greg decided that they (*have gone, will go*) to the park this Saturday. [Which of the two choices shows that the action will happen in the future?]

**7.** As an adult, our dog loves its naps, but as a puppy it (*has, had*) little interest in sleep.

**8.** Will you read the poem I (*composed, compose*) for you last night?

**9.** Martina is saying that she (*is returning, returned*) your library books yesterday.

**10.** Do you believe that this ancient organization (*had, will have*) solid founding principles?

**EXERCISE C**   Identify whether each of the following sentences uses verb tenses correctly. On the line provided, write *C* if the verb tenses are used correctly or *I* if the verb tenses are used incorrectly. Then, if the verb tenses are used incorrectly, use proofreading symbols to correct the sentence.

**Example** ___*I*__ **1.** Last night, Alfredo packed a lunch and ~~lays~~ laid out his clothes. [Both actions happened in the past, so each verb should be in the past tense.]

______**11.** Grandma promised that she and Grandpa visited us next Sunday. [Since the visit takes place in the future, what form should *visited* take?]

______**12.** Lola had discovered her love of music long before she joined the band.

______**13.** The pond is rising while the rain fell.

______**14.** As a child, Kevin watched television programs in Spanish, and he will learn the language from those programs.

______**15.** Has everyone decided what he or she orders from the menu?

# Active Voice and Passive Voice

The subject of a sentence either may perform or receive the action of the verb.

> **EXAMPLES**   **Josh lost** the hat.  [The subject *Josh* performs the action of *lost*.]
>
> The **hat was lost.**  [The subject *hat* receives the action of *was lost*.]

When a subject performs the action of the verb, the verb is in the *active voice.* When a subject receives the action, the verb is in the *passive voice.* In the passive voice, the verb phrase includes a form of *be* and the past participle of the main verb. Other helping verbs may also be included.

> **ACTIVE VOICE**   **Someone found** a ring.  [The subject *someone* performs the action of *found*.]
>
> **PASSIVE VOICE**   The ring **was found.**  [The subject *ring* receives the action of the verb phrase *was found*.]
>
> The ring **has been found.**  [The subject *ring* receives the action of the verb phrase *has been found*.]

**EXERCISE A** Identify whether each of the following sentences is in the active voice or the passive voice. Then, write *A* for *active voice* or *P* for *passive voice* on the line provided.

**Examples** ___P___ **1.** Are these egg rolls filled with vegetables?  [*Egg rolls* receives the action of *are filled,* so the sentence is in the passive voice.]

___A___ **2.** I sent flowers to my mom.  [*I* performs the action *sent,* so the sentence is in the active voice.]

_______ **1.** To her delight, Candace was treated to a surprise graduation party.  [Does the subject *Candace* perform or receive the action of *was treated*?]

_______ **2.** Has the software been updated to include the necessary changes? [Does the subject *software* perform or receive the action of *has been updated*?]

_______ **3.** At the salon, a hairstylist will cut your hair in a bold new style.

_______ **4.** Did the pilot share the flight plan with her copilot?

_______ **5.** In the bakery, the pastries are sprinkled with cinnamon.

_______ **6.** In my classroom, every student is given a turn at the board.

_______ **7.** Often, special options are offered to customers at the car lot.

_______ **8.** Ms. Hampton gives awards to many students.

_______ **9.** They were promised a fun time by their tour conductor.

_______ **10.** At dinner at my house, we pass plates of food around the table.

**GO ON**

# The Uses of the Passive Voice

Writing is usually clearer and stronger when in the active voice, so the passive voice should be used sparingly. However, there are some times when the passive voice is preferable. Use the passive voice when you do not know who performed the action, when you do not want to reveal the performer of the action, or when you want to emphasize the receiver of the action rather than the performer.

**EXAMPLES**  Several events **were cancelled.** [The performer of the action is unknown.]

The surprise **was ruined.** [The performer of the action is unrevealed.]

Ms. Li **has been given** an award. [The receiver of the action is emphasized.]

**EXERCISE B** Decide whether each of the following sentences should be rewritten using active voice. Then, on the line provided, rewrite the sentence in the active voice or explain why the sentence should remain in the passive voice.

**Example  1.** Many seniors have been admitted to colleges already. [The passive voice is

preferable.]

This sentence should remain in the passive voice to emphasize the receiver of the action.

**11.** Yesterday, new locks were installed by a skilled locksmith. [Will this sentence be stronger and

more direct if rewritten using the active voice?]

_______________________________________________________________

**12.** The traffic accident will be investigated.

_______________________________________________________________

**13.** Last Sunday, our fantastic dinner was prepared by me.

_______________________________________________________________

**14.** All stockholders have been sent their dividends.

_______________________________________________________________

**15.** Unfortunately, a lie about what happened was told by someone.

_______________________________________________________________



Sixth Course

# Troublesome Modifiers A

## *Bad* and *Badly*

*Bad* is an adjective; it describes nouns and pronouns. Usually, *bad* follows a linking verb such as *feel*, *look*, *taste*, *sound*, and *smell*. **Badly** is an adverb; it modifies verbs, adjectives, and adverbs.

**TIP** You may remember that many adverbs end in *–ly*. Use the *–ly* ending of *badly* as a reminder that this word is an adverb.

    **ADJECTIVE**    The recording sounds **bad.** [*Bad* follows the linking verb *sounds.*]

    **ADVERB**    The sound system needs repairs **badly.** [*Badly* modifies the verb *needs.*]

**NOTE** In standard, formal English, only the adjective form, *bad*, follows a linking verb. You may hear people using the expression *feel badly.* This usage is informal. In your formal writing and speaking, always use the adjective form, *bad*, after a linking verb.

    **INFORMAL**    Thelma feels badly about the mistake. [*Badly* is an adverb; it should not follow the linking verb *feels.*]

    **FORMAL**    Thelma feels **bad** about the mistake. [The adjective *bad* should follow the linking verb *feels.*]

**EXERCISE A** In each of the following items, underline the word in parentheses that is correct according to standard, formal English.

**Examples 1.** The television has (*bad, badly*) reception. It probably needs a new antenna. [The adjective *bad* describes the noun *reception.*]

    **2.** The team played (*bad, badly*). [The adverb *badly* modifies the verb *played.*]

**1.** When I keep secrets from my best friend, I feel (*bad, badly*) about it. [Which word is an adjective and should follow the linking verb *feel*?]

**2.** Champion, the horse rescued earlier today, has a (*bad, badly*) injured leg. [Which word is an adverb and should modify the adjective *injured*?]

**3.** Were the plants (*bad, badly*) damaged by the early frost?

**4.** Can I give the dog a bath? He smells (*bad, badly*).

**5.** The rowboat should be repaired; it leaks (*bad, badly*).

**6.** When I play the recording through the loudspeakers, does it sound (*bad, badly*)?

**7.** That old, flaky paint looks (*bad, badly*).

**8.** Felix wants a car of his own very (*bad, badly*).

**9.** To me, hot mustard tastes (*bad, badly*). I prefer mild mustard.

**10.** The new movie got (*bad, badly*) reviews.

## *Good* and *Well*

*Good* is an adjective; it usually describes a noun or a pronoun. *Well* may be used as an adjective or an adverb. Avoid using *good* to modify a verb. Instead, use *well* as an adverb meaning "capably" or "satisfactorily."

> **ADJECTIVE**   His drum solo sounded **good.**  [The adjective *good* follows the linking verb *sounded* and describes the noun *solo.*]

> **ADVERB**   Does the drummer usually play **well**?  [The adverb *well* modifies the verb phrase *Does play.*]

*Feel good* and *feel well* mean different things. If you feel good, you feel happy or pleased. If you feel well, you feel healthy.

> **EXAMPLES**   The soccer team felt **good** about their victory.  [The team felt pleased.]
>
> Because of the fever, Janet does not feel **well.**  [Janet does not feel healthy.]

**EXERCISE B**   In each of the following sentences, underline the word in parentheses that is correct according to standard, formal English.

**Examples 1.** Did the children behave (*good, well*) while I was gone?  [The adverb *well* modifies the verb phrase *Did behave.*]

**2.** Eve has recovered from the flu, and she feels (*good, well*).  [The expression *feel well* means "feel healthy."]

**11.** After I spilled the paint, I cleaned the floor (*good, well*).  [Which word is an adverb and should modify the verb *cleaned*?]

**12.** Doesn't Mary's new perfume smell (*good, well*)?  [Which word is an adjective and should describe the noun *perfume*?]

**13.** Because Carla sews so (*good, well*), she volunteered to make the costumes for the play.

**14.** Participating in the beach cleanup is a (*good, well*) way for our organization to help the community and have a positive impact on the environment.

**15.** I felt (*good, well*) about my performance at the recital.

**16.** The shady area is a (*good, well*) spot for a picnic.

**17.** Does my sketch for art class look (*good, well*)?

**18.** In the play, Brad performed quite (*good, well*).

**19.** Please clean your room (*good, well*) before our guests arrive.

**20.** Does a late lunch sound (*good, well*) to you?

# Troublesome Modifiers B

## *Real* and *Really*

*Real* is an adjective; it is used to describe nouns and pronouns. *Really* is an adverb meaning "truly" or "actually." *Really* can be used to modify verbs, adjectives, and adverbs.

**TIP▶** You may remember that many adverbs end in *–ly*. Use the *–ly* ending of *really* as a reminder that this word is an adverb.

> **ADJECTIVE**  Is that a **real** autograph?  [*Real* is an adjective and describes the noun *autograph*.]

> **ADVERB**  Max gave Sandy a **really** beautiful charm for her bracelet.  [*Really* is an adverb and modifies the adjective *beautiful*.]

**NOTE▶** In informal situations, you may hear people using *real* as an adverb. It is best, however, to use the adverb *really* in your formal speaking and writing.

> **INFORMAL**  Is Fredric real nervous about his solo?

> **FORMAL**  Is Fredric **really** nervous about his solo?  [The adverb *really* modifies the adjective *nervous*.]

**EXERCISE A** In each of the following sentences, underline the word in parentheses that is correct according to standard, formal English.

**Examples** **1.** Your knowledge of economics is (*real*, *really*) impressive.  [The adverb *really* modifies the adjective *impressive*.]

**2.** Is that a (*real*, *really*) plant in the aquarium?  [The adjective *real* modifies the noun *plant*.]

**1.** Thank you. Your offer of help is (*real*, *really*) thoughtful.  [Which word is an adverb and should modify the adjective *thoughtful*?]

**2.** Is that an account of (*real*, *really*) events?  [Which word is an adjective and should describe the noun *events*?]

**3.** The platypus is a (*real*, *really*) interesting animal.

**4.** Did Miranda see the (*real*, *really*) Declaration of Independence during her trip to Washington, D.C.?

**5.** Everyone should drive (*real*, *really*) slowly through school zones.

**6.** Jason practices the violin (*real*, *really*) faithfully.

**7.** Did Uncle Taylor create a (*real*, *really*) fun treasure hunt for the kids?

**GO ON ▶**

**8.** This paperweight is made of (*real, really*) granite.

**9.** Did you (*real, really*) solve the crossword puzzle without any help?

**10.** Tonight we are using (*real, really*) linen napkins instead of paper ones.

## *Slow* and *Slowly*

*Slow* can be used as an adjective or an adverb. *Slowly* is used only as an adverb. Usually, it is better to use *slowly* instead of *slow* when you need an adverb.

> **ADJECTIVE**    At the prom, they danced to several **slow** songs. [*Slow* modifies the noun *songs*.]
>
>               The climb up the mountain was **slow**. [*Slow* follows the linking verb *was* and modifies the noun *climb*.]
>
> **ADVERB**    At the prom, they danced **slowly**. [*Slowly* modifies the verb *danced*.]
>
>               We climbed **slowly** up the mountain. [*Slowly* modifies the verb *climbed*.]

**EXERCISE B**   In each of the following sentences, underline the word in parentheses that is correct according to standard, formal English. Hint: Use *slowly* as an adverb to modify verbs.

**Examples 1.** Is the traffic on the freeway moving (*slow, slowly*)? [The adverb *slowly* modifies the verb phrase *Is moving*.]

       **2.** The (*slow, slowly*), soothing music helped me relax. [The adjective *slow* describes the noun *music*.]

**11.** A firefighter must not react (*slow, slowly*) to an emergency. [Which word is an adverb and should modify the verb phrase *must react*?]

**12.** The (*slow, slowly*) snail inched its way across the sidewalk. [Which word is an adjective and should describe the noun *snail*?]

**13.** Why is the service at the drive-through so (*slow, slowly*)?

**14.** (*Slow, Slowly*), the trucker drove his rig through the mountain passes.

**15.** The feather (*slow, slowly*) fluttered to the ground.

**16.** Trish's actions were (*slow, slowly*) and careful.

**17.** Please pour the hot tea into the cups (*slow, slowly*).

**18.** In my backyard, the (*slow, slowly*) sway of the hammock relaxed me.

**19.** With so many stops, the train ride seemed incredibly (*slow, slowly*).

**20.** Breathing (*slow, slowly*) has a calming effect.

# Degrees of Comparison
## Regular Comparison

**9e.**   Modifiers change form to show comparison.

The three degrees of comparison are the *positive*, the *comparative*, and the *superlative*.

**(1)**   Most one-syllable modifiers form the comparative degree by adding *–er* and the superlative degree by adding *–est.*

|  | POSITIVE | COMPARATIVE | SUPERLATIVE |
| --- | --- | --- | --- |
| **ONE SYLLABLE** | loud | loud**er** | loud**est** |

**(2)**   Two-syllable modifiers may form the comparative degree by adding *–er* and the superlative degree by adding *–est,* or they may form the comparative degree by using *more* and the superlative degree by using *most.*

|  | POSITIVE | COMPARATIVE | SUPERLATIVE |
| --- | --- | --- | --- |
| **TWO SYLLABLES** | sunny | sunni**er, more** sunny | sunni**est, most** sunny |

**(3)**   Modifiers that have three or more syllables form the comparative degree by using *more* and the superlative degree by using *most.*

|  | POSITIVE | COMPARATIVE | SUPERLATIVE |
| --- | --- | --- | --- |
| **THREE SYLLABLES** | dramatic | **more** dramatic | **most** dramatic |

**(4)**   To show a decrease in the qualities they express, modifiers form the comparative degree by using *less* and the superlative degree by using *least.*

|  | POSITIVE | COMPARATIVE | SUPERLATIVE |
| --- | --- | --- | --- |
| **DECREASING** | fragile | **less** fragile | **least** fragile |

**EXERCISE A** Fill in the blank in each of the following sentences with the correct form of the modifier suggested in parentheses at the end of the sentence.

**Examples  1.** Please handle the eggs _____*more gently*_____. (increasing comparative form of

*gently*) [The two-syllable word *gently* uses *more* to form the increasing comparative

degree.]

**2.** Of all our cats, Weezy was the _____*least aggressive*_____. (decreasing superlative form of

*aggressive*) [*Least* is used to form the decreasing superlative degree of *aggressive*.]

**1.** Is the navy blue jacket ___________________ than the brown one? (decreasing comparative

degree of *expensive*) [What word is used to form the decreasing comparative degree?]

**2.** That was the ___________________ joke I've ever heard! (increasing superlative form of *funny*)

[How is the increasing superlative degree of a two-syllable word formed?]

**GO ON**

*Developmental Language Skills*

**3.** Although I knew the cold front would arrive in the afternoon, the temperature dropped

_____________________ than I had expected. (increasing comparative form of *rapidly*)

**4.** The mineral exhibit was _____________________ than the dinosaur exhibit. (decreasing

comparative form of *interesting*)

**5.** Who won the prize for the _____________________ costume at the party? (increasing superlative

form of *outrageous*)

**6.** Can we make the engine _____________________? (decreasing comparative form of *noisy*)

**7.** I bought the _____________________ bike I could find. (increasing superlative degree of *light*)

**8.** The teacher asked the student to speak _____________________ so that everyone could hear the

speech. (decreasing comparative form of *softly*)

**9.** I think mice are the _____________________ animals, but some of my friends are deathly afraid of

them. (decreasing superlative form of *fearsome*)

**10.** The mobile I made for my baby brother was _____________________ than the ones in the catalog.

(increasing comparative degree of *colorful*)

## Irregular Comparison

Some modifiers are *irregular.* They do not form the comparative and superlative degrees with
the usual methods.

|  | POSITIVE | COMPARATIVE | SUPERLATIVE |
| --- | --- | --- | --- |
| **EXAMPLES** | bad | worse | worst |
|  | good | better | best |
|  | many | more | most |

**EXERCISE B**  Underline the correct form of the word in parentheses in each of the following sentences.

**Example  1.** That is the (*baddest, worst*) excuse I have ever heard!  [The superlative form of *bad* is

*worst.*]

**11.** Although I found many Easter eggs, Harry found (*more, manier*).  [Which word is the correct

comparative form of the word *many*?]

**12.** Which organization raised the (*most, maniest*) money during the charity fund-raiser?

**13.** Your work on this test is (*better, gooder*) than your work on the previous test.

**14.** Which of the three options do you feel (*goodest, best*) about?

**15.** The weather today is (*worse, badder*) than it was yesterday.

# Uses of Comparisons

## Comparative and Superlative Forms

**9f.** Use the comparative degree when comparing two things. Use the superlative degree when comparing more than two things.

> **COMPARATIVE**    Both Pamela and Craig gave speeches in history class. Pamela's speech was **more interesting.** [Two speeches are being compared.]
>
> **SUPERLATIVE**    Of all the speeches in history class, Pamela's speech was **most interesting.** [More than two speeches are being compared. Pamela's speech is being compared to all of the speeches given in history class.]

**9g.** Include the word *other* or *else* when you are comparing one member of a group with the rest of the group.

> **ILLOGICAL**    Pamela worked harder than any student in the class. [Pamela is a student in the class. Logically, Pamela cannot have worked harder than herself.]
>
> **LOGICAL**    Pamela worked harder than any **other** student in the class. [One member of a group is being compared with the rest of the group, so the word *other* is used.]

**NOTE▶** When comparing one member of a group to each of the other members, use the comparative form. When comparing one member of a group to all of the members of the group, use the superlative form.

> **COMPARATIVE**    Leo swam **faster** than the other members of the team, Carl, Nina, and Ashley. [Leo is being compared to each of the other members of the team. He swam faster than Carl, he swam faster than Nina, and he swam faster than Ashley.]
>
> **SUPERLATIVE**    Leo is the **fastest** swimmer on the team. [Leo is being compared to all of the members of the group.]

**EXERCISE A** Use proofreading marks to correct any errors in the use of comparative or superlative forms. If an item is already correct, write *C* on the line provided.

**Examples** _______ **1.** When Mr. King studied the two applications, he decided Nora's was ~~best.~~ *better* [Two applications are being compared. The comparative form *better* should be used.]

    *C*    **2.** Of all the rosebushes, this one has the most blooms. [More than two rosebushes are being compared, so the superlative form *most* is correct.]

_______ **1.** My dog Fido learned the commands more quickly than any dog in the class. [Which word should be added when comparing one member of a group with the rest of the group?]

_______ **2.** The grass is greenest on the other side of the fence. [Should the comparative or the superlative degree be used when comparing two things?]

**GO ON ➡**

______ **3.** I've put together over fifty jigsaw puzzles, and this one is the more difficult.

______ **4.** Isabel has scored more points than anyone else on the team.

______ **5.** Of the two parrots, this one is most colorful.

______ **6.** I considered yellow, blue, or green paint for my bedroom. I liked yellow better.

______ **7.** Which play did you enjoy most, *Hamlet* or *The Taming of the Shrew*?

______ **8.** Tyrone collected more canned goods than anyone in the class.

______ **9.** Carrying the couch up the stairs was most difficult than carrying the chairs up the stairs.

______ **10.** Which of these two fonts is easier to read?

## Double Comparisons

**9h.**   Avoid using double comparisons.

A *double comparison* occurs when two comparative forms (usually *–er* and *more*) are used together or when two superlative forms (usually *–est* and *most*) are used together.

    **NONSTANDARD**   The curtains for the kitchen window should be more shorter than those for the dining room window. [*More shorter* is a double comparison.]

    **STANDARD**   The curtains for the kitchen window should be **shorter** than those for the dining room window. [*Shorter* is the correct comparative form.]

    **NONSTANDARD**   A cheetah can run more faster than any other land animal. [*More faster* is a double comparison.]

    **STANDARD**   A cheetah can run **faster** than any other land animal. [*Faster* is the correct comparative form.]

**EXERCISE B**   Use proofreading marks to correct double comparisons in the following items. If an item is already correct, write *C* on the line provided. Hint: There may be more than one way to correct an item.

**Example**   ______ **1.** The water in the pond was more ~~murkier~~ *murky* than it should have been. [*More murkier* is a double comparison. Changing *more murkier* to *more murky* is one way to correct the double comparison.]

______ **11.** The computer monitors in the drafting lab are more bigger than the monitors in the writing lab. [Which word can be deleted to correct the double comparison?]

______ **12.** Of all the grocery stores near my home, the one on Fourth Street has the most freshest produce.

______ **13.** Which one of these refrigerators is the most energy efficient?

______ **14.** During the camping trip, we swam, hiked, and canoed, and I liked hiking most best.

______ **15.** Mrs. Fermo is the most friendliest of the five board members.

**100**

# Placement of Modifiers A

## Misplaced Modifiers

**10a.**   Avoid using misplaced modifiers.

A *misplaced modifier* is a word, phrase, or clause that seems to modify the wrong word or word group in a sentence. To avoid misplaced modifiers, place a modifier as close as possible to the word or word group it modifies.

| | |
|---|---|
| **MISPLACED WORD** | Melting, the trees were covered with icicles. [Are the trees melting?] |
| **CLEAR** | The trees were covered with **melting** icicles. [*Melting* modifies *icicles*, so it has been placed close to the word it modifies.] |
| **MISPLACED PHRASE** | Janell finished the report that Ms. Brooks assigned during her vacation. [Did Ms. Brooks assign the report while on vacation? The phrase *during her vacation* is too far from the verb it modifies, *finished.*] |
| **CLEAR** | **During her vacation,** Janell finished the report that Ms. Brooks assigned. [This placement shows that Janell finished the report while she was on vacation.] |
| **MISPLACED CLAUSE** | James needed a break, who had been studying for an exam. [Had the break been studying for an exam? The clause *who had been studying for an exam* is too far from the noun it modifies, *James.*] |
| **CLEAR** | James, **who had been studying for an exam,** needed a break. [This placement shows that James had been studying, not the break.] |

**EXERCISE A** The underlined word or word group in each of the following sentences is misplaced. Draw an arrow to show where the underlined modifier should go in the sentence.

**Examples 1.** Determined, the steep trail did not bother the climbers. [The climbers were

determined, not the trail. *Determined* should be placed closer to the word it modifies,

*climbers.*]

**2.** This old trunk belonged to my great-grandfather, which was full of books and

papers. [The trunk was full of books and papers, not the great-grandfather. The clause

should be placed closer to the word it modifies, *trunk.*]

**1.** Delighted, the fireworks surprised the children. [Were the fireworks delighted?]

**2.** I found the book in my room that was due yesterday. [Was the room due yesterday?]

**3.** The bicycle is in the shed with a flat tire.

**4.** Escaping, the boy tried to grab the tail of the kite.

**5.** Karen's soccer team is ranked second in the state; her team has nearly won all of its games.

**6.** Ringing, I ran for the phone.

**7.** The canoe slid through the water, built by hand.

**8.** We finished reading a short story written by Mark Twain <u>during study hall</u>.

**9.** Hundreds of pumpkins lay in the fields, <u>which were almost ripe</u>.

**10.** The supervisor complimented the carpenters for working so quickly <u>as he handed out their</u>

<u>paychecks</u>.

## Squinting Modifiers

**10b.** Avoid misplacing a modifying word, phrase, or clause so that it seems to modify either of two words.

This kind of misplaced modifier is often called a *squinting,* or *two-way, modifier.*

| | |
|---|---|
| **SQUINTING** | My father promised on Saturday we would go fishing. [Did the father make the promise on Saturday, or do they plan to go fishing on Saturday?] |
| **CLEAR** | **On Saturday,** my father promised we would go fishing. [This placement clarifies that the father made the promise on Saturday.] |
| **CLEAR** | My father promised we would go fishing **on Saturday.** [This placement clarifies that they plan to go fishing on Saturday.] |
| **SQUINTING** | Annie reminded me at 6:00 P.M. we have a rehearsal. [Did Annie say that at 6:00 P.M., or will the rehearsal take place at 6:00 P.M.?] |
| **CLEAR** | **At 6:00 P.M.,** Annie reminded me we have a rehearsal. [This placement clarifies that Annie spoke at 6:00 P.M.] |
| **CLEAR** | Annie reminded me we have a rehearsal at **6:00 P.M.** [This placement clarifies that the rehearsal is at 6:00 P.M.] |

**EXERCISE B**  Decide whether the underlined modifier in each of the following sentences is clear or squinting. If the modifier is clear and correct, write *C* for *clear* on the line provided. If the modifier is squinting, write *S* for *squinting* on the line provided.

**Example** ___*S*___ **1.** The weather reporter said <u>shortly after five o'clock</u> severe weather is expect-

ed.  [The underlined modifier is squinting. Did the weather reporter speak short-

ly after five o'clock, or is the severe weather expected shortly after five o'clock?]

_______ **11.** The article in the school newspaper said <u>on March 20th</u> representatives from local

colleges will be on campus.  [Did the newspaper print the article on March 20th, or will

representatives be on campus on March 20th?]

_______ **12.** Barbara claimed she was not discouraged <u>when she saw the test scores</u>.

_______ **13.** Mark remembered <u>after dinner</u> he was supposed to wash the dishes.

_______ **14.** Mr. Fields said <u>after the mixture changed colors</u> we should turn off the Bunsen burner.

_______ **15.** <u>Before the whistle blew</u>, the coach said too many players were on the field.

# Placement of Modifiers B

## Dangling Modifiers

**10c.**  Avoid using dangling modifiers.

When a modifier does not clearly and sensibly modify any word or word group in a sentence, it is called a *dangling modifier.*

> **DANGLING**  Having decided to learn to dance, a dance studio was contacted.  [Who had decided to learn to dance?]
>
> **CLEAR**  **Having decided to learn to dance, she** contacted a dance studio.  [*Having decided to learn to dance* now clearly modifies *she.*]
>
> **DANGLING**  While shopping for groceries, the rain started.  [Was the rain shopping for groceries?]
>
> **CLEAR**  The rain started **while I was shopping for groceries.**  [The subordinate clause now makes clear *who* was shopping.]

**EXERCISE A**  Look at the underlined word group in each of the following sentences.  If the word group clearly and sensibly modifies another word or word group in the sentence, write *C* for *clear* on the line provided.  If the underlined word group is a dangling modifier, write *D* for *dangling* on the line provided.

**Examples**  __*D*__  **1.** Before making the decision, all the possibilities were considered.  [The underlined word group is dangling. Who will make the decision?]

__*C*__  **2.** Having already decorated the gym, the committee members began to set up tables and chairs.  [The underlined word group clearly modifies *members.*]

______ **1.** Having hiked for three long hours, the cabin was a welcome sight.  [Should the underlined word group modify *cabin*?]

______ **2.** Waiting for the bus, Chris and Jenny sat on the bench and talked.  [Should the underlined word group modify *Chris and Jenny*?]

______ **3.** Before leaving to get the mail, the note was taped on the door.

______ **4.** Distracted by the loud construction noise, Leonard's new earplugs helped.

______ **5.** While finishing the sketch, the pencil lead broke.

______ **6.** Sewn with care, the museum's lighting was delicate.

______ **7.** When skating, you should always wear protective gear.

______ **8.** Waking in the dark room, the smell of breakfast was appetizing.

______ **9.** Chattering excitedly, the squirrel ran from the diving blue jays.

______ **10.** After mowing the lawn and raking the leaves, his eyes itched.

**GO ON**

Most dangling modifiers come at the beginning of sentences. Two common ways to correct such dangling modifiers are as follows: (1) Add a subject to the word group that comes at the beginning of the sentence. (2) Place the word being modified closely after the comma that follows the word group at the beginning of the sentence.

| | |
|---|---|
| **DANGLING** | While researching the Industrial Revolution, the librarian helped her find several useful books. [Was the librarian researching the Industrial Revolution?] |
| **CLEAR** | **While Clara was researching the Industrial Revolution,** the librarian helped her find several useful books. [Adding a subject to the word group at the beginning of the sentence makes it clear that Clara was researching the Industrial Revolution.] |
| **DANGLING** | Resting in the shade, the tennis ball was still held in our dog's mouth. [Was the tennis ball resting in the shade?] |
| **CLEAR** | Resting in the shade, **our dog still held the tennis ball in its mouth.** [Placing the word being modified closely after the comma following the word group at the beginning of the sentence and revising the rest of the sentence makes it clear that the dog was resting in the shade.] |

**EXERCISE B** Underline the dangling modifier in each of the following sentences. Then, on the line provided, rewrite each sentence to correct the dangling modifier.

**Example  1.** Fascinated by the ants' efficiency at collecting food, the ants carried crumbs back to their anthill. [*Fascinated by the ants' efficiency at collecting food* is a dangling modifier. The sentence was rewritten to make it clear that Nick, not the ants, was fascinated by the ants' efficiency at collecting food.]

> Fascinated by the ants' efficiency at collecting food, Nick watched the ants carry crumbs back to their anthill.

**11.** While watching the sun set over the ocean, the sky turned purple, red, and orange.

 

**12.** Having run several miles, nothing is as refreshing as a cool glass of water.

 

**13.** After baking bread, the house smelled wonderful!

 

**14.** Pestered by the flies buzzing around, the cow's tail swatted at them.

 

**15.** After completing the test, the answer sheet should be placed inside the test booklet.

 

# Glossary of Usage A

***accept, except***   The verb *accept* means "to receive." *Except* may be a preposition or a verb. The preposition *except* means "excluding." The verb *except* means "to leave out" or "to excuse."

**EXAMPLES**   She would not **accept** his phone call. [You can replace *accept* with *receive*.]

Everyone **except** Jake has gone to the museum. [You can replace *except* with *excluding*.]

Are they **excepted** from duty? [You can replace *excepted* with *excused*.]

***affect, effect***   The verb *affect* means "to influence." *Effect* may be used as either a verb or a noun. The verb *effect* means "to bring about [a desired result]" or "to accomplish." The noun *effect* means "the result [of an action]."

**EXAMPLES**   Light **affects** a plant's growth. [You can replace *affects* with *influences*.]

Managers **effected** changes to the process. [You can replace *effected* with *brought about*.]

Did the praise have an **effect** on the dog's training? [You can replace *effect* with *result*.]

***all right***   *All right* should be written as two words. *All right* means "satisfactory," "unhurt," "safe," or "correct." *All right* also means "yes" when it used as a reply to a question or as an introductory remark.

**NONSTANDARD**   Ella asked me if I was allright after I scraped my leg sliding into home plate.

**STANDARD**   Ella asked me if I was **all right** after I scraped my leg sliding into home plate.

**NONSTANDARD**   Allright, we'll go camping next weekend.

**STANDARD**   **All right,** we'll go camping next weekend.

**EXERCISE A**   Underline the word or word group in parentheses that is correct according to formal, standard English.

**Example 1.** The law had an *(affect, effect)* on energy conservation requirements. [*Effect* is a noun that means "the result [of an action]." *Effect* is the correct choice.]

**1.** Everyone stood and cheered when Chris *(excepted, accepted)* the award. [Which word means "received"?]

**2.** I think I did *(all right, allright)* on the history exam.

**3.** *(Except, Accept)* for my sister, everyone in my family was born in Oregon.

**4.** High mountains *(effect, affect)* the weather in the region.

**5.** *(All right, Allright),* the speed bump on Chaucer Street has been installed.

**GO ON**

*a lot*   *A lot* is always two words and is always informal. *A lot* can be used as a noun meaning "a large number or amount" or "a great deal." *A lot* can also be used as an adverb meaning "a great deal" or "very much." Avoid using *a lot* in formal situations.

| | |
|---|---|
| **INFORMAL** | I don't have a lot of time this week. |
| **FORMAL** | I don't have **a great deal** of time this week. |

| | |
|---|---|
| **INFORMAL** | Those bats like mosquitoes a lot. |
| **FORMAL** | Those bats like mosquitoes **very much.** |

*anyways, anywheres*   Do not add an *s* to words such as *anyway, anywhere, everywhere, nowhere,* or *somewhere.*

| | |
|---|---|
| **NONSTANDARD** | Have you seen my jacket anywheres? |
| **STANDARD** | Have you seen my jacket **anywhere?** |

*at*   Don't use *at* after *where.*

| | |
|---|---|
| **NONSTANDARD** | Where are the boxes at? |
| **STANDARD** | Where are the boxes? |

*between, among*   Use *between* when referring to two individuals or items at one time. Use *among* when referring to a group rather than to separate individuals or items.

| | |
|---|---|
| **EXAMPLES** | The museum is located **between** Fifth Avenue and Sixth Avenue.  [*Between Fifth Avenue and Sixth Avenue* refers to two items.] |
| | Phyllis, Emilia, and Tamara divided the boxes **among** themselves.  [*Among themselves* refers to a group of three individuals.] |

**EXERCISE B**   Underline the word or word group in parentheses that is correct according to formal, standard English.

**Example  1.**   The birdseed was distributed (*between*, <u>*among*</u>) the five birdhouses.  [*Among the five birdhouses* refers to a group of five items.]

**6.**   (*A lot, A large number*) of students will be going to the concert.  [Which word group is formal?]

**7.**   Where did you buy your (*backpack at, backpack*)?  [Should *at* be used after *Where*?]

**8.**   I bought it at a store (*somewhere, somewheres*) in the mall.

**9.**   The bees were buzzing around (*between, among*) the many flowers.

**10.**   Our new dishwasher is (*much, a lot*) quieter than our old one.

**11.**   It may rain this weekend, but we plan to go camping (*anyway, anyways*).

**12.**   The supervisor divided the work (*between, among*) the six employees.

**13.**   I looked (*everywheres, everywhere*), but I couldn't find my keys.

**14.**   Please meet me (*among, between*) six and seven o'clock.

**15.**   Do you know where the meeting (*is, is at*)?

# Glossary of Usage B

***done*** Always use a helping verb with *done*, the past participle of the verb *do*. Do not use *done* instead of *did*.

> **NONSTANDARD** I already done the laundry.
> **STANDARD** I **have** already **done** the laundry.
> **STANDARD** I already **did** the laundry.

***don't, doesn't*** *Don't* is a contraction of *do not*. Use *don't* with plural subjects and the pronouns *I* and *you*. *Doesn't* is a contraction of *does not*. Use *doesn't* with all other singular subjects.

> **EXAMPLES** These photographs **don't** need to be retouched. [*Don't* agrees with the plural subject *photographs*.]
>
> I **don't** know how to get there. **Don't** you have the directions? [*Don't* agrees with the pronouns *I* and *you*.]
>
> My uncle **doesn't** drive a car. [*Doesn't* agrees with the singular subject *uncle*.]

**EXERCISE A** Underline the word or word group in parentheses that is correct according to formal, standard English.

**Examples 1.** She (*don't,* *doesn't*) enjoy watching football. [*Doesn't* agrees with the singular subject *She*.]

**2.** After Carl (*done,* *had done*) his errands, he went to a movie. [A helping verb is always used with *done*.]

**1.** (*Don't, Doesn't*) you play the violin? [Which contraction agrees with the pronoun *you*?]

**2.** Everyone has (*done, did*) the homework assignment. [Which form of *do* should be used with a helping verb?]

**3.** This orange (*don't, doesn't*) have many seeds.

**4.** My brothers (*don't, doesn't*) look alike.

**5.** Has everyone (*did, done*) the stretching exercises?

**6.** After I (*done, did*) my chores, I played tennis.

**7.** That radio station (*don't, doesn't*) come in well.

**8.** Have you (*done, did*) today's crossword puzzle?

**9.** If I (*doesn't, don't*) get some sleep, I'll be exhausted tomorrow.

**10.** Has everyone in Mrs. Lowen's class (*done, did*) his or her presentation?

**GO ON** ➡

*Developmental Language Skills*

*fewer, less*   *Fewer* is used with plural words and tells "how many." *Less* is used with singular words and tells "how much."

> **EXAMPLES**   This room has **fewer** chairs in it than that room.   [*Chairs* is plural.]
>
> If we leave before rush hour, it will take us **less** time to get there.   [*Time* is singular.]

*kind of, sort of*   *Kind of* and *sort of* are informal. In formal situations, use *rather* or *somewhat*.

> **INFORMAL**   The article was kind of long.
>
> **FORMAL**   The article was **rather** long.

*learn, teach*   The verb *learn* means "to gain knowledge." The verb *teach* means "to provide knowledge."

> **EXAMPLES**   Lori **learns** many sewing techniques from her aunt.   [Lori gains knowledge about sewing techniques from her aunt.]
>
> Her aunt **teaches** a sewing class.   [Her aunt provides knowledge about sewing.]

**EXERCISE B**   Underline the word or word group in parentheses that is correct according to formal, standard English.

**Examples 1.**   I wish I had brought (*fewer, less*) pieces of luggage on this trip.   [*Pieces* is plural, so *fewer* is the correct choice.]

**2.**   She acted (*somewhat, sort of*) surprised when we gave her flowers for her birthday. [*Sort of* is informal. *Somewhat* is the correct choice.]

**11.**   Mr. Kramer (*learned, taught*) the students geometry.   [Which word means "to provide knowledge"?]

**12.**   Making the quilt required (*less, fewer*) fabric than we thought it would.   [Is *fabric* singular or plural?]

**13.**   Isn't that colt looking (*kind of, rather*) sleepy?

**14.**   (*Fewer, Less*) runners entered the race this year.

**15.**   My younger brother has already (*learned, taught*) how to ride a bicycle.

**16.**   Did (*fewer, less*) people watch the program last week?

**17.**   Dr. Farrow (*learns, teaches*) French at the community college.

**18.**   Due to the construction, there were (*fewer, less*) parking spaces next to the soccer fields.

**19.**   Mary was (*sort of, somewhat*) pleased with her new haircut.

**20.**   The programs on this station have (*less, fewer*) advertisements.

# Glossary of Usage C

*of*   Do not use *of* after verbs such as *could, should, would, might, must,* and *ought [to]. Of* is a preposition and should not be substituted for *have.* Also, do not use *had of* for *had.*

> **NONSTANDARD**   The overpass should of been completed on time.
> **STANDARD**   The overpass **should have** been completed on time.

*supposed to, used to*   The past-tense forms of *suppose* and *use* always end in *–d.*

> **EXAMPLES**   Were you **supposed to** call?  [The past tense of *suppose* is *supposed.*]
> Leonard **used to** play the piano.  [The past-tense form of *use* is *used.*]

*than, then*   *Than* is a subordinating conjunction; it is used to make comparisons. *Then* is an adverb; it answers the question *when?* and usually means "at that time" or "next."

> **EXAMPLES**   This mug is bigger **than** that one is.  [*Than* is used in a comparison.]
> Jan found her seat and **then** read the program.  [*Then* means "next."]

**EXERCISE A**   Underline the word or word group in parentheses that is correct according to formal, standard English.

**Examples 1.** No one is (*suppose, supposed*) to leave before three o'clock.  [The past-tense form of

*suppose* is *supposed.*]

**2.** We have to sand the wood first, and (*than, then*) we will put a coat of primer on it.

[*Then* tells *when* the coat of primer should be put on.]

**1.** Matthew would (*have, of*) been in the play, but he became ill the day before the show.  [Which

word should be used after *would*?]

**2.** My parents and I (*used, use*) to go to the park every weekend and feed the ducks.  [How is the

past-tense form of *use* formed?]

**3.** Weren't you (*suppose, supposed*) to call me last night?

**4.** The judge examined the dogs, and (*than, then*) the trainer walked them around the ring.

**5.** We should (*of, have*) brought our camera.

**6.** If I finish earlier (*than, then*) you do, I'll wait for you outside.

**7.** If you (*had, had of*) secured the lid to the cage, the hamster would not have escaped.

**8.** (*Than, Then*) what do you want to do?

**9.** All of the volunteers were (*supposed, suppose*) to receive free T-shirts.

**10.** Do you like this shade of blue better (*than, then*) that one?

**GO ON**

***try and, try to***   Use *try to*, not *try and*.

> **INFORMAL**   Try and shut the door more quietly next time.
>
> **FORMAL**   **Try to** shut the door more quietly next time.

***this here, that there***   Do not use *here* or *there* after *this* or *that*.

> **NONSTANDARD**   This here door is locked.
>
> **STANDARD**   **This** door is locked.

***who, which, that***   *Who* is used to refer to people. *Which* is used to refer to things. *That* can be used to refer to either people or things.

> **EXAMPLES**   He is the man **who** [or **that**] lost his keys.  [*Who* or *that* can be used to refer to people.]
>
> The table, **which** is made of solid wood, was expensive.  [*Which* is used to refer to things.]
>
> Is that the bicycle **that** your aunt bought you?  [*That* can be used to refer to things.]

**EXERCISE B**  Underline the word or word group in parentheses that is correct according to formal, standard English.

**Examples  1.** Do you know who owns (*that, that there*) car?  [*That there* is nonstandard.]

**2.** Do you know anyone (*who, which*) can fix a bicycle chain?  [*Who* is used to refer to people.]

**11.** My uncle, (*who, which*) lives in Hawaii, is a pilot.  [Does the pronoun refer to a person or to a thing?]

**12.** When you go to the store, (*try to, try and*) find this new brand of shampoo.  [Should *and* or *to* be used after *try*?]

**13.** (*This here, This*) computer monitor is broken.

**14.** This book, (*who, which*) was recommended to me, is really good.

**15.** Isn't (*that, that there*) fish a neon tetra?

**16.** You can (*try to, try and*) walk the cat on a leash, but I don't think you'll get very far.

**17.** Does anyone understand the instructions (*who, that*) she gave us?

**18.** Are you finished with (*this, this here*) section of the newspaper?

**19.** Mr. Chan is a teacher (*that, which*) is always ready to help students.

**20.** Maria should (*try to, try and*) be more patient with her younger sister.

# Glossary of Usage D
## Double Negatives

Using two or more negative words for one negative idea creates a ***double negative.*** Some common negative words include *barely, but* (meaning "only"), *hardly, neither, never, no, nobody, none, no one, not (–n't), nothing, nowhere, only,* and *scarcely.* Avoid using double negatives.

| | |
|---|---|
| **NONSTANDARD** | I couldn't barely reach the top shelf.  [The contraction *–n't* and the word *barely* are both negative. When they are used together to express one negative idea, they form a double negative.] |
| **STANDARD** | I could **barely** reach the top shelf.  [Deleting the negative contraction *–n't* eliminates the double negative.] |
| **STANDARD** | I could**n't** reach the top shelf.  [Deleting the negative word *barely* eliminates the double negative.] |
| **NONSTANDARD** | She doesn't need no help.  [The contraction *–n't* and the word *no* are both negative. When they are used together to express one negative idea, they form a double negative.] |
| **STANDARD** | She needs **no** help.  [Deleting the negative contraction *–n't* eliminates the double negative.] |
| **STANDARD** | She **doesn't** need **any** help.  [Substituting *any* for the negative word *no* eliminates the double negative.] |

**EXERCISE A**  Each of the following sentences contains a double negative. Use proofreading marks to delete or change words to correct the double negative. Hint: There may be more than one way to correct each double negative.

**Examples 1.** My cousins ~~haven't~~ *have* never learned to swim.  [*Haven't never* is a double negative. Changing *haven't* to *have* is one way to correct the double negative.]

**2.** We couldn't ~~hardly~~ stay away!  [*Couldn't hardly* is a double negative. Deleting *hardly* is one way to correct the double negative.]

**1.** Don't you have no manners?  [Which two words or word parts are negative?  Which word could you change to correct the double negative?]

**2.** My little sister can't hardly talk yet.  [Which two words or word parts are negative?  Which word could you change to correct the double negative?]

**3.** Did hardly no residents vote for the new property tax?

**4.** Couldn't Sarah find no shoes she liked?

**5.** Don't never leave the car's engine running while you're at the gas pump!

**6.** Without a good light, I can't barely read comfortably.

**7.** There isn't scarcely time to finish the test.

**8.** I don't want nothing for dessert.

**9.** We haven't bought scarcely enough flour for the recipe.

**10.** Permanent marker shouldn't never be used on the white board.

---

## Nonsexist Language

*Nonsexist language* applies to people in general, whether they are male or female. Often these words refer to occupations or professions. Usually you can replace words that refer to only one gender with words that apply to all people. You should use nonsexist language rather than gender-specific language when you are referring to people in general.

| GENDER-SPECIFIC | NONSEXIST |
| --- | --- |
| stewardess, steward | flight attendant |
| fireman | firefighter |
| policeman | police officer |
| man-made | synthetic, manufactured |
| mailman | mail carrier |

**GENDER-SPECIFIC**  For additional assistance, please contact one of our salesmen.  [*Salesmen* is a gender-specific term.]

**NONSEXIST**  For additional assistance, please contact one of our **salesclerks.**  [*Salesclerks* is a nonsexist term.]

**NOTE▶** If a pronoun's antecedent may be either masculine or feminine, use both the masculine and the feminine pronouns to refer to that antecedent.

**EXAMPLE**  **No one** worked on **his or her** project last weekend.  [*No one* may be either masculine or feminine, so both *his* and *her* are used to refer to *No one*.]

---

**EXERCISE B** Use proofreading symbols to revise each of the following sentences to eliminate gender-specific terms.

**Example  1.** When will ~~mankind~~ learn to work out differences peacefully?  [*Mankind* is gender-specific. The word *humanity* or *people* can be used instead.]

**11.** My cousins Jack and Ann are training to become airline stewards.  [Which nonsexist term can be used in place of the gender-specific word *stewards*?]

**12.** Ask the deliveryman to leave the package outside.

**13.** Mrs. Sims was elected president of that businessmen's organization.

**14.** Is the material in this rug man-made or natural?

**15.** Aunt Deborah found a part-time job as a watchman at the factory.

# Capitalization A

## First Words

**12a.** Capitalize the first word of every sentence.

> **EXAMPLE** **B**luebirds flew in circles around the tree. [*Bluebirds* is the first word of the sentence.]

Begin a quoted sentence with a capital letter, even when the quoted sentence begins in the middle of a longer sentence.

> **EXAMPLES** "**A**re we going to the movies tonight?" asked Josh. [*Are* is capitalized because it is the first word of a quoted sentence. *Are* is also the first word of the longer sentence.]
>
> Gina said, "**W**e should leave now, or we will be late for school." [*We* is capitalized because it is the first word of a quoted sentence.]

**EXERCISE A** Circle the letter that should be capitalized in each of the following sentences.

**Examples** **1.** (n)ew employees are being asked to report to the cafeteria at one o'clock. [The *n* in *new* should be capitalized because it is the first word of the sentence.]

    **2.** Tom asked, "(a)re you auditioning for *Our Town*?" [The *a* in *are* should be capitalized because it is the first word of the quoted sentence.]

**1.** Jessica said, "let's go out for lunch today." [Is the first word of the quoted sentence capitalized?]

**2.** our teacher was promoted to vice principal. [Is the first word of the sentence capitalized?]

**3.** this computer runs slowly when the network is busy.

**4.** Alicia whispered, "when are the reports due?"

**5.** the cat stretched out its paw and swatted at the ball.

**6.** "where are we supposed to set these cases of juice?" asked Devon.

**7.** the spider has woven its web across the opening in the fence.

**8.** Grandma muttered, "well, I guess the bulb needs to be changed."

**9.** a mouse has been scratching around behind the walls of the storage shed.

**10.** Hey! there's a quarter lying next to the curb.

**GO ON**

## The Pronoun *I*

In English the pronoun *I* is always capitalized, even if it is not the first word of a sentence.

**EXAMPLES**   Do you think **I** will like this lasagna?  [*I* is always capitalized.]

She knows that **I**'m joining the drama club next year.  [*I* is capitalized even when it is used as part of a contraction.]

**EXERCISE B** Circle the letter that should be capitalized in each of the following sentences.

**Example  1.**  "If I were you," he said, "I'd ask Dad for advice."  [*I* should always be capitalized.]

**11.** If you set the table, i'll wash the dishes tonight.  [Should *I* be capitalized when used in contractions?]

**12.** For the past two summers, i've volunteered at the animal shelter.

**13.** Jason and i rode our bicycles around Town Lake this weekend.

**14.** "This fall," Marta told us, "i'm going to visit my sister in Nevada."

**15.** I've decided that i should take the shuttle to the fairgrounds.

## Salutations and Closings

**12c.**   Capitalize the first word in both the salutation and the closing of a letter.

A *salutation* is a short line of greeting that begins a letter. A *closing* is a short line at the end of a letter, right before a signature.

**SALUTATIONS**   **D**ear Mr. Tamayo:      **M**y dearest grandson,

**CLOSINGS**   **V**ery truly yours,      **S**incerely,

**NOTE▶** Except for names and titles, the first word is the only word that is capitalized in a salutation or closing. In the examples, *Mr.* is capitalized because it is a title. *Tamayo* is capitalized because it is a name.

**EXERCISE C** Circle each letter that should be capitalized in each closing or salutation.

**Example  1.**  Regards,  [*Regards* is the first word in a closing.]

**16.** yours truly,  [Should the first word of a closing be capitalized?]

**17.** dear Aunt Teresa,

**18.** my darling Rebecca,

**19.** dear Professor Hanami:

**20.** sincerely yours,

# Capitalization B

## Proper Nouns and Proper Adjectives

**12d.** Capitalize proper nouns and proper adjectives.

A *proper noun* is the name of a particular person, place, thing, or idea. Proper nouns are capitalized. A **common noun** is the name of a type of person, place, thing, or idea. A common noun generally is not capitalized unless it begins a sentence or is part of a title.

|  |  |  |  |
|---|---|---|---|
| **PROPER NOUNS** | Eric Clapton | Reyes Park | Buddhism |
| **COMMON NOUNS** | guitarist | park | religion |

A *proper adjective* is an adjective formed from a proper noun. Proper adjectives are capitalized. Some proper adjectives are formed by adding an ending, such as *–ish, –ic, –ese, –ian,* or *–an,* to a proper noun.

> **EXAMPLES**  Gulf moisture [same form as the proper noun]
>
>               Italian lace [formed from the proper noun *Italy*]
>
>               Icelandic heritage [formed from the proper noun *Iceland*]

**EXERCISE A**  Circle each letter that should be capitalized in each of the following sentences.

**Examples 1.** Leticia named her new kitten fiona. [*Fiona* is the name of a particular kitten.]

      **2.** How far is the atlantic shoreline from that campground? [*Atlantic* is a proper adjective describing *shoreline*.]

**1.** Will the company cookout be held at brentwood park? [What words are the name of a particular place?]

**2.** My friend mario is playing center in tonight's basketball game. [What word is the name of a particular person?]

**3.** Ms. samuels is making a speech to the committee.

**4.** I am visiting boston this summer.

**5.** Today's lecture is on the origin of arabic numerals.

**6.** One of the highest mountains in the world is nanga parbat.

**7.** Mr. Jesse and his dog once hiked across much of south carolina.

**8.** Doesn't a portuguese man-of-war have stinging cells in its tentacles?

**9.** That simple cabin was kentuckian Winslow Carter's birthplace.

**10.** The island of cuba gained its independence from Spain in 1898.

**GO ON**

**TIP▶** To tell whether a noun is common or proper, try placing the article *a, an,* or *the* in front of the noun. If *a, an,* or *the* makes sense, the noun is probably a common noun. If *a, an,* or *the* does not make sense, the noun is probably a proper noun.

| | |
|---|---|
| **NOUN** | Houston |
| **NOUN + ARTICLE** | **a** Houston, **the** Houston  [When placed in front of the noun *Houston*, the articles *a* and *the* do not make sense. *Houston* is a proper noun.] |
| **NOUN** | city |
| **NOUN + ARTICLE** | **a** city, **the** city  [When placed in front of the noun *city*, the articles *a* and *the* make sense. *City* is a common noun.] |

**EXERCISE B** Write a proper noun for each of the common nouns given below. Be sure to capitalize the proper nouns that you write. Hint: You may make up any names you need.

**Example 1.** hamster    *Frankie*

**11.** state    __________

**12.** lake    __________

**13.** school    __________

**14.** team    __________

**15.** month    __________

## Persons and Animals

Capitalize the names of people and animals, including initials and abbreviations that either precede or follow names.

| | | | |
|---|---|---|---|
| **PERSONS** | Claude Monet | E. W. Roosevelt | Simon Osborne, Jr. |
| **ANIMALS** | Lassie | Checkers | Mr. Ed |

**EXERCISE C** Underline the correctly capitalized word group in each pair below.

**Example 1.** Jarrel d. keating    <u>Jarrel D. Keating</u>

       [*Jarrel D. Keating* is the name of a specific person.]

**16.** her puppy Jack       her puppy jack

    [Should the name of a specific puppy be capitalized?]

**17.** Juanita F. Garcia       Juanita f. garcia

**18.** Francis Riggs, jr.       Francis Riggs, Jr.

**19.** marcella l. ward       Marcella L. Ward

**20.** my horse Barney       my horse barney

for **CHAPTER 12: CAPITALIZATION**   pages 345–349

# Capitalization C

## Geographical Names

**12d.** Capitalize proper nouns and proper adjectives.

Geographical names are proper nouns and should be capitalized. Geographical names include places such as countries, states, street names, and natural landmarks.

    **EXAMPLES**  **J**apan [country]      **K**ansas [state]

                  **R**ichmond **A**venue [street]    **L**uray **C**averns [natural landmark]

When words such as *north, south, eastern,* or *southwest* are used as the name of a region, they are capitalized. When you use these words to show a direction, don't capitalize them.

    **EXAMPLES**  The library is being built **north** of the high school. [*North* is used to tell direction, so it is not capitalized.]

                  Shelly has lived in the **North** for most of her life. [*North* is used as the name of a region, so it is capitalized.]

**NOTE▶** Words such as *lake, park,* and *street* are capitalized only when used as part of a name.

    **EXAMPLES**  He went to the **park** today.

                  We met at **Woodlawn Park.**

**EXERCISE A**  Circle each letter that should be capitalized in each of the following sentences.

**Examples 1.** Lucy has lived in **B**aytown for six years. [*Baytown* is the name of a specific town.]

      **2.** We sailed on **L**ake **A**ustin. [*Lake Austin* is the name of a specific lake.]

**1.** Adam voted that we visit the grand canyon this year. [What words are the name of a specific landmark?]

**2.** We made a map of argentina for geography class. [What word is the name of a specific country?]

**3.** My friend Enrique lives in maine.

**4.** The new high school is on raines road.

**5.** The continent of europe is one of the smallest continents in the world.

**6.** Julia rode her bike around rosedale park.

**7.** A series of earthquakes began near mount st. helens in 1980.

**8.** Captain James Cook's ship ran aground on the great barrier reef in 1770.

**9.** We are moving to kentucky next year.

**10.** Kingsville, Texas, is in kleberg county.

**GO ON ➡**

# Organizations, Teams, Institutions, and Government Bodies

The names of organizations, teams, institutions, and government bodies are proper nouns and should be capitalized.

**EXAMPLES**   Mothers Against Drunk Driving  [organization]

Bell High School Chargers  [team]

Trenton Heights Memorial Hospital  [institution]

Congress  [government body]

**NOTE▶** Abbreviations of the names of organizations, institutions, and government bodies are often a set of capital letters.

**EXAMPLES**   PAL        Police Activities League

NATO        North Atlantic Treaty Organization

**EXERCISE B** Circle each letter that should be capitalized in each of the following sentences.

**Examples 1.** The humane society of the united states provides tips on how to keep squirrels out of bird feeders.  [*Humane Society of the United States* is the name of an organization.]

**2.** Is she really applying for a job with the fbi?  [*FBI* is the abbreviation of a name of an organization, *the Federal Bureau of Investigation*.]

**11.** My cousin is joining the united states air force when she graduates.  [What words are the name of an organization?]

**12.** Our state elected members of the house of representatives.  [What words are the name of a government body?]

**13.** The reporter wrote, "The Carrolton cougars cruised to an easy victory," but the game was tough!

**14.** Dr. Frye is a member of the american medical association.

**15.** This facility complies with the directives of osha and other regulatory agencies.

**16.** The interstate commerce commission regulated railroads.

**17.** Be sure to get on one of the buses that has "molltown isd" printed on its side.

**18.** The muscular dystrophy association educates the public about muscular dystrophy.

**19.** Did you apply to the university of pennsylvania?

**20.** Aren't we playing the hornets tomorrow?

# Capitalization D

## Historical Events and Periods, Dates, Holidays

**12d.** Capitalize proper nouns and proper adjectives.

Be sure to capitalize the names of important events and periods in history. The names of other kinds of special events are also capitalized.

| | |
|---|---|
| **EXAMPLES** | **G**reat **D**epression  [historical period] |
| | **W**orld **W**ar II  [historical event] |
| | **W**imbledon **C**hampionships  [sporting event] |

Always capitalize days of the week, months, and holidays. The names of the seasons of the year are not usually capitalized.

| | |
|---|---|
| **WEEKDAY** | **M**onday |
| **HOLIDAY** | **F**ourth of **J**uly |
| **SEASON** | spring |

**EXERCISE A** Circle each letter that should be capitalized in each of the following sentences.

**Examples 1.** Is your grandfather coming for a visit on thanksgiving?  [*Thanksgiving* is the name of a holiday.]

**2.** Arturo's saving up to go to the olympic games someday.  [*Olympic Games* is the name of a sporting event.]

**1.** The algebra test is on monday.  [What word is the name of a day of the week?]

**2.** I am watching the british open, my favorite golf tournament, this Sunday.  [What words name a specific sporting event?]

**3.** Why did the ming dynasty last for more than 250 years?

**4.** Marilyn, Maya, and I are cleaning up the park on arbor day this year.

**5.** Traditionally, seniors hold their formal banquet in early april.

**6.** This saturday is the day of the Expo.

**7.** This summer, Paul's birthday falls on a thursday.

**8.** We studied the battle of waterloo in history class today.

**9.** Why do the British celebrate guy fawkes day?

**10.** Our little brother Owen turns seven in january.

**GO ON**

## Nationalities, Races, and Peoples

Words that name nationalities, races, or peoples begin with a capital letter.

    **NATIONALITY**   Canadian
          **RACE**   Caucasian
      **PEOPLE**   Choctaw

**EXERCISE B** Circle each letter that should be capitalized in each of the following sentences.

**Example 1.** Maureen's ancestry is Irish. [*Irish* is capitalized because it is the name of a nationality.]

**11.** The greek chef cooked a delicious meal. [What word names a nationality?]

**12.** I am taking a course in asian studies next year.

**13.** The painting in the waiting area is by a little-known japanese artist.

**14.** The curator's lecture concerned the history of the iroquois peoples.

**15.** Mara and David are studying indian culture in sociology class.

## Religions, Holy Days, Holy Writings, and Specific Deities

Capitalize the names of religions and their followers, holy days and celebrations, holy writings, and specific deities.

    **EXAMPLES**   Judaism [religion]
               Catholic [follower of a religion]
               Ramadan [religious event]
               Juno [specific deity]

**EXERCISE C** Circle each letter that should be capitalized in each of the following sentences.

**Example 1.** Emma is celebrating passover. [*Passover* is the name of a religious event.]

**16.** The commemoration of the birth of Jesus is called christmas. [What word is the name of a holy

     day?]

**17.** We read selections from the torah, the five books of Moses, in world religions class.

**18.** Muslims study the koran, a book said to contain Allah's revelations to Mohammed.

**19.** One god in the Hindu religion is vishnu.

**20.** A goddess of the ancient Greeks, athena was thought to be wise.

# Capitalization E

## Businesses and the Brand Names of Business Products

**12d.**  Capitalize proper nouns and proper adjectives.

The names of businesses and brand names are capitalized. Do not capitalize the name of a type of product.

> **EXAMPLES**  **K**ellogg **C**ompany  [business name]
> **P**ost **B**ran **F**lakes  [brand name]
> cereal  [type of product]

**EXERCISE A** Circle each letter that should be capitalized in the following sentences. Draw a slash through each letter that is capitalized but should be lowercase.

**Example 1.** If I owned a store that sold Software, I'd name it Software Giant.  [*Software* should not be capitalized because it is the name of a type of product.  *Software Giant* should be capitalized because it is the name of a business.]

1. The new Computers in the library were made by dell.  [What word is the name of a type of product?  What word is the name of a business?]

2. She drives a ford Pickup Truck.

3. We took a Flight on northwest airlines when we visited Grandma.

4. Would you like some Oatmeal—quaker oats—for breakfast?

5. The brand of Juice in the ice chest is ocean spray.

## Ships, Trains, Aircraft, Spacecraft, and Other Vehicles

The names of ships, trains, aircraft, spacecraft, and other vehicles should be capitalized.

> **SHIP**  *Atlantic Dragon*
> **TRAIN**  *Mountain Skipper*
> **AIRCRAFT**  the *Doyle*
> **SPACECRAFT**  *Discovery*

**EXERCISE B** Circle each letter that should be capitalized in each of the following sentences.

**Examples 1.** We saw a replica of the Spirit of St. Louis at the exhibition.  [*Spirit of St. Louis* should be capitalized because it is the name of a specific aircraft.]

2. Wasn't the command capsule named Odyssey?  [*Odyssey* should be capitalized because it is the name of a specific spacecraft.]

**GO ON**

**6.** She named her hot-air balloon *roswell*. [What word is the name of a specific aircraft?]

**7.** We rode on a train called the *lowland flyer*. [What words are the name of a specific train?]

**8.** The hubble space telescope's optics were repaired in 1993.

**9.** One of Christopher Columbus's ships was named the *pinta*.

**10.** According to the story, the time machine *counterclock* visited ancient Rome.

**11.** On their quest for the Golden Fleece, the argonauts sailed aboard the *argo*.

**12.** Has *galileo*'s mission been completed?

**13.** The USS *forrestal* sailed out of this port.

**14.** Footage of the launch of the space shuttle *columbia* was shown in a documentary last night.

**15.** It's fun to sit on the balcony listening to the sound of the train *newcastle express* as it roars past

our apartments.

---

## Buildings and Other Structures

The names of buildings and other structures are capitalized. Do not capitalize the name of a
type of building unless the word is part of the building's name.

    **EXAMPLES**  **R**ialto **B**ridge [*Bridge* is part of the structure's name.]

               **S**ears **T**ower [*Tower* is part of the building's name.]

---

**EXERCISE C**  Circle each letter that should be capitalized in each of the following sentences.

**Example 1.** Andreas brought pictures of the (g)reat (w)all of China to class. [*Great Wall* should be

capitalized because it is the name of a structure.]

**16.** My aunt visited Chaucer's grave, which is inside westminster abbey, when she was in

London. [What words are the name of a building?]

**17.** The senior prom was held at the driskill hotel.

**18.** Meet us at the paramount theater at 7:00 P.M.

**19.** The riverside animal park opened today.

**20.** The turner wildflower center was full of flowers in bloom.

*for* **CHAPTER 12: CAPITALIZATION**   *pages 352–353*

# Capitalization F

## Monuments, Memorials, and Awards

**12d.**  Capitalize proper nouns and proper adjectives.

The names of monuments and memorials, which are often buildings or structures, are capitalized. The names of special awards and prizes also should begin with a capital letter.

> **EXAMPLES**  Cape Krusenstern National Monument
>
> Lincoln Memorial
>
> Purple Heart

**NOTE** Some proper nouns have more than one word. In these names, short prepositions (those of fewer than five letters) and articles (*a, an, the*) are generally not capitalized. Some common short prepositions are *at, in, from, of, on, to,* and *with.*

> **EXAMPLE**  Medal of Freedom [The short preposition *of* in the proper noun *Medal of Freedom* is not capitalized.]

**EXERCISE A** Circle each letter that should be capitalized in each of the following sentences.

**Example  1.**  Each year, the Academy of Motion Picture Arts and Sciences awards an Oscar for best actress.  [*Oscar* is the name of an award.]

**1.** Who won the pritzker prize this year?  [What words are the name of an award?]

**2.** On our trip to Washington, D.C., we saw the washington monument.

**3.** The civil rights memorial was dedicated in Montgomery, Alabama.

**4.** In Japan, the sengen shrine has been used in the worship of Mount Fuji.

**5.** Someday, Brook hopes to win an avery fisher prize.

## Planets, Stars, Constellations, and Other Heavenly Bodies

Be sure to capitalize the names of planets, stars, constellations, and other heavenly bodies. Generally, the words *sun* and *moon* are not capitalized. The word *earth* is not capitalized unless it is used along with the name of another heavenly body that is capitalized.

> **PLANET**  Jupiter
>
> **STAR**  Antares
>
> **CONSTELLATION**  Ursa Major

**EXERCISE B** Circle each letter that should be capitalized in each of the following sentences.

**Example  1.**  Did you see andromeda last night?  [*Andromeda* is the name of a constellation.]

**6.** Is neptune the planet farthest from the sun?  [What word is the name of a planet?]

**GO ON**

*Developmental Language Skills*

**7.** Studies of biela's comet helped support the idea that some meteors are pieces of comets.

**8.** The star proxima centauri is part of a triple star system.

**9.** The moon is too bright tonight for us to see the pleiades.

**10.** Like the moon, the planet mercury exhibits phases.

## School Subjects

Capitalize the names of language classes or course names that include a number. Otherwise, the names of school subjects are not capitalized.

> **EXAMPLES**   **m**ath  [school subject]
>
> **G**erman  [name of a language class]
>
> **C**reative **W**riting II  [course name that includes a number]

**NOTE▶** Do not capitalize the word *freshman, sophomore, junior,* or *senior* unless it is part of a name.

> **EXAMPLES**   Is Deven a **j**unior or a **s**enior this year?  [*Junior* and *senior* are not capitalized.]
>
> Tomorrow is **F**reshman **S**pirit **D**ay.  [*Freshman* is capitalized because it is part of a name.]

**EXERCISE C**   Circle each letter that should be capitalized in each of the following sentences. Draw a slash through each letter that is capitalized but should be lowercase.

**Example 1.** I am planning to take Math and Latin classes next year.  [*Math* should not be

capitalized because it is the name of a class but does not have a number. *Latin* should be

capitalized because it is the name of a language.]

**11.** Do you enjoy your geometry II class?  [What word is the name of a class followed by a course

number?]

**12.** I finished my Chemistry homework last night.

**13.** Mr. Durand is a good french teacher.

**14.** I wrote an essay for my Language Arts class.

**15.** Mrs. Garcia is teaching physical education II next year.

# Capitalization G

## Titles of Persons

**12f.** Capitalize titles.

Always capitalize the title of a person when the title comes before the person's name. Even if the title is abbreviated, capitalize it.

> **EXAMPLES**  These orders should go directly to **C**aptain Knight.  [The title *Captain* comes before a person's name.]
>
> Did you make an appointment with **D**r. Ramirez?  [*Dr.,* an abbreviation for the title *Doctor,* comes before a person's name.]
>
> The **p**rofessor claimed that birds were actually dinosaurs.  [The word *professor* is not capitalized because it does not come before a person's name.]

**EXERCISE A**  Circle each letter that should be capitalized in each of the following sentences. Draw a slash through each letter that is capitalized but should be lowercase.

**Example  1.**  We followed the instructions of ⓜr. Blake, our piano I̸nstructor.  [*Mr.* should be capitalized because it is a person's title and comes before a person's name.]

**1.** The Mayor spoke to the town council.  [What word is a title? Does it come before a person's name?]

**2.** My mother wrote a letter to sen. Maria Ochoa.

**3.** That sprained ankle may need a Doctor's care.

**4.** The army troop was under the command of sergeant Jefferson.

**5.** Shelley was elected President of the student council.

A word that shows a family relationship is capitalized when the word comes before the person's name or is used in place of the person's name.

> **EXAMPLES**  Ask **D**ad if he would like a sandwich, too.  [*Dad* is used in place of someone's name.]
>
> Do you think **U**ncle Robert will play the fiddle at the family reunion?  [*Uncle* comes before a person's name.]

Do not capitalize a word showing a family relationship when a possessive comes before the word. Possessives are words such as *my, your, his, her, its, our,* and *their.*

> **EXAMPLES**  My **a**unt Veronica is a very good chef.  [*My* comes before a word showing a family relationship; therefore, *aunt* is not capitalized.]
>
> What time is your **g**randma arriving from Spain?  [*Your* comes before a word showing a family relationship; therefore, *grandma* is not capitalized.]

**GO ON** ➡

**EXERCISE B**   Circle each letter that should be capitalized in each of the following sentences. Draw a slash through each letter that is capitalized but should be lowercase.

**Example 1.** I think that Cousin Fred is coming to the birthday party for my Father. [*Cousin* should be capitalized because it comes before a person's name. *Father* should not be capitalized because it follows the possessive word *my*.]

**6.** Remember that grandma needs a ride to the airport at 3:00 P.M. [What word is used in place of someone's name?]

**7.** Is your Mother coming to the talent show tonight?

**8.** I didn't know that your Uncle Mike was in the Peace Corps.

**9.** This afternoon, dad, I have a guitar lesson.

**10.** My Aunt Kelly was a country-western singer.

## Titles of Creative Works

Whenever you write the title of a book, a poem, or any other creative work, be sure to capitalize the first word, the last word, and all other important words. Capitalize these words in subtitles, too. Do not capitalize an article (*a, an,* or *the*) or a short preposition (such as *of, in,* or *with*) unless the article or preposition is the first or last word in the title or subtitle.

|  |  |
|---|---|
| **BOOK** | *Frankenstein: or, the Modern Prometheus* |
| **CHAPTER** | "The Great Depression" |
| **POEM** | "Ode on a Grecian Urn" |
| **PAINTING** | *Sidewalk and Grate* |

**EXERCISE C**   Circle each letter that should be capitalized in each of the following sentences.

**Example 1.** Have you finished reading *hamlet, prince of denmark*? [*Hamlet, Prince of Denmark* is the name of a play.]

**11.** The *times* was founded in 1851. [What word is the name of a newspaper?]

**12.** My doctor keeps a copy of the book *middlemarch* on her desk.

**13.** Miguel told us that he found the painting *subway angels: a study in blue* very beautiful.

**14.** For Christmas, Ms. Kostas is writing a play called *a yuletide visitor.*

**15.** Have you finished reading the short story "the last bus"?

# End Marks

An *end mark* is a period, question mark, or exclamation point used to indicate the purpose of a sentence.

## Sentences

**13a.** A statement (or declarative sentence) is followed by a period.

> **EXAMPLE**    Buster is the dog with the brown spots. [The sentence is a statement, so it is followed by a period.]

**13b.** A question (or interrogative sentence) is followed by a question mark.

> **EXAMPLE**    What time is your guitar lesson? [The sentence is a question, so it is followed by a question mark.]

Sometimes a sentence may sound like a question but be a statement. Use a period when a sentence is a statement.

> **EXAMPLES**    Did you get the correct answer to question five? [The sentence is a question, so it is followed by a question mark.]
>
> Jacob asked if we got the correct answer to question five. [The sentence is a statement, not a question, so it is followed by a period.]

**EXERCISE A** Use proofreading symbols to add either a period or a question mark as needed to each of the following sentences.

**Examples 1.** Austin is the capital of Texas⊙ [The sentence is a statement, so it should be followed by a period.]

     **2.** Did you water the plants this morning? [The sentence is a question, so it should be followed by a question mark.]

**1.** Maya said that it was nice being at home again  [Is the sentence a question or a statement?]

**2.** Are you finished with your essay for history class  [Is the sentence a question or a statement?]

**3.** Do you think your father will give us a ride to the movies

**4.** We gathered research at the library on Saturday for our essays

**5.** The newspaper was delivered early this morning

**6.** What do you think of my handmade quilt

**7.** Is it time for the baby's bath

**8.** I would like more asparagus, please

**GO ON** ➡

**9.** Is Michael's specialty spaghetti with marinara sauce

**10.** Allison asked Teresa if Teresa could tutor her after school

---

**13c.** An exclamation (or exclamatory sentence) is followed by an exclamation point.

> **EXAMPLE**   Look out for that step! [The sentence is an exclamation, so it is followed by an exclamation point.]

An interjection is followed by an exclamation point or comma. If the interjection expresses mild surprise or excitement, it is followed by a comma. If the interjection expresses strong surprise or excitement, it is followed by an exclamation point.

> **EXAMPLES**   Oh, I'm glad you are feeling better. [The interjection *Oh* expresses mild excitement, so it is followed by a comma.]
>
> Wow! That model airplane can fly high! [The interjection *Wow* expresses strong surprise, so it is followed by an exclamation point.]

**13d.** A request or a command (an imperative sentence) is followed by either a period or an exclamation point.

If the request or command is mild, it is followed by a period. If the request or command is strong, it is followed by an exclamation point.

> **EXAMPLES**   Please clean your room. [The request is a mild command, so it is followed by a period.]
>
> Don't touch that hot oven! [The command is strong, so it is followed by an exclamation point.]

**EXERCISE B**   Use proofreading symbols to add a period, comma, or exclamation point where it is needed in each of the following sentences.

**Example  1.**  Ah, that is what he meant. [*Ah* is a mild interjection, so it should be followed by a comma.]

**11.** No Don't bring that spider near me!  [What word is an interjection expressing strong surprise?]

**12.** Don't climb any higher

**13.** My what a beautiful garden that is.

**14.** That television is far too loud

**15.** Hey Turn that music down!

# Abbreviations A

**13e.**   Many abbreviations are followed by a period.

## Personal Names

Abbreviate names if a person is commonly known by the abbreviated form of the name. Place a period after each initial, leaving a space between two initials, but not between three or more.

> **EXAMPLES**   Thomas **A.** Edison     Ida **B.** Wells-Barnett
>
>                **T. S.** Eliot         **M.F.K.** Fisher

**EXERCISE A** Use proofreading symbols to add periods where they are needed in each of the following sentences.

**Example 1.** My uncle, Reilly J⊙Ward, established the first hotel in Riverside.   [*J* is an initial that stands for someone's name, so it should be followed by a period.]

**1.** Did you read that book by F Scott Fitzgerald?   [What letter stands for someone's name?]

**2.** My father is known as E E J Serafini.

**3.** One of the U.S. presidents on the list is Ulysses S Grant.

**4.** When Roberta becomes an author, her pen name will be R N McIntyre.

**5.** Of all the authors we have studied, I like E M Forster the best.

## Titles

Abbreviate social titles (*Mr., Mrs., Ms., Sr., Sra., Dr.*) whether they are used before the full name or before the last name alone. Abbreviate civil and military titles used before full names or before initials and last names. Spell out civil and military titles when they are used before last names alone.

> **EXAMPLES**   **Dr.** Michelle L. Rodriquez   [Social titles are abbreviated.]
>
>                **Sen.** Mary Janowitz   [Civil titles are abbreviated before full names.]
>
>                **Prof.** J. Garcia   [Civil titles are abbreviated before initials and last names.]
>
>                **Senator** Thomas   [Civil titles are spelled out before last names alone.]

Abbreviate titles and academic degrees that come after names.

> **EXAMPLES**   John Andrews, **Jr.**      Janet Meyerson, **M.D.**

**NOTE▶** Do not use the abbreviations *Mr., Mrs., Ms.,* or *Dr.* with a title or degree that appears after a name.

> **INCORRECT**   Dr. Robert Agarwal, M.D.
>
> **CORRECT**   **Dr.** Robert Agarwal      Robert Agarwal, **M.D.**

**GO ON ▶**

**EXERCISE B** Circle the letter of the item that is correctly abbreviated in each of the following pairs.

**Example** 1. **a.** Mrs. Mary Park    **b.** Missus Mary Park

[Social titles should be abbreviated.]

**6. a.** General Markowitz    **b.** Gen. Markowitz

[Should military titles be abbreviated before last names alone?]

**7. a.** Owen Ward, Jr    **b.** Owen Ward, Jr.

**8. a.** Dr. Ann Bernini, M.D.    **b.** Ann Bernini, M.D.

**9. a.** Professor McDonald    **b.** Prof. McDonald

**10. a.** Senator Jerry Jacobsen    **b.** Sen. Jerry Jacobsen

## Agencies, Organizations, and Acronyms

Many agencies and organizations are known by their acronyms. An *acronym* is formed from the first (or first few) letters of a series of words. When writing, spell out the first use of the name of the agency or organization. After that, you may use the acronym. Do not use periods in acronyms.

**EXAMPLES** **PBS** **P**ublic **B**roadcasting **S**ervice

**HSUS** **H**umane **S**ociety of the **U**nited **S**tates

**EXERCISE C** Circle the letter before the item that is correct in each of the following pairs.

**Example** 1. **a.** The EPA is investigating the spill. Environmental Protection Agency personnel soon will begin arriving at the contaminated site.

**b.** The Environmental Protection Agency is investigating the spill. EPA personnel soon will begin arriving at the contaminated site. [The first use of the name of an agency or organization should be spelled out rather than abbreviated.]

**11. a.** HUD    **b.** H.U.D. [Should an acronym contain periods?]

**12. a.** The Department of Public Safety is expanding. DPS officials are calling for applicants.

**b.** The DPS is expanding. Department of Public Safety officials are calling for applicants.

**13. a.** MDA    **b.** M.D.A.

**14. a.** Volunteers for MADD handed out Mothers Against Drunk Driving brochures today.

**b.** Volunteers for Mothers Against Drunk Driving handed out MADD brochures today.

**15. a.** O.S.H.A.    **b.** OSHA

# Abbreviations B

**13e.**   Many abbreviations are followed by a period.

## Geographical Terms

Spell out names of states and political units in regular text. Abbreviate names of states and political units in tables, notes, and bibliographies.

**TEXT**   Have you ever been to Portland, **Oregon,** or Memphis, **Tennessee**?

**TABLE OR NOTE**   Portland, **Ore.**      Memphis, **Tenn.**

Spell out the words of an address in regular text. Words in a letter address or in tables and notes may be abbreviated. Use two-letter state abbreviations only when the ZIP Code is included.

**TEXT**   My sister moved to 4523 Woodlawn Avenue, Seattle, Washington.

**ENVELOPE**   4523 Woodlawn Ave.

Seattle, **WA** 78564

**TABLE**   Westlake **Dr.**        |   Albuquerque, **N. Mex.**   |

**EXERCISE A** Circle the letter of the item that is correct in each of the following pairs.

**Examples** 1. **a.** They've lived in Phoenix, Arizona, and San Diego, California.

**b.** They've lived in Phoenix, Ariz., and San Diego, Calif.

[The names of states should be spelled out in regular text.]

1. **a.** 4782 Anderson Lane          **b.** 4782 Anderson Ln.

Riverdale, CA                Riverdale, CA 89753

[When should a two-letter abbreviation of the name of a state be used?]

2. **a.** The university library is located in Nashville, Tennessee.

**b.** The university library is located in Nashville, TN.

3. **a.** The invitation said that the party is at 332 Cameron Dr.

**b.** The invitation said that the party is at 332 Cameron Drive.

4. **a.** My grandmother's luggage was sent to Paris, France, not Paris, Tex.

**b.** My grandmother's luggage was sent to Paris, France, not Paris, Texas.

5. **a.** 784 Prairie Ln.          **b.** 784 Prairie Ln

Oklahoma City, OK 78843          Oklahoma City, Ok 78843

**GO ON**

*Developmental Language Skills*                                                         **131**

## Time

Always abbreviate A.D. (*anno Domini*), B.C. (before *Christ*), A.M. (*ante meridiem*), and P.M. (*post meridiem*). Spell out the names of months and days in regular text. The names of months and days can be abbreviated in tables, notes, and bibliographies.

> **EXAMPLES**   This tomb was sealed in 1355 B.C., and it was opened in A.D. 1786.
>
> The bridge will open at 9:00 A.M. tomorrow, **Monday, August** 21.
>
> **NOTE**   Fri., Oct. 12

## Units of Measurement

Spell out the names of units of measurement in regular text. They may be abbreviated in tables and notes following a number. Abbreviations for units of measurement are usually written without periods, but *in.*, the abbreviation for *inch*, always has a period to avoid confusion with the word *in*.

> **TEXT**   The room measured seven **feet** by twelve **feet.** [The unit of measurement *feet* is spelled out in regular text.]
>
> **TABLE OR NOTE**   26 **in.**     2 **c** water     1 **doz** eggs [Abbreviated measurements are written without periods, except for *in.* for *inch*.]

**EXERCISE B**   Circle the letter of the item that is correct in each of the following pairs.

**Example**   **1.** **a.** The meteor shower will peak at 3:00 A.M.

     **b.** The meteor shower will peak at 3:00 *ante meridiem*.

     [*Ante meridiem* and *post meridiem* should always be abbreviated.]

**6. a.** Is the dance scheduled for Wed., Nov. 20?

   **b.** Is the dance scheduled for Wednesday, November 20?

   [Should days and months be abbreviated in regular text?]

**7. a.** We need three yds of material for this dress.

   **b.** We need three yards of material for this dress.

**8. a.** These scattered stones, in 1500 BC, were part of a wall.

   **b.** These scattered stones, in 1500 B.C., were part of a wall.

**9. a. NOTE**     5 tsp basil

   **b. NOTE**     5 teaspoons basil

**10. a. NOTE**     Sat., May 31

   **b. NOTE**     Saturday, May 31

for **CHAPTER 13: PUNCTUATION**    *pages 379–381*

# Commas A

## Items in a Series

**13f.**   Use commas to separate items in a series.

Do not use a comma before the first item or after the last item in a series.

> **WORDS**   The cups, saucers, glasses, and dishes have been washed. [Each of the nouns in the list is a separate item, so commas separate the nouns.]
>
> **PHRASES**   The dog ran down the street, across the yard, and through the gate. [Each of the phrases in the list is a separate item, so commas separate the phrases.]
>
> **CLAUSES**   The heater is on, the doors are closed, and the room is warm. [Each of the clauses in the list is a separate item, so commas separate the clauses.]

When *and, or,* or *nor* joins all the items in a series, do not use commas to separate them.

> **EXAMPLES**   Paul **and** Roger **and** Margaret were all selected for the leads in the play. [*And* joins all the items in the series, so commas do not separate the items.]
>
> The missing keys must be on the counter **or** in the cabinet **or** under the sofa. [*Or* joins all the items in the series, so commas do not separate the items.]

**EXERCISE A** Use proofreading symbols to add commas where they are needed in each of the following sentences. If a sentence doesn't need additional commas, write *C* on the line provided.

**Examples**   ______   **1.** Rita went to the optometrist, got an eye exam, and selected a pair of glasses. [Commas should separate items in a series.]

  __*C*__   **2.** The kitten stretched and yawned and napped. [*And* joins all the items in the series, so no commas are needed.]

______   **1.** Were Robert and Marcia and Janet the finalists in the talent show? [Do items in a series joined by *and* need commas?]

______   **2.** My favorite kinds of books are mysteries thrillers and the classics. [Do commas separate each of the nouns in this series?]

______   **3.** We rode our bikes swam in the creek and fished for trout.

______   **4.** Aunt Sally sewed and washed and pressed the curtains.

______   **5.** I wrote my essay and completed my math problems and planned my science project.

______   **6.** Did Anna write produce and direct her own play?

______   **7.** The cows grazed in the field mooed loudly and stood blinking in the sunlight.

**GO ON** ▶

_______  **8.** My father planted the flowers mulched the garden and watered the plants.

_______  **9.** Vincent chopped the vegetables and stirred the stew and baked the bread.

_______ **10.** The parrot squawked rustled its feathers and asked for a cracker.

---

**13g.**  Use a comma to separate two or more adjectives preceding a noun.

> **EXAMPLE**  The green, lush hills were beautiful against the blue, clear sky.  [*Green* and
> *lush* describe *hills* and are separated by a comma. *Blue* and *clear* describe
> *sky* and are separated by a comma.]

Don't place a comma before the last adjective in a series if the adjective is so closely related to
the noun that it is thought of as part of the noun.

> **EXAMPLE**  A small, new French restaurant is on Richmond Avenue.  [*Small* and *new* are
> both adjectives describing *French restaurant*, so a comma separates them.
> *French* and *restaurant* are thought of as part of the same noun, so no
> comma comes before *French*.]

An adverb may modify an adjective that comes before a noun. Do not use a comma between
the adverb and adjective.

> **EXAMPLE**  It was a bright, sunny morning.  [*Bright* and *sunny* are adjectives describing
> *morning*, so a comma separates them.]
>
> He's wearing a **bright green** jacket.  [*Bright* describes the adjective *green*, so
> *bright* is an adverb. No comma is needed between *bright* and *green*.]

**EXERCISE B**  Use proofreading symbols to add commas where they are needed in each of the following
sentences. If a sentence doesn't need commas, write *C* on the line provided.

**Example** _______  **1.** Don't you like that fancy new grocery store?  [*Fancy* and *new* describe *grocery*

*store*, which is thought of as one item.]

_______ **11.** I like those light yellow curtains.  [Is *light* an adverb describing the adjective *yellow*?]

_______ **12.** Lucy is a gentle intelligent dog.

_______ **13.** Today was a beautiful windy spring day.

_______ **14.** Dad prepared a light tasty lunch.

_______ **15.** Mario is a hungry tired boy.

# Commas B

## Independent Clauses

**13h.** Use a comma before a coordinating conjunction *(and, but, for, nor, or, so,* or *yet)* when it joins independent clauses.

> **EXAMPLES**    Sandy skated to the park**, and** Marcus rode his bike. [The two groups of words are independent clauses that are joined by *and*.]
>
> Dad repaired the fence**, but** Mom mowed the lawn. [The two groups of words are independent clauses that are joined by *but*.]

> **REMINDER**   An *independent clause* is a group of words that has a subject and a verb, expresses a complete thought, and can stand by itself as a sentence.

**EXERCISE A** Use proofreading symbols to add commas where they are needed in each of the following sentences.

**Examples 1.** Joshua played the guitar and Susan sang a song. [A comma should be placed before the coordinating conjunction *and,* which joins two independent clauses.]

    **2.** The room had been painted but the floor still needed to be repaired. [A comma should be used before the coordinating conjunction *but,* which joins two independent clauses.]

**1.** Are you studying or are you sleeping? [Does a comma separate two independent clauses joined by *or*?]

**2.** Patrick painted the shutters and Felicia painted the eaves. [Does a comma separate two independent clauses joined by *and*?]

**3.** He didn't feel well yet he went to the concert.

**4.** My uncle built a boat but he isn't sure it will float.

**5.** We could go to the library or we could study at home.

**6.** Veronica wasn't prepared for class but she promised herself that it wouldn't happen again.

**7.** The kitten played with the toy mouse all day so he took a long afternoon nap.

**8.** The book *The Hobbit* was very good so I am reading *The Lord of the Rings*.

**9.** We went to the baseball game and my little brother caught a fly ball.

**10.** I enjoyed the art gallery and Mom enjoyed the wildflower center.

**GO ON**

A *compound sentence* has two or more independent clauses. Do not confuse a compound sentence with a simple sentence that has a compound verb. A *compound verb* is two or more verbs that are joined by a conjunction and share the same subject. A simple sentence does not need a comma before the conjunction that joins its verbs.

**EXAMPLES**    The chipmunk grabbed the pecan, and he shelled it with his paws. [This compound sentence has two independent clauses joined by the conjunction *and,* so a comma is used before *and.*]

The dog jumped in the air and caught the ball. [This simple sentence has only one subject and a compound verb, *jumped* and *caught.* The sentence has only one independent clause. No comma is needed.]

**EXERCISE B**   Use proofreading symbols to add commas where they are needed in each of the following sentences. If a sentence doesn't need commas, write *C* on the line provided.

**Examples**    *C*    **1.** The butterfly floated through the air and landed on the coneflower. [The simple sentence has a compound verb, *floated* and *landed.* It does not need a comma.]

**2.** My father jogged past the bridge and then he rested on the park bench. [This sentence has two independent clauses joined by the coordinating conjunction *and.* A comma should be placed before the coordinating conjunction.]

**11.** The snake sunned itself on the patio and then slithered away. [Are there two independent clauses joined by a coordinating conjunction in this sentence?]

**12.** The movie was long and dull but my aunt stayed until the end. [Are there two independent clauses joined by a coordinating conjunction in this sentence?]

**13.** Has Janet combined the colors and brushed paint on the canvas?

**14.** The newspaper flew from the delivery person's hand and landed right on the porch.

**15.** The leaf fell from the tree and tumbled in the wind.

**16.** Little Sara swam the length of the pool so her father cheered for her.

**17.** I rode my bike to the bus stop but I took a cab to the museum.

**18.** Julian mixed the ingredients and his mother baked the casserole.

**19.** Did Victoria kick the soccer ball and run down the field?

**20.** I read the article and wrote a review of it.

for **CHAPTER 13: PUNCTUATION**     *pages 384–386*

# Commas C

## Nonessential Elements

**13i.**   Use commas to set off nonessential subordinate clauses and nonessential participial phrases.

A ***nonessential subordinate clause*** adds information to a sentence but is not necessary to the meaning of the sentence. A nonessential subordinate clause can be removed from the sentence without changing its basic meaning.

> **EXAMPLE**   Our teacher**, who is an author,** helped us begin our essays. [*Who is an author* is a nonessential subordinate clause. It adds information about *teacher* and can be removed from the sentence without changing the basic meaning of the sentence.]

> **REMINDER▶**  A *subordinate clause* is a group of words that has both a verb and its subject but does not express a complete thought.

An ***essential*** subordinate clause contains information that is necessary to the meaning of the sentence. An essential subordinate clause is not set off by commas.

> **EXAMPLE**   The boys **that are standing by the lockers** are my cousins. [*That are standing by the lockers* is an essential subordinate clause that tells which boys are being discussed.]

**EXERCISE A**  The subordinate clause in each of the following sentences is underlined. If the clause is nonessential, use proofreading symbols to insert commas where they are needed. If the clause is essential and does not need commas, write *C* on the line provided.

**Examples**    ______ **1.** My little brother who is wearing the blue shirt is a very fast runner. [*Who is wearing the blue shirt* is a nonessential subordinate clause adding information about *brother*. It should be set off from the rest of the sentence by commas.]

   __*C*__ **2.** Is the book that is on the sofa Joshua's favorite? [The essential subordinate clause *that is on the sofa* does not need commas.]

______ **1.** This pack which was left on the table belongs to Nancy. [Is the subordinate clause necessary to the meaning of the sentence?]

______ **2.** Is this one of the lakes where migrating geese gather? [Does the meaning of the sentence change if the subordinate clause is removed?]

______ **3.** Chip who always worked hard at his studies won a scholarship to Harvard.

______ **4.** My bicycle which needs a new tire is leaning against the fence.

______ **5.** Lyle whose family lives in New York plans to visit the city soon.

______ **6.** Holly is the only tennis player from Bayside High School who made it to the finals.

**GO ON ▶**

______ **7.** Jennifer wrote the article that was printed in the school newspaper.

______ **8.** We shouldn't try to paint the car's hood while the wind is blowing.

______ **9.** That team which is in our division was last year's regional champion.

______ **10.** The store manager is the person whom we first contacted.

---

A *nonessential participial phrase* adds information to a sentence but is not necessary to the meaning of the sentence. A nonessential participial phrase can be removed from the sentence without changing its basic meaning.

> **EXAMPLE**   **Warmed by the sun,** the streets steamed after the rain. [The participial phrase *Warmed by the sun* adds information about *streets* but can be removed from the sentence without changing the basic meaning of the sentence.]

**REMINDER** A *participial phrase* is a group of words that begins with a present or past participle. The entire phrase is used as an adjective.

An *essential* participial phrase contains information that is necessary to the meaning of a sentence. Essential participial phrases are not set off by commas.

> **EXAMPLE**   The man **jogging around the park** is my father. [The participial phrase *jogging around the park* is necessary to the meaning of the sentence. The phrase is not set off by commas.]

**EXERCISE B** The participial phrase in each of the following sentences is underlined. If the phrase is nonessential, use proofreading symbols to insert commas where they are needed. If the phrase is essential and does not need commas, write *C* on the line provided.

**Example** ______ **1.** Thrown into the stands, the football bounced into Zack's hands. [The participial phrase *Thrown into the stands* is not necessary to the basic meaning of the sentence, so it is set off by a comma.]

______ **11.** How many of the parts worn by friction can be replaced quickly? [Does the basic meaning of the sentence change if the participial phrase is removed?]

______ **12.** The snail creeping slowly finally made it to the garden.

______ **13.** Citizens needing information about where to vote should visit the city's Web site.

______ **14.** Polished with wax the car looked as if it were new.

______ **15.** The boy speaking with the teacher about the essay is Robert.

# Commas D

## Introductory Elements

**13j.** Use a comma after certain introductory elements.

Use a comma to set off introductory words such as *yes, no, well,* or *why* at the beginning of a sentence.

   **EXAMPLES** **No,** the plants haven't been watered yet.

       **Well,** I think it is time to leave.

**EXERCISE A** Use proofreading symbols to add commas where they are needed in the following sentences.

**Example 1.** No I didn't see that bird.  [*No* is an introductory element, so it should be set off by a

    comma.]

**1.** Well Sheila said that it might happen.  [What word is an introductory element?]

**2.** Why that is the prettiest bouquet of flowers I have ever seen!

**3.** Yes I will meet you at the movies at 7 P.M.

**4.** Oh that was a complete surprise!

**5.** Yes I agree with you completely.

Use a comma after an introductory participle or participial phrase.

**REMINDER** A *participle* is a verb form usually ending in *–ing* or *–ed* that is used as an adjective. A *participial phrase* is a group of words that begins with a participle and is used as an adjective.

   **EXAMPLES** **Pouncing,** the cat landed on the toy mouse.  [The introductory participle *Pouncing* is set off from the rest of the sentence by a comma.]

       **Frozen by the winter cold,** the lawn had turned yellow.  [The introductory participial phrase *Frozen by the winter cold* is set off from the rest of the sentence by a comma.]

**EXERCISE B** Use proofreading symbols to add a comma where it is needed in each of the following sentences.

**Example 1.** Reading the boy stumbled over the chair.  [*Reading* is an introductory participle, so it

    should be set off from the rest of the sentence by a comma.]

**6.** Proofreading his essay for the last time Julio felt happy about his work.  [What words are an

   introductory participial phrase?]

**7.** Blushing Maura thanked the student council for their compliments.

**8.** Made from scratch the casserole tasted delicious.

**9.** Smiling the mayor, wearing his best suit, announced that the resolution had passed.

**10.** Trimmed the bushes along the front sidewalk looked good again.

---

Use a comma after two or more introductory prepositional phrases or after one long introductory prepositional phrase.

> **EXAMPLES**   **In the fields next to the school,** we found a jacket.  [The two introductory prepositional phrases are followed by a comma.]
>
> **After hard work and perseverance,** we won the championship.  [The long introductory prepositional phrase is followed by a comma.]

Use a comma after an introductory adverb clause. An **adverb clause** is a group of words that has a subject and a verb, cannot stand alone as a sentence, and tells *where, when, how,* or *to what extent* about another word in the sentence. An adverb clause begins with a subordinating conjunction such as *as soon as, although, after, because, if, when,* or *while.*

> **EXAMPLES**   **As soon as Ashley gets here,** we will leave for the recital.  [The introductory adverb clause is followed by a comma.]

---

**EXERCISE C** Insert commas where they are needed in each of the following sentences.

**Examples 1.** While I waited for my mother, I read part of Chapter 27.  [The introductory adverb clause *While I waited for my mother* should be followed by a comma.]

**2.** Under the umbrella over the picnic table, we ate our lunch.  [A comma should follow the two prepositional phrases *Under the umbrella* and *over the picnic table.*]

**11.** After warming up on the violin for the next several minutes Frederick will perform.  [Should a comma follow two or more introductory prepositional phrases?]

**12.** When you get home will you please let the dog out?  [Should a comma follow an introductory adverb clause?]

**13.** Although we didn't think we would win the game we won by five points.

**14.** Near the edge of the lake the ducks quacked happily.

**15.** Once the dog had drunk its water did it bound off after the ball?

**16.** After we wash the dishes we can ride our bikes to the park.

**17.** By the time the game is over my mother should be here.

**18.** Since I have been exercising regularly I feel healthier and stronger.

**19.** As soon as we feed the baby we can leave for the picnic.

**20.** Beneath the books on the table you will find the letter.

# Commas E

## Interrupters

**13k.** Use commas to set off an expression that interrupts a sentence.

Use commas to set off nonessential appositives and appositive phrases. An *appositive* is a word that is placed beside another word to explain or describe it. An *appositive phrase* is a group of words that includes an appositive and any of the modifiers of the appositive.

A *nonessential* appositive or appositive phrase adds information to a sentence but is not necessary to the basic meaning of the sentence.

> **EXAMPLE**  My cousin**, the athlete,** draws very well. [The appositive phrase *the athlete* adds information about *cousin* but is not necessary to the meaning of the sentence.]

An *essential* appositive or appositive phrase adds information that is necessary to the meaning of the sentence. An essential appositive or appositive phrase is not set off from the rest of the sentence by commas.

> **EXAMPLE**  My friend **Carmen** invited me to dinner. [The essential appositive *Carmen* is not set off from the rest of the sentence by commas.]

**EXERCISE A**  The appositives and appositive phrases in the following sentences are underlined. If the appositive or appositive phrase is nonessential, use proofreading symbols to add commas where they are needed. If the appositive or appositive phrase is essential and the sentence is correct without commas, write *C* on the line provided.

**Examples**  _______ **1.** Teresa, the oldest girl in our family, is graduating from high school

tomorrow.  [The nonessential appositive phrase *the oldest girl in our family* should be set off by commas.]

_______ **2.** My brother Tom came for a visit this weekend.  [The essential appositive *Tom* should not be set off by commas.]

_______ **1.** Your aunt the one that lives in Mexico is a talented artist.  [Will the basic meaning of the sentence change if the appositive phrase is removed?]

_______ **2.** Does the store Kodie's sell hand-crafted shelves?  [Is the appositive necessary to the basic meaning of the sentence?]

_______ **3.** Barney my little brother's hamster runs on its wheel for hours.

_______ **4.** These tools some wrenches and screwdrivers are probably all we'll need to finish the project.

_______ **5.** The assignment a five-page essay on wildlife is due on Monday.

_______ **6.** My teacher Ms. Janowitz offered extra help on this algebra problem.

**GO ON** ➡

_______ **7.** The quilt the one with the gingham and clouds was sewn by my great-grandmother.

_______ **8.** Is that dress the white chiffon the one you want?

_______ **9.** My dog Barkley is the smartest dog on the whole block.

_______ **10.** The dentist Dr. Nobles always kids me out of being afraid.

---

Words used in direct address are set off by commas. *Direct address* names the person or persons spoken to in a sentence.

> **EXAMPLE**  **Marcellus,** could you come here please?  [*Marcellus* is direct address, so it is set off from the rest of the sentence by a comma.]

---

**EXERCISE B** Use proofreading symbols to add commas where they are needed in the following sentences.

**Example  1.** What are you doing after school, Sarah?  [*Sarah* is direct address, so it should be set off from the rest of the sentence by a comma.]

**11.** This pasta primavera Dad is the best I have ever tasted.  [What word is direct address?]

**12.** Your poem Mr. Reyes is inspirational.

**13.** Suzi what do you think of our science project?

**14.** I will decorate for the party Lee if you bring the plates and cups.

**15.** What time does the movie start Francis?

---

Parenthetical expressions are set off by commas. **Parenthetical expressions** are side remarks that add information or show relationships between ideas in a sentence. Some common parenthetical expressions are *after all, by the way, for instance, however, meanwhile,* and *therefore.*

> **EXAMPLE**  He was, **after all,** an excellent violinist.  [*After all* is a parenthetical expression, so it is set off from the rest of the sentence by commas.]

---

**EXERCISE C** Use proofreading symbols to add commas where they are needed in the following sentences.

**Example  1.** The new girl at school, by the way, is quite nice.  [The parenthetical expression *by the way* should be set off by commas.]

**16.** David went home I believe.  [What words are a parenthetical expression?]

**17.** In the first place I never said that I could attend.

**18.** The tires however still need to be rotated.

**19.** She was incidentally the best cook in Springfield.

**20.** I agree with you of course.

**142**

# Commas F

## Conventional Uses

**13l.**  Use commas in certain conventional situations.

Use commas to separate items in dates and addresses. Do not use commas to separate a month from the day of the month, the day from the month when the day comes before the month, or the month from the year when no day is given.

>**EXAMPLES**  The graduation ceremony will be on Friday, May 18, 2009.  [Commas are used to separate items in the dates, but a comma does not separate the month from the day of the month.]
>
>The reunion is scheduled for 19 November, 2010.  [A comma separates the month from the year, but no comma separates the day from the month.]
>
>The new bridge should be completed by July 2010.  [Commas are not used between the month and the year when no day is given.]

Do not use commas to separate a house number from a street name, a state name or abbreviation from a ZIP Code, or items joined by prepositions.

>**EXAMPLES**  We once lived at 1325 Newcreek Lane.  [Commas are not used between the house number and a street name.]
>
>Send the package to 4217 Woodrow Avenue, Raleigh, NC 44873.  [Commas are not used between the two-letter state abbreviation and the ZIP Code.]
>
>The new museum is at 637 Karen Avenue in Manchester.  [*At* and *in* are prepositions. No commas are used between items separated by the prepositions.]

**EXERCISE A**  Use proofreading symbols to add commas where they are needed in each of the following sentences.  Draw a slash through each comma that should not be in the sentence.

**Example  1.**  In December, 2019, my grandparents will celebrate their fiftieth anniversary.  [A comma is not needed between the month and the year when no date is given.]

**1.**  The observatory will be built on Fifth Street, in Weston.  [Are commas needed between items joined by a preposition?]

**2.**  The address on the envelope read 234 Anderson Avenue, New York, NY, 65342.

**3.**  Stop by my house at 875, Beechwood Avenue.

**4.**  The wellness center is at 543 Bluebonnet Lane Marshall TX 74652.

**5.**  On January 30 2018 my baby nephew will be eighteen years old.

**GO ON**

Use a comma after the salutation of a personal letter and after the closing of any letter. The *salutation* is the short line at the top of a letter in which you greet the person you are writing. The *closing* is the short line at the bottom telling the person that the letter is about to end.

    **EXAMPLES**  Dear Macy,     Yours truly,

**EXERCISE B** Use proofreading symbols to add commas where they are needed in each of the following items.

**Example 1.** Dear Grandma, [The salutation of a personal letter should have a comma.]

**6.** Sincerely  [Should the closing of a letter have a comma?]

**7.** Dear James

**8.** Very truly yours

**9.** Regards

**10.** Dear Aunt Janet

Use a comma to set off a title, such as *Jr., Sr.,* or *Ph.D.,* that follows a person's name.

    **EXAMPLE**  Roger Baldwin, Jr.

**EXERCISE C** Use proofreading symbols to add a comma where it is needed in each of the following items.

**Example 1.** Michael Morris, Sr.  [A comma should set off a title after a person's name.]

**11.** Maria Cypress M.D.  [Should a comma set off a title after a person's name?]

**12.** Patrick Matthews Jr.

**13.** Antonio Martinelli Jr.

**14.** Frederick Jefferson Sr.

**15.** Anna Bledsoe Ph.D.

# Semicolons A

**14a.** Use a semicolon between independent clauses that are closely related in thought and are not joined by a coordinating conjunction *(and, but, for, nor, or, so,* or *yet).*

> **EXAMPLE**  The wooden bridge groaned; a heavy truck was driving across.  [The clause *The wooden bridge groaned* is connected to the related clause *a heavy truck was driving across* by a semicolon.]

An independent clause has a subject and a verb and can stand alone as a sentence. Two independent clauses with similar ideas may be joined with a semicolon. Use a semicolon only if the ideas are closely related.

> **EXAMPLE**  The Sahara was once wet and green; climate changes have made it a vast desert.  [The two independent clauses are closely related. The clauses are not joined by a coordinating conjunction, so a semicolon separates them.]

**EXERCISE A**  Insert a semicolon between the independent clauses in the following sentences.

**Example 1.** The ring slipped down the drain; Nora immediately turned off the faucet.  [*The ring slipped down the drain* is an independent clause, and *Nora immediately turned off the faucet* is an independent clause that tells what Nora did when the ring slipped.]

**1.** I reached into my pocket the horse nuzzled me for a treat.  [Where should these two independent clauses be separated?]

**2.** The ice cubes must be ready they have been in the freezer for an hour.  [Where should these two independent clauses be separated?]

**3.** Patrick glanced at his watch the plane was actually early.

**4.** The thermometer showed it was 100 degrees outside Carla went back for her hat.

**5.** The player kicked toward the net the goalie sprang toward the ball.

**6.** Dusk fell on the neighborhood porch lights flicked on.

**7.** The school bus came to a stop children poured out.

**8.** Margo felt relieved her exam was over at last.

**9.** The probe landed on the planet computers soon lit up with incoming information.

**10.** Sunshine Café is famous people come from miles around for the food.

**GO ON** ▶

**14b.** **Use a semicolon between independent clauses joined by a conjunctive adverb or a transitional expression.**

A *conjunctive adverb* or a *transitional expression* tells how two clauses are related in meaning. Always set off conjunctive adverbs and transitional expressions with commas because conjunctive adverbs and transitional expressions are extra information in the sentence. You can place a conjunctive adverb or transitional expression right after the semicolon or put it within the second clause.

> **EXAMPLES**   Camels have very thick skin**;** **otherwise,** blowing desert sand would hurt them. [The clause *Camels have very thick skin* is connected to the related clause *blowing desert sand would hurt them* by a semicolon and the conjunctive adverb *otherwise*.]
>
> Jan looked at the radios**;** she did not**, however,** buy one. [The clause *Jan looked at the radios* is connected to the related clause *she did not buy one* by a semicolon and the conjunctive adverb *however*. Conjunctive adverbs do not always come at the beginning of the second independent clause.]

**EXERCISE B** Insert a semicolon between the independent clauses in the following sentences.

**Example 1.** The batteries were dead **;** as a result, the flashlight was useless. [The transitional expression *as a result* directly follows the semicolon. The expression is set off by one comma.]

**11.** Laurie worked all summer consequently, she started a savings account. [What conjunctive adverb joins the two independent clauses? Where should the semicolon go?]

**12.** The nest we were observing was unusual for instance, a hair ribbon was wound through it. [What transitional expression joins the two independent clauses? Does the transitional expression come at the beginning of the second clause?]

**13.** One team took the mountain route meanwhile, our team took the river route.

**14.** The woven rug had a snag it began to unravel, in fact.

**15.** The class was almost over the students, therefore, put away the lab materials.

**16.** The weather forecast predicted rain Miss Rose, accordingly, decided to bring her umbrella.

**17.** Don't throw that paper away instead, put it in the recycling bin.

**18.** Linda was never a stranger for very long in other words, she was very friendly.

**19.** It's getting dark out besides, it's freezing outside!

**20.** That bird feeder is popular sparrows, for example, flock around it every day.

# Semicolons B

**14c.** You may need to use a semicolon (rather than a comma) before a coordinating conjunction to join independent clauses that contain commas.

Think of a semicolon as "stronger" than a comma. A comma tells readers to pause, but a semicolon helps readers make a bigger pause when too many commas make a sentence long and confusing.

**EXAMPLE**   The toolbox held nails, a hammer, screws, and a screwdriver; **but** a wrench, a ruler, and a saw were missing. [Both independent clauses contain several commas. A semicolon is needed with the coordinating conjunction *but* to join the clauses without confusion.]

**REMINDER**  The coordinating conjuctions are *and, or, for, nor, but, so,* and *yet.*

---

**EXERCISE A**  Insert a semicolon between the independent clauses in the following sentences.

**Examples 1.** The store was out of paper towels, laundry soap, and dish soap; nor did it have milk, orange juice, or eggs. [These clauses contain commas, so a semicolon and the coordinating conjunction *nor* join the two independent clauses.]

      **2.** We walked the dogs, watered the plants, and mowed the lawn; and Frank painted the mailbox, washed the dishes, and mended the fence. [These clauses contain commas, so a semicolon and the coordinating conjunction *and* join the two independent clauses.]

**1.** The suitcase contained shirts, lots of socks, pants, and a tie but it had no identification card, tag, or paper inside. [What coordinating conjunction joins the two independent clauses? Does the sentence need a semicolon to help make a stronger pause?]

**2.** Mr. Snyder will go on vacation June 16 through June 20, and then take off June 25 or he will take off June 6 through June 15. [What coordinating conjunction joins the two independent clauses? Does the sentence need a semicolon to help make a stronger pause?]

**3.** A stage costume may have feathers, sequins, and several flounces yet bright colors and a simple design will show up more onstage.

**4.** Stock your pantry with noodles, cans of fruit, dried beans, and rice for you can use these inexpensive and healthy foods in so many quick meals.

**5.** The cave tour wound through low walkways, tight tunnels, and cramped turns but then, at the end, we reached an open, large cavern.

**GO ON**

**6.** The children gathered strawberries, blueberries, and raspberries but the strawberries, sweet and juicy, were their favorites.

**7.** Mrs. Bird had stocked the cabinet with paper, envelopes, and pens so the faculty, staff, and students did not run out of supplies.

**8.** Today's mail had two flyers, a few bills, and a catalog yet no letters, postcards, or packages arrived.

**9.** On the lunch special you can order a main dish, two side dishes, and a drink or a main dish, three side dishes, and fruit can be ordered.

**10.** The tournament runs Thursday, Friday, and Saturday but Monday, and possibly Tuesday, will also be game days.

---

**14d.** Use a semicolon between items in a series if the items contain commas.

> **EXAMPLE**   The dance team included Lila Keys, the captain; Sandra Davis, the co-captain; and Nina Nichols, the lieutenant. [Each item in this series contains commas. A semicolon between items keeps the items separate and makes the list of items easier to read.]

**EXERCISE B** Circle the commas that should be semicolons between items in the following series.

**Example 1.** The art show winners were Alice James, for oil painting, Bob Tiller, for watercolors, Yin Parks, for murals, and Roy Long, for drawing. [The four items in this series contain commas, so they should be separated by semicolons.]

**11.** The museum displayed a mummy, from Egypt, a kimono, from Japan, and a statue, from Italy. [Find each item in the series. Does each item have a semicolon to separate it from the other items?]

**12.** The band was made up of Shari Bolt, on piano, Chris Lee, on saxophone, Jon Burk, on guitar, and Cam Smith, on drums.

**13.** A baseball catcher wears a mask, to protect his face, a mitt, to protect his hand, and leg pads, to protect his knees.

**14.** My grandfather has lived in London, England, Berlin, Germany, and Dublin, Ireland.

**15.** The hit songs now are "Hello You," by Kate Katz, "Summer Song," by The Urchins, and "Salza Waltz," by Lemon-Aide.

# Colons

## Lists

**14e.**  Use a colon to mean "note what follows."

**(1) Use a colon before a list of items, especially after expressions such as *as follows* and *the following*.**

> **EXAMPLES**  The stew had several ingredients**:** potatoes, carrots, and celery.  [The colon tells a reader that a list follows.]
>
> The recipe was **as follows:** brown the onions, add the broth, and stir in the chopped vegetables.  [The phrase *as follows* and the colon tell the reader that a list follows.]

**NOTE▶** Do not use a colon immediately after a verb or immediately after a preposition.

> **INCORRECT**  The school offered: fencing, archery, and karate.  [The colon after the verb *offered* cuts off the verb from its complements *fencing, archery,* and *karate.*]
>
> **CORRECT**  The school offered fencing, archery, and karate.

**EXERCISE A**  Circle the colons that are used correctly in the following sentences.  Put a slash (/) through colons that are not used correctly.

**Example  1.**  The bank teller counted the following coins**:** nickels, dimes, and quarters.  [The colon appears after the phrase *the following* to signal that a list of coins follows.]

**1.**  The dentist had the following three openings: Tuesday morning, Thursday morning, or Friday afternoon.  [Is the list correctly set off by a colon?]

**2.**  The Colorado River crosses through: Colorado, Utah, and Arizona.

**3.**  The client jotted down: the name, the address, and the phone number of the company.

**4.**  The past club presidents were as follows: Mr. Samson, Miss Gonzales, and Mrs. Lee.

**5.**  The trainer recommended several exercises as follows: sit-ups, curls, and pull-ups.

## Quotations and Explanations

**(2) Use a colon before a long, formal statement or quotation.**

> **EXAMPLE**  Jane Austen opens *Pride and Prejudice* with a view of marriage**:** "It is a truth universally acknowledged, that a single man in possession of a good fortune, must be in want of a wife."  [A colon sets off the long quotation.]

**(3) Use a colon between independent clauses when the second clause explains or restates the idea of the first.**

> **EXAMPLE**  Gina grimaced suddenly**:** The kitten had attached itself to her ankle.  [The second clause is set off with a colon because it explains the first clause.]

**GO ON ➡**

**EXERCISE B** Insert a colon where needed in the following sentences.

**Example  1.** Our team has a code of honor **:** We will play hard, play smart, and play against the other team, not against ourselves.  [The colon sets off the second sentence, which explains the first sentence.]

**6.** My father lives by these simple words "You should not live your life as an explanation but live it as an exclamation."  [Does the quotation need a colon before it?]

**7.** That puppy was on a mission Trashing the couch, chewing shoes, and shredding newspapers seemed its goal in life.

**8.** The store has a rigid policy They accept no returns without a receipt and a price tag.

**9.** The novel *Lord Jim* begins with a description of Jim "He was an inch, perhaps two, under six feet, powerfully built, and he advanced straight at you with a slight stoop of the shoulders, head forward, and a fixed from-under stare which made you think of a charging bull."

**10.** There's just one problem with this map It is missing a section.

## Conventional Situations

| **14f.** | Use a colon in certain conventional situations. |

Use a colon between the hour and the minute, between chapter and verse when referring to a passage from the Bible, between a title and a subtitle, and after the salutation of a business letter.

**EXAMPLES**   10:30 P.M.                                    John 3:16
             *Paw Prints: The Life of a Clever Cat*  [book]      Dear Mr. Jones:

**EXERCISE C** Insert a colon where needed in the following sentences.

**Example  1.** Dear Store Manager **:** [*Dear Store Manager* is a business letter salutation that needs a colon.]

**11.** I believe that verse is from Mark 4 1–15 in the Bible.  [Should a colon separate the chapter from the verses when referring to passages from the Bible?]

**12.** Sasha calls this painting *Hours of the Day Siesta.*

**13.** The shuttle leaves at exactly 4 00 P.M. each day.

**14.** Books-Mart has a copy of *Mind Benders Puzzles for Kids.*

**15.** Dear Madam Justice

# Italics

**14g.** Use italics (underlining) for the titles and subtitles of books, plays, long poems, periodicals, works of art, films, radio and television series, long musical works and recordings, videos, video and computer games, and comic strips.

Italics are printed letters that *slant to the right*. If you are not using a computer, you can show italicized words by underlining them: I read <u>The Cave</u> this summer.

> **EXAMPLES**  *Cry, the Beloved Country*  [book]
>
> *Smithsonian*  [magazine]
>
> *Mona Lisa*  [painting]

**NOTE▶** Italicize the articles *a*, *an*, and *the* in the title of a periodical (something published at regular intervals, like a magazine or a newspaper) only if the article is part of the official title. Check the title page, front page, or table of contents of a periodical to find the official title.

> **EXAMPLE**  The article appeared in *The New York Times,* but it was not in **the** *USA Today* that I bought.  [*The* is part of the official title of *The New York Times,* so it is italicized. *USA Today* does not have *the* in its official title, so *the* is not italicized.]

**EXERCISE A**  Underline the words, letters, or numbers that should be italicized in the following sentences.

**Examples 1.** <u>You Can't Take It with You</u> will be the spring play for the drama club.  [*You Can't Take It with You* is italicized because it is the name of a play.]

**2.** Did you find the stock quotes in <u>The Wall Street Journal</u>?  [*The Wall Street Journal* is italicized because it is the title of a periodical (newspaper).]

**1.** We finally got tickets to the musical The Producers.  [Should the title of a long musical work be italicized?]

**2.** Which part of the long poem The Rime of the Ancient Mariner did you enjoy most?  [Should the title of a long poem be italicized?]

**3.** During my drive from work, I listen to Fresh Air with Terry Gross on the radio.

**4.** Have you seen my copy of Time magazine?

**5.** I'm learning sign language from the CD-ROM Speaking with Your Hands.

**6.** Will we rent Antz or some other movie this weekend?

**7.** Louisa always carries a tattered copy of Jane Eyre when she travels.

**8.** I get a laugh out of The Far Side cartoons on my desk calendar.

**GO ON ➡**

**9.** Is my costume for A Midsummer Night's Dream ready yet?

**10.** The new television series Danger Mountain should be a hit.

---

| **14h.** | Use italics (underlining) for the names of trains, ships, aircraft, and spacecraft. |

> **EXAMPLES**  *Orient Express* [train]  *Lusitania* [ship]
>
> *The Flyer* [aircraft]  *Discovery* [spacecraft]

| **14i.** | Use italics (underlining) for words, letters, symbols, and numerals referred to as such, and for foreign words that have not been adopted into English. |

> **EXAMPLES**  Aunt Cora uses the word ***pince-nez*** to describe her oddly shaped eyeglasses.
> [*Pince-nez* is italicized because the writer is calling attention to it as a
> word. If the writer did not want to call attention to *pince-nez* as a word,
> the sentence would not contain italics: Aunt Cora asked for her
> pince-nez.]
>
> I stamped the box with an ***E*** for express mail.  [The letter *E* is italicized
> because it is referred to as a letter.]
>
> The typewriter's ***6*** key doesn't seem to work.  [The number *6* is italicized
> because it is referred to as a number.]
>
> The hotel clerk in Montreal answered the phone with a cheerful ***bonjour.***
> [*Bonjour* is italicized because it is a foreign word that has not been
> adopted into English.]

---

**EXERCISE B**  Underline the words, letters, or numbers that should be italicized in the following sentences.

**Example  1.**  What do the letters km stand for on this ruler?  [The letters *km* are italicized because

they are referred to as letters.]

**11.**  A replica of the Mayflower is on display in the harbor.  [Should the names of ships be italicized?]

**12.**  Carmen wrote 60 on the box, but I find only fifty candles in here.

**13.**  We saw gorgeous scenery as we chugged along on the California Zephyr.

**14.**  In Hawaii, we were greeted with the word aloha wherever we went.

**15.**  Did I put an extra s in *Mississippi*?

# Quotation Marks A

**14j.**   Use quotation marks to enclose a *direct quotation*—a person's exact words.

When you write exactly what a person says, you are directly quoting that person. Quotation marks show when that person's exact words begin and when the words end. The first word of a direct quotation generally begins with a capital letter. Words that indicate the speaker are set off with a comma or commas.

> **EXAMPLES**   "My hobby," Joe said, "is disk golf." [Joe's exact words are enclosed in a set of quotation marks.]
>
> The Australian laughed, "You ought to try a boomerang." [The Australian's exact words are enclosed in a set of quotation marks. Notice that the first word of the quoted sentence is capitalized.]

When you write what someone said without using his or her exact words, you are using an *indirect quotation.* Indirect quotations do not have quotation marks.

> **EXAMPLE**   The historian said that people did not use forks much until the 1700s. [The words *people did not use forks much until the 1700s* retell what the historian said. They are not the historian's exact words, so they do not need quotation marks.]

**EXERCISE A**   Revise the following sentences by adding quotation marks.

**Examples 1.** "Mom, I'm looking for my backpack," Dinah called. [Dinah's exact words *Mom, I'm looking for my backpack* should be set off with quotation marks.]

    **2.** Mom replied, "Look in your closet." [Mom's exact words are *Look in your closet.* The first quoted word, *Look,* is capitalized because it is the first word of the quoted sentence.]

**1.** The secret to light biscuits is sticky dough, the cook confessed. [Where are the cook's exact words?]

**2.** I ride every day, the cyclist said, and I eat a lot of high-energy meals. [Where are the cyclist's exact words?]

**3.** Let's try that scene again, said the director.

**4.** Try a scarf with that jacket, the salesperson suggested.

**5.** The salesperson suggested, That red scarf would match best.

**6.** Race cars, said the mechanic, need a lot of maintenance.

**7.** Do not stand up in a canoe, our river guide warned.

**GO ON**

**8.** The innkeeper apologized, I'm afraid we are full tonight.

**9.** Get your cold drinks right here, called the vendor.

**10.** I think it's odd, Gene remarked, how the newspaper always ends up in the doghouse.

---

In general, a comma belongs inside the closing quotation marks. A period also belongs inside the quotation marks if the quotation is at the end of the whole sentence.

 **EXAMPLE** "Your car needs an oil change." the mechanic advised, "or you could ruin the engine." [A comma tells the reader to switch from quoted words to the rest of the sentence. The comma goes inside the closing quotation mark. The period at the end of the sentence also goes inside the closing quotation mark.]

Question marks and exclamation points generally go inside the quotation marks if they belong to the quoted sentence. When question marks and exclamation points are not part of the quoted sentence, then they belong outside the quotation marks.

 **EXAMPLES** "What's wrong with my car?" Curran asked. [The quoted sentence is a question, so the question mark is inside the quotation marks.]

    Did the mechanic say, "The oil level is really low"? [The overall sentence is a question about what the mechanic said. The question mark goes outside the quotation marks because it is not part of the quotation.]

**EXERCISE B** Revise the following sentences by adding quotation marks and appropriate punctuation.

**Example 1.** "Bring that rake to me," Mr. Evans called. [The words *Bring that rake to me* are enclosed in quotation marks because they are Mr. Evans' exact words. A comma goes inside the closing quotation marks to separate the quotation from the explanation of who was talking.]

**11.** Is it going to rain Ivan wondered. [Where are Ivan's exact words? Where does the question mark belong?]

**12.** The sky this morning Eva wrote is pearly gray.

**13.** This book Kayla remarked says that pandas aren't actually bears.

**14.** Don't forget to lock the door called Dad.

**15.** May I have another serving, please the guest asked.

for **CHAPTER 14: PUNCTUATION**   *pages 415–416*

# Quotation Marks B

**14k.** Use quotation marks to enclose titles (including subtitles) of short works, such as short stories, short poems, essays, articles and other parts of periodicals, songs, episodes of radio and television series, and chapters and other parts of books.

> **EXAMPLES**  "The Gift of the Magi" [short story]
>
>              "Harlem" [poem]
>
>              "On Liberty" [essay]
>
>              "The New Century" [article]

When you use the title of a short work within another quotation, use single quotation marks (') for the title.

> **EXAMPLE**  Starla asked, "Don't you love the song 'Space Race' by Alien Invasion?" [The song title *'Space Race'* has single quotation marks around it because it is within a quotation.]

**TIP** You may find it easier to remember when to use quotation marks or italics with titles if you keep in mind that long works that use italics, such as books and long musical works, usually stand alone. Short works that use quotation marks, such as chapters and songs, are usually part of some larger work.

> **EXAMPLE**  My favorite song from the album ***Rubber Soul*** is **"Norwegian Wood (This Bird Has Flown)."**

**EXERCISE A** Revise the following sentences by adding quotation marks to titles of short works.

**Examples 1.** Ms. Little assigned the chapter "Modern Art" in our textbook. [*"Modern Art"* is enclosed with quotation marks because it is the title of a book chapter.]

      **2.** I found Pam's Pizzaria listed in the "Restaurant Review" section of the December city guide. [*"Restaurant Review"* is the title of a part of a periodical.]

**1.** Ann Smith appeared in the episode Edge of Night of *Mummies and Mommies.* [Is the title of an episode set off by quotation marks?]

**2.** One of Elvis Presley's first hits was the song Heartbreak Hotel in 1956. [Is the title of a song set off by quotation marks?]

**3.** Every senior should read the article Packing for College in *On the Move* magazine.

**4.** Set the VCR to record the episode Eleanor Roosevelt of *The Lives of First Ladies.*

**5.** I made copies of the essay My Certain Slant of Light.

**6.** Check the chapter Fast Fish Recipes in that cookbook.

**7.** Mrs. Forest read aloud Wallace Stevens' poem Anecdote of the Jar to the class.

**8.** The speaker in Lucille Clifton's poem Island Mary is a woman.

**9.** Do you understand that chapter called Fire and Ice in this novel?

**10.** Wishing Star is my favorite song on this CD.

---

**14l.** Use quotation marks to enclose slang words, invented words, technical terms, dictionary definitions of words, and any expressions that are unusual in standard English.

> **EXAMPLES**   Hold out your hand so I can "pony up" your allowance. [*Pony up* is slang for "pay money owed."]
>
> We call Tim's car the "Joltswagon." [*Joltswagon* is an invented term.]
>
> "Scud" is a sailing term meaning "sail with a strong wind." [*Scud* is a technical term in the sailing profession.]
>
> The rancher rounded up the "dogies," or orphaned calves. [*Dogie* is a slang word for a motherless calf.]
>
> Mina needed plenty of time to get "dolled up" for the prom. [*Dolled up* is an informal term for "dressed up" in standard English.]

**EXERCISE B**   Revise the following sentences by adding quotation marks around slang words, invented words, technical terms, dictionary definitions of words, and any expressions that are unusual in standard English.

**Examples 1.** I always delete "spam" from my e-mail messages. [The word *spam* belongs in quotation marks because it is an invented term for unwanted Internet messages.]

**2.** This old novel refers to nickels as "jitneys." [The word *jitneys* belongs in quotation marks because it is slang for a type of money.]

**11.** Does your brother really prefer snail-mail to electronic communication? [Is the word *snail-mail* a standard term for traditional postal service?]

**12.** The pilot radioed roger when he'd gotten our message. [Is the term *roger* a technical term in communications?]

**13.** In Canada, a toonie is a two-dollar coin.

**14.** The headings in the beautiful, old manuscript were set in a swash style of type.

**15.** Dan said he was a spelunker, which means cave explorer.

**16.** The newspaper called the unsuccessful track meet an Uh-Oh-lympics.

**17.** Gina loves to put little emoticons (smiling face symbols) in her e-mails.

**18.** *Voyage to Mars* was the sleeper hit of the summer movie season.

**19.** Dad's lawn mower is so advanced that we call it the Robomower.

**20.** I think our cat is the original couch potato.

**156**

# Ellipsis Points

**14m.** Use *ellipsis points* to mark omissions from quoted material and pauses in a written passage.

When you leave out words in a direct quotation, you must use three ellipsis points (three periods with spaces between them) to show where the words were left out. You can use ellipsis points for words left out at the beginning, middle, or end of a quotation.

> **ORIGINAL**    Mr. Conrad explained, "Not all birds can fly. Penguins have wings, but they cannot fly. Instead, penguins swim underwater by using their wings."

> **OMISSION**    Mr. Conrad explained, "Not all birds can fly. Penguins have wings, but they . . . swim underwater by using their wings." [Three ellipsis points show where the words *cannot fly. Instead, penguins* have been left out of the quotation.]

**NOTE**   When you omit the first word of a sentence, capitalize the new first word of the sentence. Then, put brackets around the capital letter to show that the word was not capitalized in the original sentence.

> **EXAMPLE**    "Not all birds can fly. . . . [P]enguins swim underwater by using their wings."

**EXERCISE A**   Rewrite the following sentences by crossing out the words in parentheses. Then, draw ellipsis points above the crossed out words. If a sentence will begin with a new first word, put the capital letter in brackets after the ellipsis points.

**Examples 1.** The journalist claimed, "~~The background for~~ *. . . [T]* this article came from court records and interviews." (The background for) [Three ellipsis points show where words were omitted at the beginning of the quotation. The word *this* has a capital *T* in brackets to show it is not the first word of the original sentence.]

**2.** "You must go ~~far, far~~ *. . .* into the country to see lots of stars clearly," advised the astronomer. (far, far) [Three ellipsis points show where words were omitted from the middle of the quotation.]

**1.** The skater cautioned, "The ice is thin over there near the trees." (near the trees) [Where will you need ellipsis points?]

**2.** Rachel told the store manager, "I've read all the books in this mystery series. I especially liked the first two mysteries. Now I'm waiting for the next book to come out." (I especially liked the first two mysteries.) [When you leave out a whole sentence, where do the ellipsis points belong?]

**3.** As Amy opened the mailbox, she thought, "Please, let there be a letter from Greenwood College telling me I'm accepted at the college." (from Greenwood College)

**GO ON ▶**

**4.** The coach yelled, "Take your time. That's it. Nice shot!" (That's it.)

**5.** The skier asked, "Is it true snow can turn pink when it has red bacteria in it?" (Is it true)

**6.** The naturalist wrote in his journal, "At midnight the coyotes began to howl. Their chorus of yips and yowls kept me awake for hours. It was music to my ears." (kept me awake for hours. It)

**7.** "That cloud up there looks full of rain," Sam noticed warily. (up there)

**8.** The artist murmured, "I think a touch of red makes a sunset more realistic." (I think a touch of)

**9.** "Watch my black Labrador Cinder catch this ball," Ron called. (my black Labrador)

**10.** Darcy shivered, "Turn up the heat. It's too cold in here. I'm turning into an ice cube!" (It's too cold in here.)

---

Use three ellipsis points ( . . . ) with spaces between them to indicate a pause in written dialogue. Speakers sometimes pause for dramatic effect or because they are hesitating. When you write dialogue, ellipsis points show a dramatic or hesitant pause by the speaker.

> **EXAMPLE**   "So . . . you decided to cut your hair?" Greg remarked. [The pause between Greg's words is shown by three ellipsis points.]

---

**EXERCISE B**   Find the most likely place for a pause in the following sentences. Then, draw a caret (^) where the pause should be and write ellipsis points above it.

**Example 1.** "Oĥ I thought you were my date," Chrissy said in surprise when she opened the door. [Ellipsis points show that the speaker paused.]

**11.** "I think your drawing is very creative," Maria carefully commented. [Where is the most likely or effective place for a pause?]

**12.** Mrs. Parks sighed wearily, "Well at least *that's* over for another year."

**13.** After Tim drove for an hour, Keri asked, "Um do you know where you're going?"

**14.** Lance told Mrs. Ramirez, "That's right the dog ate my homework."

**15.** "No but you're getting warmer," Emma teased as Josie tried to guess her surprise.

# Apostrophes A

## Forming Possessives

**14n.** Use an apostrophe to form the possessives of singular nouns and indefinite pronouns.

A noun or pronoun is "possessive" when it shows ownership or possession. An apostrophe signals that a word is possessive. In general, you can add an apostrophe and an *s* to singular nouns to make them possessive.

> **EXAMPLES**   Kelly's microscope is focused now.  [That the microscope belongs to Kelly is shown by an *'s* added to *Kelly*.]
>
> A zebra's stripes make it unique.  [That the stripes belong to the zebra is shown by an *'s* added to *zebra*.]

A plural noun that ends in an *s* needs only the apostrophe to make the noun possessive. A plural noun that does not end in *s* needs both the apostophe and an *s*.

> **EXAMPLES**   the Sims' home  [*Sims* is a plural noun ending in *s*. An apostrophe alone makes the word possessive.]
>
> the men's team  [*Men* is a plural noun that does not end in *s*. An apostrophe and an *s* make the word possessive.]

**EXERCISE A** Write the possessive form of each of the following words on the lines provided.

**Examples 1.** river  ______*river's*______  [The possessive form of the singular noun *river* is made by adding an apostrophe and an *s*.]

**2.** children  ______*children's*______  [The word *children* is a plural noun that does not end in *s*. The possessive is formed by adding an apostrophe and an *s*.]

**1.** volcano  ________________

**2.** pioneers  ________________

**3.** windows  ________________

**4.** Odysseus  ________________

**5.** Jerry  ________________

**6.** trees  ________________

**7.** player  ________________

**8.** hive  ________________

**9.** peacock  ________________

**10.** women  ________________

**GO ON**

Possessive personal pronouns do not need an apostrophe or an *s*.

> **EXAMPLES**  I bought **my** ticket. [*My* is the possessive form of the pronoun *I*.]
>
> David parked **his** bicycle. [*His* is the possessive form of the pronoun *he*.]
>
> The stamp lost **its** stickiness. [*Its* is the possessive form of the pronoun *it*.]
>
> Snakes shed **their** skin. [*Their* is the possessive form of the pronoun *they*.]

Indefinite pronouns need both an apostrophe and an *s* to make them possessive.

> **EXAMPLES**  Is this anybody's map?
>
> I think I have someone's jacket.

**EXERCISE B**  Complete the following sentences by using the directions following the sentence to write the correct possessive noun or pronoun on the line provided.

**Examples  1.** Jenna phoned in _____*her*_____ order. (belonging to Jenna)  [The word *her* is a

possessive personal pronoun that refers to *Jenna*.]

**2.** _____*Someone's*_____ letter is on your desk. (belonging to someone)  [The possessive of

*someone* is formed by adding an apostrophe and *s*.]

**11.** Lizards can regrow ________________ tails after they are damaged. (belonging to lizards)

[Which plural possessive pronoun can refer to *lizards*?]

**12.** The library offers books for ________________ tastes. (belonging to anybody)  [How do you form

the possessive of an indefinite pronoun?]

**13.** ________________ home was damaged in the storm. (belonging to nobody)

**14.** Larry put ________________ speech notes in his briefcase. (belonging to Larry)

**15.** The wolves raised ________________ voices to howl at the moon. (belonging to wolves)

**16.** Toby checked that ________________ name was missing from the list. (belonging to no one)

**17.** You, Abby, and I must finish the decorations before the party for ________________ mother

begins. (belonging to you, Abby, and I)

**18.** Would you collect ________________ tickets now? (belonging to everybody)

**19.** ________________ watch is two minutes fast. (belonging to you)

**20.** ________________ car alarm is going off. (belonging to somebody)

# Apostrophes B

## Contractions

**14o.**  Use an apostrophe to show where letters, numerals, or words have been omitted in a contraction.

A contraction is a shortened form of a word or a number. When you want to shorten a long word, a group of words, or a number, use an apostrophe to show where a letter, word, or number has been left out.

> **EXAMPLES**   we'd (we would)     it's (it is)
>
> '96 (1996)     o'clock (of the clock)
>
> won't (will not)     shouldn't (should not)

**TIP▶** Do not confuse contractions with possessive pronouns. Most possessive pronouns do not use apostrophes.

> **CONTRACTIONS**   **It's** an ad for a summer job.  [*It's* is the contraction of *It is*.]
>
> **You're** looking for a job?  [*You're* is the contraction of *You are*.]
>
> **POSSESSIVES**   **Its** pay is really high.  [*Its* is a possessive pronoun.]
>
> **Your** job application is finished?  [*Your* is a possessive pronoun.]

**EXERCISE A** Write the contraction of the underlined words or numbers in each of the following sentences.

**Examples**   ___'42___   **1.** This picture was taken in 1942.  [The contraction for the number *1942* is '42.]

___won't___   **2.** This tire will not go flat.  [The contraction for *will not* is *won't*.]

__________   **1.** That is my old elementary school.  [Which letter is left out to form the contraction for *that is?*]

__________   **2.** Leigh Ann graduated from high school in 2008.  [How is the number *2008* made into a contraction?]

__________   **3.** What will the new fence cost?

__________   **4.** We had better make our reservations now.

__________   **5.** The movie starts at 3 of the clock this afternoon.

__________   **6.** Carlos should not need a coat today.

__________   **7.** The heavy truck could not get up the hill.

__________   **8.** Let us ride to the game together.

__________   **9.** I am so thrilled you won an award.

__________   **10.** Has not the package arrived yet?

**GO ON ▶**

## Plurals

**14p.** Use an apostrophe and an *s* to form plurals of all lowercase letters, of some capital letters, of numerals, of symbols, and of words referred to as words.

> **EXAMPLES**    The word *Massachusetts* has four **s's** in it. [To show more than one *s*, an *'s* is added after the *s*.]
>
> Write ***'s** on the items you're putting in the garage sale. [To show more than one * symbol, the writer put an *'s* after the *.]
>
> The phone number has three **9's** in it. [More than one nine is shown by adding *'s* to the numeral 9.]
>
> The vote was decided by two **no's.** [More than one *no* is shown by adding an *'s* to *no*.]

> **NOTE** To form the plural of abbreviations that end with a period, add an apostrophe and an *s*. To form the plurals of abbreviations that do not end with periods, add either an *'s* or just an *s*.
>
> **EXAMPLES**    Dr.'s      Ph.D.'s
>                    RPM's     SASEs

**EXERCISE B** Complete the following sentences by writing on the line provided the plural of the letters, symbols, numbers, and words in parentheses.

**Examples** 1. Hannah spells her name with two _____*h's*_____. *(h)* [The lowercase letter *h* is made plural by adding an apostrophe and an *s*.]

2. The actress' speech had five _____*thank you's*_____ in it. *(thank you)* [A word referred to as a word is made plural by adding an apostrophe and an *s*.]

**11.** The menu needs _____________ beside each price. *($)* [How is the plural of the *$* symbol shown?]

**12.** As a snake in the play, I use lots of _____________ in my speech. *(s)* [How is the plural of a lowercase letter shown?]

**13.** Does the word *roommate* have two _____________ or one? *(m)*

**14.** We received six _____________ to our invitation. *(yes)*

**15.** Using _____________ and *thank you*'s at the dinner table is common courtesy. *(please)*

**16.** Mrs. Carr is in charge of processing the _____________ *(COD)*

**17.** So many prices have two _____________ in them. *(9)*

**18.** Rowan plans to make all _____________ this semester. *(A)*

**19.** Please use _____________ to fill in your ballot. *(X)*

**20.** All e-mail addresses have _____________ in them. *(@)*

# Hyphens

**14q.**   Use a hyphen to divide a word at the end of a line.

A hyphen (-) tells a reader that a word you began on one line will continue on the next line. Hyphens should be used only between the syllables of a word.

> **EXAMPLE**   After playing for an hour, the chess players reached a stale-
> mate.  [*Stalemate* divides into two syllables, *stale-mate.* The hyphen
> belongs between the two syllables.]

**NOTE** Do not hyphenate a word that has only one syllable. Also, do not leave a letter standing alone when you divide a word.

> **INCORRECT**   When we arrived, the play was just a-
> bout to start.  [The word *about* divides into two syllables, *a-bout.*
> However, the *a* by itself is awkward.]
>
> **CORRECT**   When we arrived, the play was just
> about to start.  [The whole word *about* goes on the second line because it
> cannot be divided.]

If you aren't sure whether a word is two or more syllables, check a dictionary. Dictionaries show exactly where words divide into syllables.

**EXERCISE A** Each of the following sentences has one word underlined. Draw a vertical line in the word showing where the word could be hyphenated. If the underlined word cannot be hyphenated, write *none* on the line provided. Hint: One of the words may be hyphenated in more than one place. Draw a line for each place the word can be hyphenated.

**Example** _______ **1.** Luke gave the audience a stunning smile.  [*Stunning* can be divided between

the double consonants *n.*]

_______ **1.** Cassie looked all around for poison ivy.  [Can *around* be divided?]

_______ **2.** The raccoon was busily rummaging through the picnic area.

_______ **3.** The bay held boats from all over the world.

_______ **4.** Chef Garza agreed to prepare omelets for breakfast.

_______ **5.** The school board hired a new football coach this year.

Some words are always hyphenated. Use hyphens with the following: compound numbers from *twenty-one* to *ninety-nine;* fractions used as modifiers; the prefixes *ex–, self–, all–,* and *great–;* the suffixes *–elect* and *–free;* prefixes before proper nouns and adjectives; and compound adjectives that precede the nouns they modify.

> **EXAMPLES**   Pedro planted **twenty-six** trees in the park.  [*Twenty-six* is a compound
> number.]
>
> The recipe calls for **one-third** cup of chopped chives.  [The fraction *one-third*
> is used to modify *cup.*]

**GO ON** ➡

> Has Kimi been officially named **treasurer-elect** for next year?  [Use a hyphen with the suffix *–elect*.]
>
> Most **pre-Elizabethan** playwrights have been overshadowed by Shakespeare.  [The prefix *pre–* is hyphenated before a proper adjective.]
>
> These sturdy, **well-insulated** houses should be inexpensive to maintain.  [The compound adjective is hyphenated because it comes before the word it modifies.]

**NOTE▶** Do not use a hyphen if one of the modifiers before a noun ends in *–ly*.

> **EXAMPLE**   These **fully insulated** houses should be inexpensive to maintain.  [The first modifier ends in *–ly*, so no hyphen is needed.]

**EXERCISE B** Rewrite the underlined word in each of the following sentences, adding hyphens where needed. Write the words on the lines provided. If an underlined word does not need a hyphen, write *C* on the line.

**Examples 1.** Li's great grandmother sang opera. ___great-grandmother___ [The prefix *great–* is

hyphenated when it is connected to a word.]

**2.** Two thirds of the school board members must agree to pass a new attendance

policy. _________*C*_________ [In this sentence, *Two thirds* is not used as an adjective,

so it does not need a hyphen.]

**6.** The sack with the hole lost three fourths of the sugar. ___________________ [Does *three*

*fourths* modify anything here? If not, do you need a hyphen?]

**7.** Engineers have designed a two way bridge. ___________________ [Is *two way* a compound

adjective?]

**8.** Mama Maria's is a world famous brand of pasta. ___________________

**9.** The newspaper ran a picture of the mayor elect. ___________________

**10.** The radio announced an all points weather bulletin. ___________________

**11.** It's so hard to find foods that are salt free. ___________________

**12.** The collector has many pre Civil War artifacts. ___________________

**13.** Explorers need warm gear for the trans Alaskan hike. ___________________

**14.** *Crisscross* is a highly rated new novel. ___________________

**15.** This job requires a five eighths inch bolt. ___________________

# Dashes, Parentheses, and Brackets

## Dashes

**14v.** Use a dash to indicate an abrupt break in thought or speech.

> **EXAMPLE** The hurricane—it was massive—did not come on land.  [The information *it was massive* is set off with dashes because it breaks into the sentence.]

**14w.** Use a dash to mean *namely, in other words,* or *that is* before an explanation.

> **EXAMPLE** Claire is more than a sister—she is my best friend.  [The dash here means *that is*. The words *she is my best friend* further explain Claire's opinion of her sister.]

**EXERCISE A** Place a caret (∧) in the following sentences where dashes should be placed. Then, draw the dash above the caret.

**Example  1.**  The mural‸it covered the whole wall‸showed the state's history.  [Dashes around *it covered the whole wall* indicate an abrupt break in thought.]

**1.** Only one word can describe the dance fantastic!  [Does the word *fantastic* explain the first part of this sentence?]

**2.** Those salmon look at them go are swimming upstream.

**3.** Chen didn't just win any old award he won the *top* award.

**4.** Then, a limousine drove up and but I won't give away the show's end.

**5.** Ben Franklin or was it William Shakespeare? said the world is a stage.

## Parentheses

**14x.** Use parentheses to enclose informative or explanatory material of minor importance.

> **EXAMPLE** Florence Nightingale (known as "The lady with the lamp") began the modern nursing profession.  [The information *known as "The lady with the lamp"* goes in parentheses because it is extra, minor information that does not affect the overall meaning of the sentence.]

**EXERCISE B** Add parentheses around the informative or explanatory words in the following sentences.

**Example  1.**  People in cities can see very few stars (about 2 percent) compared to people in the country.  [The information *about 2 percent* is extra information that is not necessary to the sentence's meaning.]

**6.** Glenda Jones formerly an actress directed the movie *Modern Poetry*.  [What extra information is given in this sentence?]

**GO ON** →

**7.** The menu offers two choices I like either one of vegetables.

**8.** Black bears see their range map on page 50 still live in North America.

**9.** Polynesia which means "many islands" lies in the Pacific Ocean.

**10.** Friday's assembly I won't be able to attend it will be in the gym.

## Brackets

**14y.**   Use brackets to enclose an explanation within quoted or parenthetical material.

> **EXAMPLES**   "Our bodies need three to four hours of deep sleep **[called "orthodox" sleep]** each night," said Dr. Ross.   [*Called "orthodox" sleep* is in brackets to show that it is not part of the original quotation.]
>
> Easter Island (2,200 miles west of Chile **[3,540 kilometers]**) has mysterious stone statues.   [*3,540 kilometers* is in brackets because it is an explanation within parenthetical information.]

Another use of brackets is to insert the Latin word *sic* into a quotation to show that an error exists in the original quotation.

> **EXAMPLE**   Susan's report began, "James Joyce's novel *The* **[sic]** *Portrait of the Artist as a Young Man* is unique."   [The correct title of the novel is *A Portrait of the Artist as a Young Man.* Adding the word *sic* in brackets shows that the mistake was made in Susan's report, not in this quotation from it.]

**EXERCISE C**   Each of the following sentences is followed by information in brackets. Draw a caret in each sentence to show where the information should be added.

**Example 1.** A Russian ballerina (Anna Pavlova) is the focus of my report. *[1881–1931]*

> *[1881–1931* is in brackets because it is part of the parenthetical information about Anna Pavlova.]

**11.** According to this article, "Few people expressed any opinion about President Tafft." *[sic]* [*Taft* is misspelled in this quotation. Where would you put the bracketed information?]

**12.** Chariot races (run on an oval track) were a popular event in ancient Rome. *[called a "hippodrome"]*

**13.** The skateboard (first developed in California) was originally used for surfing practice. *[in the 1930's]*

**14.** The story of Frankenstein (created by Mary Shelley) is a popular movie theme. *[who published it in 1818]*

**15.** "Franklin Roosevelt (who made public radio broadcasts) was president for twelve years," explained the tour guide. *[called 'fireside chats']*

# Words with *ie* and *ei*

**15a.** Write *ie* when the sound is long *e*, except after *c*.

The long *e* sound is what you hear in words such as *need*, *grief*, and *leaf*.

> *i* **before** *e*   ach**ie**ve, p**ie**ce, s**ie**ge, th**ie**f
>
> *ei* **after** *c*   c**ei**ling, conc**ei**ve, dec**ei**t, rec**ei**pt

Some exceptions to the rule include the following words: **ei**ther, **n**ei**ther**, l**ei**sure, prot**ei**n.

**15b.** Write *ei* when the sound is not long *e*, especially when the sound is long *a*.

The long *a* sound is what you hear in words such as *gate*, *braid*, *sleigh*, and *bay*.

> *ei* **pronounced** *ay*   fr**ei**ght, n**ei**ghbor, r**ei**n, w**ei**gh

Some exceptions to the rule include the following words: *anc**ie**nt, pat**ie**nce, misch**ie**f, fr**ie**nd*.

**EXERCISE A**  Underline the word in parentheses that is spelled correctly in each of the following sentences.

**Examples 1.** Would you like a (*peice*, *piece*) of fruit?  [The sound is a long *e*, and the letters do not

follow *c*, so the correct spelling is *piece*.]

**2.** Is this blood vessel a (*vein*, *vien*) or an artery?  [The sound is a long *a*, so the correct

spelling is *vein*.]

**1.** Did she (*receive*, *recieve*) a reward for finding the lost kitten?  [Is the sound a long *e* or a long *a*?

Do the letters follow *c*?]

**2.** The judge (*beleived*, *believed*) that the defendant was innocent.  [Is the sound a long *e* or a long *a*?

Do the letters follow *c*?]

**3.** (*Weigh*, *Wiegh*) each test tube and its contents.

**4.** The fort was badly damaged during the long (*seige*, *siege*).

**5.** Late at night, they heard the whistle of a (*freight*, *frieght*) train.

**6.** Your graduation represents a major (*acheivement*, *achievement*).

**7.** That building is at least (*eight*, *ieght*) hundred feet high.

**8.** Have you ever seen a horse-drawn (*sleigh*, *sliegh*)?

**9.** The knight's (*sheild*, *shield*) protected him from injury.

**10.** Let me know when you find the missing (*piece*, *peice*) of the puzzle.

**GO ON** ➡

**TIP▶** The old rhyme "*i* before *e*, except after *c* or when sounded as *ay*, as in *neighbor* and *weigh*," may help you remember these spelling rules. However, there are several exceptions to the rule, so be sure to use a dictionary if you are uncertain about a word's spelling.

**EXERCISE B** Underline the word in parentheses that is spelled correctly in each of the following sentences.

**Examples**  **1.** Everyone was (*releived*, *relieved*) when the storm was over. [The sound is a long *e*, and the letters do not follow *c*, so the correct spelling is *relieved*.]

     **2.** Where do (*reindeer*, *riendeer*) live? [The sound is a long *a*, so the correct spelling is *reindeer*.]

**11.** Mr. Kelly's (*niece*, *neice*) moved here from Arizona. [Is the sound a long *e* or a long *a*? Do the letters follow *c*?]

**12.** The earth's magnetic (*feild*, *field*) causes compass needles to point north. [Is the sound a long *e* or a long *a*? Do the letters follow *c*?]

**13.** Please help me (*retreive*, *retrieve*) the papers that scattered in the wind.

**14.** The door frame in the kitchen is marked with all of our (*heights*, *hieghts*).

**15.** I thought that movie was (*weird*, *wierd*).

**16.** What (*foriegn*, *foreign*) language are you studying this year?

**17.** The teacher asked each group to give a (*breif*, *brief*) report about its progress.

**18.** Ask the salesperson to give you a (*receipt*, *reciept*).

**19.** Jake sold his prize (*heifer*, *hiefer*) at the livestock fair.

**20.** The kingdom prospered during the monarch's (*reign*, *riegn*).

# Prefixes and Suffixes

A *prefix* is a letter or group of letters added to the beginning of a word to change its meaning.
A *suffix* is a letter or group of letters added to the end of a word to change its meaning.

**15d.**  When adding a prefix, do not change the spelling of the original word.

> **EXAMPLES**  un + important = un**important**     mis + spell = mis**spell**

**15e.**  When adding the suffix *–ness* or *–ly*, do not change the spelling of the original word.

> **EXAMPLES**  careless + ness = **careless**ness     love + ly = **love**ly

If a word ends in *y*, you may need to change the *y* to *i* before adding *–ness* or *–ly*. For most
words that have two or more syllables and end in *y*, change the *y* to *i* before adding *–ness*
or *–ly*.

> **EXAMPLES**  messy + ness = **messi**ness     happy + ly = **happi**ly

**EXERCISE A**  Add the given prefix or suffix to each of the following words. Write the new word on the
line provided.

**Example 1.**  dis + cover = ___*discover*___  [Adding the prefix *dis–* does not change the spelling

of the word *cover.*]

**1.** careful + ly = ______________  [Does adding     **3.** semi + circle = ______________

the suffix *–ly* change the spelling of the word?]     **4.** lonely + ness = ______________

**2.** re + write = ______________     **5.** over + achieve = ______________

**15f.**  Drop the final silent *e* before adding a suffix that begins with a vowel.

**15g.**  Keep the final silent *e* before adding a suffix that begins with a consonant.

A silent *e* is not pronounced when you say the word.

> **EXAMPLES**  imagine + able = **imagin**able  [The suffix *–able* begins with a vowel, so
> the final silent *e* is dropped.]
> awe + some = **awe**some  [The suffix *–some* begins with a consonant, so
> the final silent *e* is not dropped.]

**EXERCISE B**  Add the given suffix to each of the following words. Write the new word on the line
provided.

**Example 1.**  lone + some = ___*lonesome*___  [The suffix begins with the consonant *s*, so the final

silent *e* is kept.]

**6.** conspire + ing = ______________  [Does     **8.** drive + er = ______________

the suffix begin with a vowel or a consonant?]     **9.** retrieve + al = ______________

**7.** excite + ment = ______________     **10.** same + ness = ______________

**GO ON** ➡

*Developmental Language Skills*     **169**

for **CHAPTER 15: SPELLING**   pages 444–447   *continued*

**15h.**  For words ending in *y* preceded by a consonant, change the *y* to *i* before adding any suffix that does not begin with *i*.

>  **EXAMPLES**  steady + ly = **steadi**ly  [The suffix –*ly* does not begin with *i*.]
>  classify + ing = **classify**ing  [The suffix –*ing* begins with *i*.]

**15i.**  For words ending in *y* preceded by a vowel, keep the *y* when adding a suffix.

>  **EXAMPLE**  employ + ment = **employ**ment  [The *y* follows the vowel *o*.]

**EXERCISE C**  Add the given suffix to each of the following words. Write the new word on the line provided.

**Example  1.**  fly + ing = ______*flying*______  [The letter before *y* is the consonant *l*, but the suffix begins with *i*, so the *y* does not change to *i*.]

**11.**  ally + ed = _____________  [Is the letter          **13.**  rely + able = _____________

before *y* a consonant or a vowel?]                       **14.**  delay + ing = _____________

**12.**  try + ed = _____________                          **15.**  empty + ness = _____________

**15j.**  Double the final consonant before adding a suffix that begins with a vowel if the word both (1) has only one syllable or has the accent on the final syllable and (2) ends in a single consonant preceded by a single vowel.

>  **EXAMPLES**  swim + ing = swim**ming**  [*Swim* has only one syllable and ends in a single consonant preceded by a single vowel. The final consonant is doubled.]
>  break + able = break**able**  [*Break* has only one syllable, but it does not end in a single consonant preceded by a single vowel. The final consonant is not doubled.]

**EXERCISE D**  Add the given suffix to each of the following words. Write the new word on the line provided.

**Example  1.**  excel + ed = ______*excelled*______  [*Excel* has the accent on the final syllable and ends in a single consonant preceded by a single vowel. The *l* should be doubled.]

**16.**  select + ed = _____________  [Does the          **18.**  control + able = _____________

word end in a single consonant preceded                   **19.**  bright + est = _____________

by a single vowel?]                                       **20.**  drop + ed = _____________

**17.**  trim + ed = _____________

**170**

# Plurals of Nouns A

**15k.**  Remembering the following rules will help you spell the plural forms of nouns.

**(1)** For most nouns, add *s*.

| | | | | | |
|---|---|---|---|---|---|
| **SINGULAR** | brick | eye | lizard | Smith | word |
| **PLURAL** | brick**s** | eye**s** | lizard**s** | Smith**s** | word**s** |

**(2)** For nouns ending in *s, x, z, ch,* or *sh*, add *es*.

| | | | | | |
|---|---|---|---|---|---|
| **SINGULAR** | boss | mix | Gomez | church | wish |
| **PLURAL** | boss**es** | mix**es** | Gomez**es** | church**es** | wish**es** |

**TIP** If the plural form of a word has one more syllable than the singular form, then the plural word is probably spelled with *es*.

> **EXAMPLE**  The singular word *pinch* has one syllable. The plural word *pinches* has two syllables: *pinch•es*. The plural word *pinches* is formed by adding *es* to the singular word *pinch*.

**EXERCISE A**  Write the plural form of each of the following words on the line provided.

**Examples  1.** father _____*fathers*_____ [The plural of *father* is formed by adding *s*.]

**2.** box _____*boxes*_____ [*Box* ends in *x*, so the plural is formed by adding *es*.]

**1.** ring _____________ [Does the plural form of *ring* end in *s* or *es*?]

**2.** trench _____________ [Do words that end in *ch* add *s* or *es* to form the plural?]

**3.** fox _____________

**4.** impression _____________

**5.** guess _____________

**6.** physician _____________

**7.** fire _____________

**8.** canyon _____________

**9.** dish _____________

**10.** moon _____________

**(3)** For nouns ending in *y* preceded by a vowel, add *s*.

| | | | |
|---|---|---|---|
| **SINGULAR** | boy | journey | tray |
| **PLURAL** | boy**s** | journey**s** | tray**s** |

**(4)** For nouns ending in *y* preceded by a consonant, change the *y* to *i* and add *es*.

| | | | |
|---|---|---|---|
| **SINGULAR** | mutiny | penny | sky |
| **PLURAL** | mutin**ies** | penn**ies** | sk**ies** |

**GO ON**

**EXERCISE B**  Write the plural form of each of the following words on the line provided.

**Examples  1.** alley ______*alleys*______ [The letter before *y* is a vowel, so the plural is formed by

adding *s*.]

**2.** possibility ___*possibilities*___ [The letter before *y* is a consonant, so the plural is formed

by changing the *y* to *i* and adding *es*.]

**11.** enemy _____________ [Is the letter

before *y* a consonant or a vowel?]

**12.** key _____________ [Is the letter

before *y* a consonant or a vowel?]

**13.** pantry _____________

**14.** Monday _____________

**15.** decoy _____________

**16.** candy _____________

**17.** valley _____________

**18.** harmony _____________

**19.** attorney _____________

**20.** victory _____________

---

**(5)**  For some nouns ending in *f* or *fe*, add *s*.  For others, change the *f* or *fe* to *v* and add *es*.

| | | | | | |
|---|---|---|---|---|---|
| **SINGULAR** | roof | sa**fe** | lea**f** | wi**fe** | whar**f** |
| **PLURAL** | roo**fs** | sa**fes** | lea**ves** | wi**ves** | whar**fs** *or* whar**ves** |

**TIP▶** If you are unsure how to form the plural of a word, consult a dictionary.

---

**EXERCISE C**  Write the plural form of each of the following words on the line provided.

**Example  1.** thief ______*thieves*______ [The *f* in *thief* changes to *v* before *es* is added.]

**21.** life _____________ [Does the *fe* change to *v* before *es* is added?]

**22.** giraffe _____________

**23.** belief _____________

**24.** hoof _____________

**25.** shelf _____________

# Plurals of Nouns B

**15k.**   Remembering the following rules will help you spell the plural forms of nouns.

**(6)** For nouns ending in *o* preceded by a vowel, add *s*.

| | | | | |
|---|---|---|---|---|
| **SINGULAR** | igloo | patio | radio | stereo |
| **PLURAL** | igloo**s** | patio**s** | radio**s** | stereo**s** |

**(7)** For many nouns ending in *o* preceded by a consonant, add *es*.

| | | | | |
|---|---|---|---|---|
| **SINGULAR** | hero | potato | tomato | veto |
| **PLURAL** | hero**es** | potato**es** | tomato**es** | veto**es** |
| **EXCEPTIONS** | piano**s** | solo**s** | ego**s** | photo**s** |

**NOTE▶** Most words that refer to music and end in *o* form the plural by adding *s*. If you are unsure of how a word forms the plural, look the word up in a dictionary.

**EXERCISE A** Write the plural form of each of the following words on the line provided.

**Example 1.** ratio _____ratios_____ [*Ratio* ends in *o* preceded by a vowel, so the plural is formed by adding *s*.]

**1.** rodeo _____________ [Is the letter before *o* a consonant or a vowel?]

**2.** torpedo _____________

**3.** trio _____________

**4.** cameo _____________

**5.** echo _____________

**(8)** The plurals of a few nouns are formed irregularly.

| | | | | |
|---|---|---|---|---|
| **SINGULAR** | child | louse | tooth | woman |
| **PLURAL** | child**ren** | **lice** | te**eth** | wom**en** |

**(9)** For a few nouns, the singular and the plural forms are the same.

| | | | | |
|---|---|---|---|---|
| **SINGULAR** | aircraft | deer | pliers | sheep |
| **PLURAL** | aircraft | deer | pliers | sheep |

**EXERCISE B** Write the plural form of each of the following words on the line provided.

**Example 1.** tooth _____teeth_____ [The letters *oo* change to form the plural form *teeth*.]

**6.** foot _____________ [What letters change to make the plural form?]

**7.** spacecraft _____________

**8.** man _____________

**9.** pants _____________

**10.** series _____________



**GO ON ▶**

**(10)** For most compound nouns, form the plural of only the last word of the compound.

> **SINGULAR**  doorbell  picture window  five-year-old
> **PLURAL**  doorbell**s**  picture window**s**  five-year-old**s**

**(11)** For compound nouns in which one of the words is modified by the other word or words, form the plural of the noun modified.

> **SINGULAR**  brother-in-law  editor in chief  bird-watcher
> **PLURAL**  brother**s**-in-law  editor**s** in chief  bird-watcher**s**

**EXERCISE C** Write the plural form of each of the following words on the line provided.

**Example 1.** teenager  *teenagers*  [The plural form of *teenager* is formed by adding *s*.]

**11.** runner-up ________________ [Which word  **13.** bookshelf ________________

is being modified by the  **14.** window box ________________

other word?]  **15.** great-grandmother ________________

**12.** baby sitter ________________

**(12)** For some nouns borrowed from other languages, the plural is formed as in the original language.

A few nouns borrowed from other languages have two acceptable plural forms.

> **SINGULAR**  alumnus  criterion
> **PLURAL**  alumn**i**  criteria *or* criterion**s**

**(13)** To form the plurals of numerals, most uppercase letters, symbols, and most words referred to as words, add an *s* or both an apostrophe and an *s*.

> **SINGULAR**  20  C  $  *if*
> **PLURAL**  20**s** *or* 20**'s**  C**s** *or* C**'s**  $**s** *or* $**'s**  *if***s** *or* *if***'s**

**EXERCISE D** Write the plural form of each of the following words, numerals, letters, or symbols on the line provided. Hint: The plurals may be formed in more than one way.

**Example 1.** radius  *radii or radiuses*  [The plural form of *radius* is *radii* or *radiuses*.]

**16.** *although* ________________ [What is  **18.** 1870 ________________

added to form the plural of words  **19.** @ ________________

used as words?]  **20.** *W* ________________

**17.** formula ________________

# Writing Numbers

**15l.** Spell out a *cardinal number*—a number that states how many—if it can be expressed in one or two words. Otherwise, use numerals.

Cardinal numbers are the numbers you use when you count: *1, 2, 3,* and so on.

> **EXAMPLES**  **one hundred** cats    **twelve** hours
>               **294** chairs        **5,280** feet

> **NOTE▶** When two or more cardinal numbers are in the same sentence, be consistent. Do not spell out one number and use numerals for the other.

> **INCONSISTENT**  Of **1,550** tickets, we sold only **two hundred.**
> **CONSISTENT**  Of **1,550** tickets, we sold only **200.**

**15m.** Spell out a number that begins a sentence.

> **EXAMPLE**  **Ten thousand** people attended the concert.  [The number should be spelled out because it begins the sentence.]

A long number at the beginning of a sentence is difficult to read. You may need to revise a sentence if the spelled-out number will be longer than two or three words.

> **EXAMPLES**  **One thousand seven hundred sixty** yards equal one mile.  [The spelled-out number is quite long.]
>              One mile equals **1,760** yards.  [The sentence was rewritten so that numerals could be used.]

**EXERCISE A** In the following sentences, underline any number that should be spelled out. If all the numbers in a sentence are written correctly, write *C* on the line provided.

**Example** _______ **1.** <u>2,000</u> posters were printed.  [*2,000* should be spelled out because it begins

             the sentence and can be written as two words.]

_______ **1.** There are 29 rows in this section.  [Can the number be written in one or two words?]

_______ **2.** We need at least 375 more cups.

_______ **3.** 2 or 3 hours from now, we'll be leaving for the beach.

_______ **4.** The flower garden has over 25 different types of flowers.

_______ **5.** 475 actors tried out for the play.

**15n.** Spell out an *ordinal number*—a number that expresses order.

Ordinal numbers are the numbers you use when you describe the position or order of something: *first, second, third,* and so on.

> **EXAMPLE**  No one remembers the **third** verse of the song.

**GO ON ➡**

**EXERCISE B** In the following sentences, underline any number that should be spelled out. If all the numbers in a sentence are written correctly, write *C* on the line provided.

**Example** _______ **1.** Frank answered the 2nd problem correctly.  [The ordinal number *second* should be spelled out.]

_______ **6.** The two runners tied for 3rd place.  [Should ordinal numbers be spelled out?]

_______ **7.** She is the sixth person from the right in that photograph.

_______ **8.** Jupiter, the 5th planet from the sun, is larger than the 6th planet from the sun, Saturn.

_______ **9.** 1st, put away your books and take out a pencil.

_______ **10.** The game was boring until the bottom of the 8th inning.

---

**15o.**  Use numerals to express numbers in conventional situations.

Use numerals to identify roads, television channels, page numbers, and line numbers. The numbers in street addresses and dates are also written as numerals. Always use numerals to express measurements or statistics.

>**EXAMPLES**  U.S. Highway **66**   Interstate **95**   Channel **2**
>
>pages **9–29**   lines **6–9**   November **11, 1919**
>
>**604** Stateline Street, Apt. **12,** Houston, TX **77002**

Dates and times of day are usually written with numerals, with a few exceptions. You should spell out a number before *o'clock*, and you should not use *A.M.* or *P.M.* with a spelled-out number.

>**EXAMPLES**  **9:25** P.M.    **3:00** A.M.    **1500** B.C.    A.D. **275**    **2001**
>
>**nine** o'clock **in the morning**  [The number is spelled out because it is used with *o'clock*. The phrase *in the morning*, rather than the abbreviation A.M., is used to tell the period of the day.]

**EXERCISE C** In the following sentences, underline any number that is spelled out but should not be. If all the numbers in a sentence are written correctly, write *C* on the line provided.

**Example** _______ **1.** By 5 o'clock, the temperature had fallen to 30 degrees.  [The time should be spelled out because it comes before *o'clock*. The temperature is correctly written as a numeral because it is a measurement.]

_______ **11.** The ruins date to about five hundred B.C.  [Which number expresses a date?]

_______ **12.** U.S. Highway Five runs from the Canadian border to the Mexican border.

_______ **13.** Were you born in nineteen ninety-five?

_______ **14.** The rooster began to crow shortly after five o'clock in the morning.

_______ **15.** Who can paraphrase lines nine–twelve of the poem?

**176**

*for* **CHAPTER 15: SPELLING**    **pages 456–458**

# Words Often Confused A

People often confuse the following words. Some of these words are *homonyms*—that is, their pronunciations are the same. However, these words have different meanings and spellings. Other words in the following groups have the same or similar spellings yet have different meanings.

*all ready*   [adjective] *all prepared*
The students were **all ready** for summer vacation.

*already*   [adverb] *previously*
Have they **already** announced the winner?

*all together*   [adverb] *in unison; at the same time*
At the signal, the runners will start **all together.**
[adjective] *in the same place*
The family will be **all together** at the wedding.

*altogether*   [adverb] *entirely*
The line for the movie is **altogether** too long.

**EXERCISE A**   Underline the word or word group in parentheses that correctly completes the sentence.

**Example 1.** Is everyone (<u>*all ready*</u>, *already*) to leave? [The meaning is *all prepared,* so the correct answer is *all ready.*]

**1.** The traffic has become (*altogether, all together*) frustrating. [Is the meaning *entirely,* or is the meaning *in unison?*]

**2.** The herd stood (*altogether, all together*) under a tree in the center of the field.

**3.** Has Nick (*all ready, already*) painted the walls?

**4.** Mix the first five ingredients (*all together, altogether*) in a bowl.

**5.** Are we (*already, all ready*) for the morning hike?

*brake*   [verb] *to slow down or stop*
Jerry **braked** when the ball rolled in front of the car.
[noun] *a device for slowing down or stopping*
Those steep hills are hard on the **brakes.**

*break*   [verb] *to cause to come apart; to shatter*
That kind of plastic may bend, but it should not **break.**
[noun] *a fracture*
The **break** happened when he fell off the bicycle.

**GO ON** ➡

*Developmental Language Skills*                                      **177**

    ***capital***   [noun]  *a city that is the seat of government of a state or country; money or property*

    The **capital** of Germany is Berlin.

    He invested all his **capital** in his business.

    [adjective]  *punishable by death; of major importance; uppercase*

    What is your position on **capital** punishment?

    Increasing attendance at our meetings is a **capital** concern.

    Proper nouns begin with **capital** letters.

    ***capitol***   [noun]  *a building in which a legislature meets*

    The **Capitol** is beautiful at night.  [*U.S. Capitol* is always capitalized.]

    ***coarse***   [adjective]  *rough; crude*

    The road was covered with **coarse** gravel.

    ***course***   [noun]  *path of action; part of a meal; series of studies*

    This path follows the **course** of the river.

    The first **course** at the banquet was asparagus soup.

    How many **courses** are required for graduation?

    [also used in the expression *of course,* meaning *naturally* or *certainly*]

    Of **course,** we meant to invite you!

**EXERCISE B**   Underline the word in parentheses that correctly completes the sentence.

**Examples 1.** Which math *(coarse, course)* was your favorite?  [The meaning is *a unit of study,* so the correct answer is *course.*]

**2.** We took our cousins on a tour of the dome of the *(capital, capitol).*  [The meaning is *a building in which a legislature meets,* so *capitol* is the correct choice.]

**6.** How did he *(break, brake)* his leg?  [Is the meaning *to fracture,* or is the meaning *to stop*?]

**7.** The bag is made of *(coarse, course)* cloth.  [Is the meaning *rough,* or is the meaning *path of action*?]

**8.** That crime may be a *(capital, capitol)* offense.

**9.** The sailor set a *(coarse, course)* for the distant island.

**10.** Apply the *(break, brake)* slowly on an icy road.

**11.** Did the investors refuse to provide more *(capital, capitol)*?

**12.** Her ankle is badly sprained, but she didn't *(break, brake)* it.

**13.** This poet doesn't use many *(capital, capitol)* letters.

**14.** Over the *(coarse, course)* of a year, our garden produced enough food for three families.

**15.** Olympia, not Seattle, is the *(capital, capitol)* of Washington.

**178**

# Words Often Confused B

People often confuse the following words. Some of these words are *homonyms*—that is, their pronunciations are the same. However, these words have different meanings and spellings. Other words in the following groups have the same or similar spellings yet have different meanings.

**complement**   [noun] *something that makes whole or complete*

Is angle ABC the **complement** or the supplement of angle CBD?

[verb] *to make whole or complete*

A glass of water **complements** any meal.

**compliment**   [noun] *praise; a courteous act or expression*

She meant that comment as a **compliment.**

[verb] *to express praise or respect*

The children were **complimented** on their behavior.

**desert**   [noun, pronounced *des′ • ert*] *a dry region*

This overgrazed area may become a **desert** one day.

**desert**   [verb, pronounced *de • sert′*] *to leave or abandon*

Why did you **desert** me when I needed you?

**dessert**   [noun, pronounced *des • sert′*] *the sweet, final course of a meal*

I don't want any **dessert,** thank you.

**EXERCISE A**   Underline the word in parentheses that correctly completes the sentence.

**Example  1.** This thorny plant grows only in the (<u>desert</u>, dessert).  [The meaning is *a dry region*, so the correct word is *desert*.]

**1.** The clarinet's part (*complements, compliments*) the oboe's part.  [Is the meaning *something that makes whole or complete*, or is the meaning *praise*?]

**2.** Even the rats (*desert, dessert*) a sinking ship.

**3.** Please send our (*complements, compliments*) to the designers; these costumes look great!

**4.** Would anyone like pumpkin pie for (*desert, dessert*)?

**5.** Sunset in the (*desert, dessert*) is spectacular.

**GO ON**

    ***its***   [possessive form of the pronoun *it*]   *belonging to it*
         The cat yawned and stretched **its** back.

    ***it's***   [contraction of *it is* or *it has*]
         **It's** not cold outside today.

    ***lead***   [verb, rhymes with *feed*]   *to go first; to guide*
         The park ranger will **lead** us to the campground.

    ***led***   [verb, past form of *lead*]   *went first*
         The drum major **led** the marching band.

    ***lead***   [noun, rhymes with *red*]   *a heavy metal; graphite used in a pencil*
         Are those old pipes made from **lead** or copper?
         The **lead** in this pencil keeps breaking.

    ***loose***   [adjective, rhymes with *noose*]   *free; not close together; not firmly fastened*
         The hamsters escaped from the cage, so they may be **loose** in the house.
         When there is **loose** gravel on the road, you should slow down.
         One of the buttons on my jacket is **loose.**

    ***lose***   [verb, rhymes with *shoes*]   *to suffer loss of*
         Did you **lose** the phone number?

**EXERCISE B**   Underline the word in parentheses that correctly completes the sentence.

**Examples**   **1.** I'll be home before (*its, it's*) dark. [The meaning is *it is*. The correct word is *it's.*]

         **2.** The phone may (*loose, lose*) the signal in the elevator. [The meaning is *to suffer loss of,*
         so the correct word is *lose.*]

**6.** The dog found (*its, it's*) way home again. [Is the meaning *belonging to it* or a contraction for *it has*?]

**7.** My little brother has another (*loose, lose*) tooth. [Is the meaning *not firmly fastened,* or is the meaning *to suffer loss*?]

**8.** Was (*led, lead*) used in the glaze on this piece of pottery?

**9.** (*Its, It's*) been several weeks since the last rain.

**10.** How dark is the (*led, lead*) in this pencil?

**11.** Did the volleyball team win or (*loose, lose*) the game last night?

**12.** Last weekend we repainted the shed because (*its, it's*) paint had begun to crack and peel.

**13.** Sometimes an internship (*leds, leads*) to a well-paying job.

**14.** When did the cat (*loose, lose*) its collar?

**15.** With all (*its, it's*) might, the hurricane slammed into the coast.

# Words Often Confused C

People often confuse the following words. Some of these words are *homonyms*—that is, their pronunciations are the same. However, these words have different meanings and spellings. Other words in the following groups have the same or similar spellings yet have different meanings.

> ***passed*** [verb, past form of *pass*] *went beyond*
> Did you see me when I **passed** your house?
>
> ***past*** [noun] *time gone by*
> The incident happened in the **past.**
> [adjective] *of a former time*
> In the **past** few minutes, I've made five phone calls.
> [preposition] *beyond*
> Craig drove **past** the school and turned around.
>
> ***quiet*** [adjective] *still; silent*
> After Labor Day, the beach is peaceful and **quiet.**
>
> ***quite*** [adverb] *completely; rather; very*
> The merry-go-round was **quite** old and rickety.

**EXERCISE A** Underline the word in parentheses that correctly completes the sentence.

**Example 1.** The marchers (*past, passed*) the courthouse. [The meaning is *went by*, so the correct

    answer is *passed*.]

**1.** Watching the squirrels chase each other was (*quiet, quite*) entertaining. [Is the meaning *silent*, or

is the meaning *rather?*]

**2.** A library is supposed to be a place for (*quiet, quite*) reading.

**3.** Just (*past, passed*) the drugstore is a mailbox.

**4.** Do animals have any memories of the (*past, passed*)?

**5.** You'll have to get up (*quiet, quite*) early tomorrow morning.

> ***than*** [conjunction, used for comparisons]
> It's windier today **than** it was yesterday.
>
> ***then*** [adverb] *at that time; next*
> When everyone is seated, **then** we can start the movie.

**GO ON**

> ***their***   [possessive form of *they*] *belonging to them*
> The lizards have shed **their** skins again.
> ***there***   [adverb] *at that place*
> One of the skins is over **there,** next to that rock.
> [expletive, used to begin a sentence]
> **There** is something fascinating about this process.
> ***they're***   [contraction of *they are*]
> The hinges need to be oiled again because **they're** starting to creak.
>
> ***who's***   [contraction of *who is* or *who has*]
> Do you know **who's** living in that house?
> ***whose***   [possessive form of *who*] *belonging to whom*
> **Whose** artwork was included in the book?

**EXERCISE B**   Underline the word in parentheses that correctly completes the sentence.

**Examples 1.** The twins opened *(their, they're)* birthday presents together. [The meaning is

*belonging to them,* so the correct answer is *their.*]

    **2.** *(Who's, Whose)* turn is it to take out the trash? [The meaning is *belonging to whom,* so

the correct answer is *Whose.*]

**6.** Kim would rather lead *(then, than)* follow. [Is the meaning *next,* or is the sentence making a

comparison?]

**7.** If there is no way to determine *(whose, who's)* backpack that is, please bring it to the front desk.

[Is the meaning *belonging to whom,* or is it a contraction of *who has*?]

**8.** Nearly all bats search for *(their, there)* food at night.

**9.** *(Who's, Whose)* responsible for this mess?

**10.** These tomatoes are ripening faster *(than, then)* those are.

**11.** Someone *(who's, whose)* dog is missing has put up posters.

**12.** *(There, They're)* are three primary colors and three secondary colors.

**13.** Write a draft first, and *(than, then)* read and revise it.

**14.** *(There, They're)* rehearsing in the theater.

**15.** I spent more *(than, then)* twenty dollars on school supplies.

# Common Errors Review

## Common Usage Errors

Be sure to proofread your writing before you turn it in. Errors in your writing can confuse and distract your readers, and readers may form a poor impression of a writer who makes careless errors. Look for mistakes by asking yourself these questions:

| | |
|---|---|
| Do subjects and verbs agree? | Are modifiers used and placed correctly? |
| Are verb forms and tenses correct? | Are troublesome words used correctly? |
| Are pronouns used correctly? | Is usage appropriate for audience and purpose? |
| Are pronoun references clear? | |

After you make corrections or changes to your writing, read your writing again. Sometimes a change you make will create a new problem in another part of your writing.

**EXERCISE A** Use the list of questions above to help you find and correct common errors in usage in the following items. Use proofreading symbols to make your corrections.

**Example 1.** Rapid Repair, a garage in Mark's town, ~~need~~ *needs* a junior mechanic to work during the summer. [*Rapid Repair* is singular, so the verb should be singular too. *Needs* agrees with the singular subject.]

**1.** As graduation approaches, me and many of my classmates have started to look for jobs. [Does *me have started* sound right? What pronoun would sound better as the subject of the sentence?]

**2.** I would like to work at Rapid Repair during the summer and gain most experience fixing cars than I have at this time. [Which word should be used when comparing two things?]

**3.** I am taking a course at my high school, which covers advanced topics in automotive repair, currently.

**4.** I can do basic tune-ups real good, and I have alot of experience replacing brake pads and shoes.

**5.** Everyone which works on late model cars needs to know their way around computer diagnostics, and I would like to learn more about using computer diagnostics.

**6.** My experience and my desire to learn more automotive repair makes me the perfect candidate for the job opening at Rapid Repair garage.

**7.** Because I have did so well in my automotive repair classes, my teacher, Mr. Calhoun, has written me a letter of recommendation for this job.

**GO ON**

**8.** I have included his letter, and you had ought to call him if you have any questions about them.

**9.** I will graduate at the end of this month, and than I will be available for work.

**10.** I can't hardly wait to hear from you and begin my career as a mechanic. Thank you for taking the time to look over my application.

## Common Mechanics Errors

Always check your capitalization, punctuation, and spelling. Use a dictionary if you are not sure of a spelling or how to divide a word. Make sure you haven't confused two words that sound alike but are spelled differently. These details make a big difference in your writing! Ask yourself the following questions as you proofread your work:

Does every sentence begin with a capital letter and end with an appropriate end mark?
Are all proper nouns and proper adjectives capitalized?
Are words spelled and divided correctly?
Have you placed commas and apostrophes where they are needed?
Are direct quotations and titles capitalized and punctuated correctly?

**EXERCISE B**   Correct the errors in capitalization, punctuation, and spelling in the following items. Use proofreading symbols to make your corrections.

**Example 1.** While Joanne was camping in the Great Smoky mountains she kept a journal of her daily *activities* ~~activity~~. [A comma should set off the introductory clause from the rest of the sentence. *Mountains* should be capitalized because it is part of a proper noun. The plural form of *activity* is *activities*.]

**11.** After driving for six hours we arrived at the campsite and managed to set up camp before nightfall, now everything is quite. [Is the introductory phrase set off from the rest of the sentence with a comma? Can a comma separate two complete sentences? Is *quite* spelled correctly?]

**12.** Its so beautiful hear The early-morning fog makes me feel as though Im waking in an enchanted land.

**13.** Ms. hughes, our Trail Guide, said that "she hopes all of us will leave with a greater appreciation of nature and its beauty."

**14.** I have learned several new skills; how to set up a tent how to read a compass and how to identify different animals tracks.

**15.** What a great time Im having on this trip?

**184**